The Way of the House Husband

KOUSUKE OONO

10

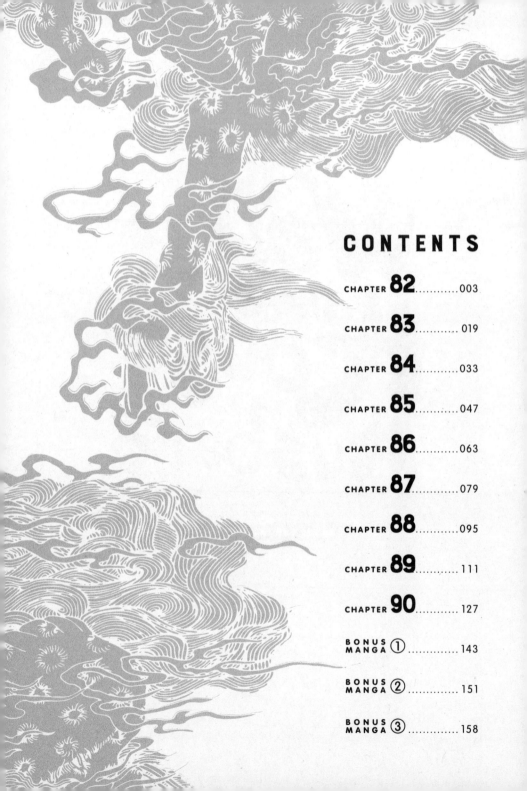

CONTENTS

CHAPTER 82

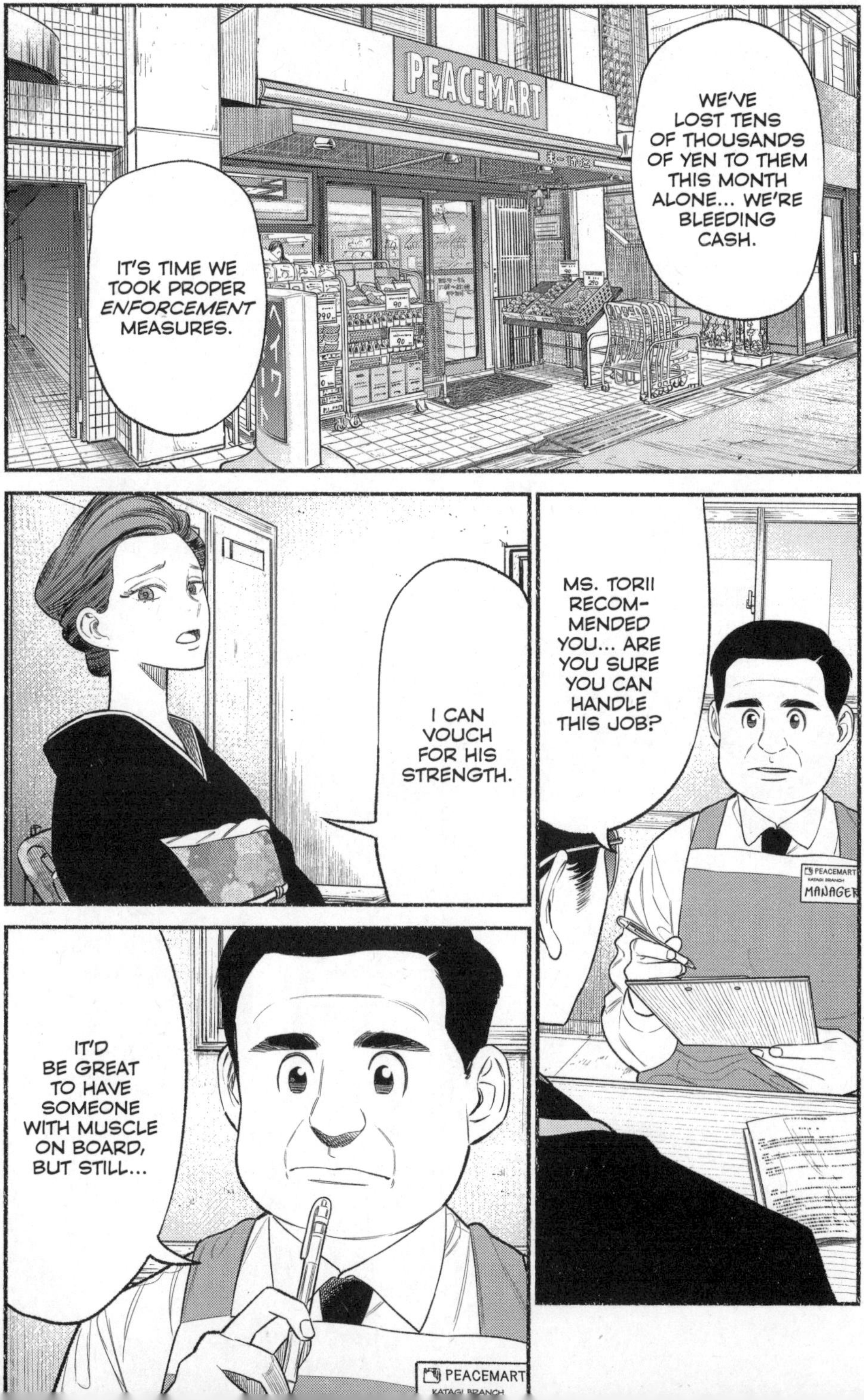
PEACEMART
WE'VE LOST TENS OF THOUSANDS OF YEN TO THEM THIS MONTH ALONE... WE'RE BLEEDING CASH.
IT'S TIME WE TOOK PROPER *ENFORCEMENT* MEASURES.
MS. TORII RECOMMENDED YOU... ARE YOU SURE YOU CAN HANDLE THIS JOB?
PEACEMART KATAGI BRANCH MANAGER
I CAN VOUCH FOR HIS STRENGTH.
IT'D BE GREAT TO HAVE SOMEONE WITH MUSCLE ON BOARD, BUT STILL...
PEACEMART KATAGI BRANCH

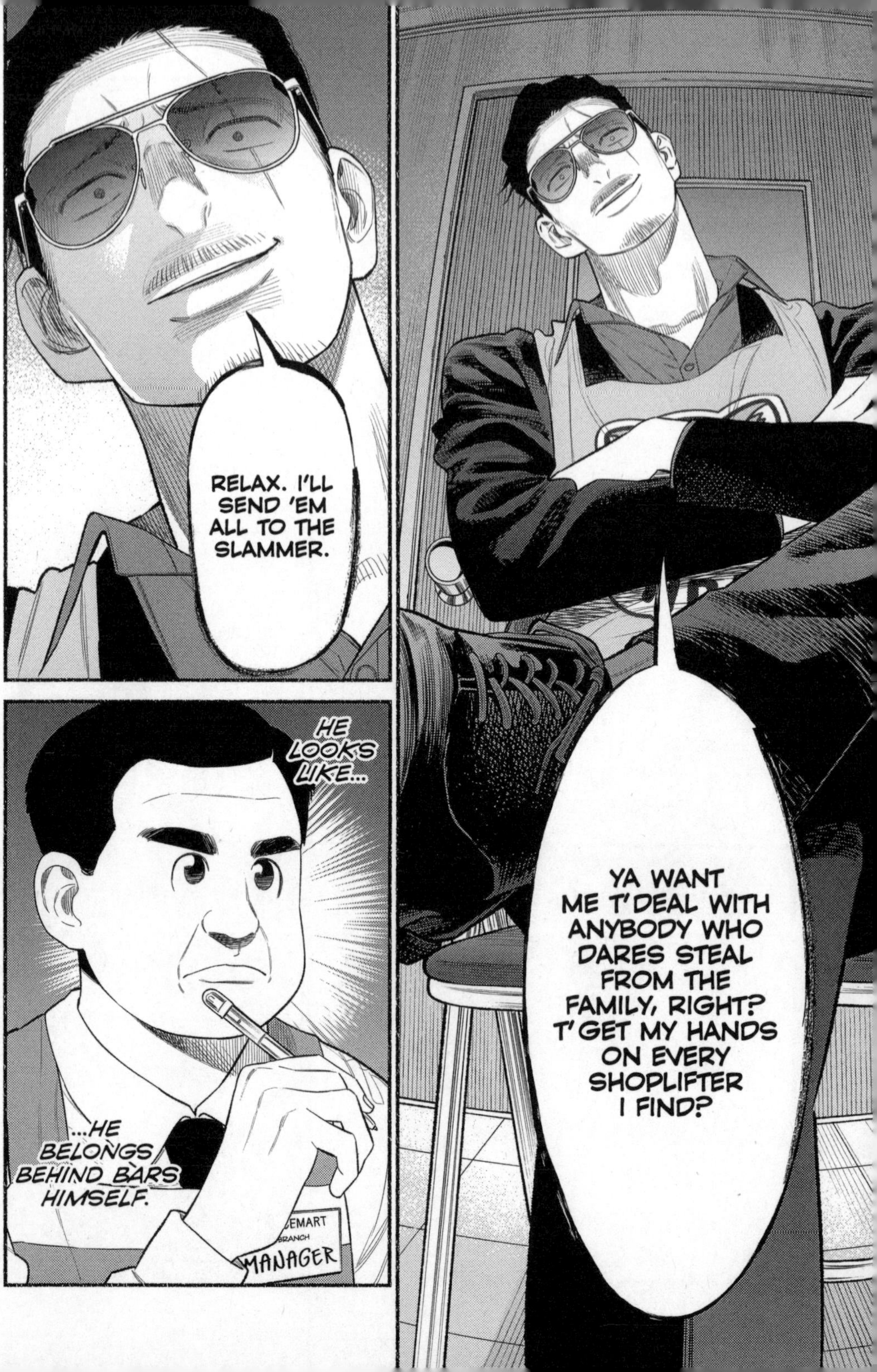
YA WANT ME T'DEAL WITH ANYBODY WHO DARES STEAL FROM THE FAMILY, RIGHT? T'GET MY HANDS ON EVERY SHOPLIFTER I FIND?
RELAX. I'LL SEND 'EM ALL TO THE SLAMMER.
HE LOOKS LIKE...
...HE BELONGS BEHIND BARS HIMSELF.
MANAGER

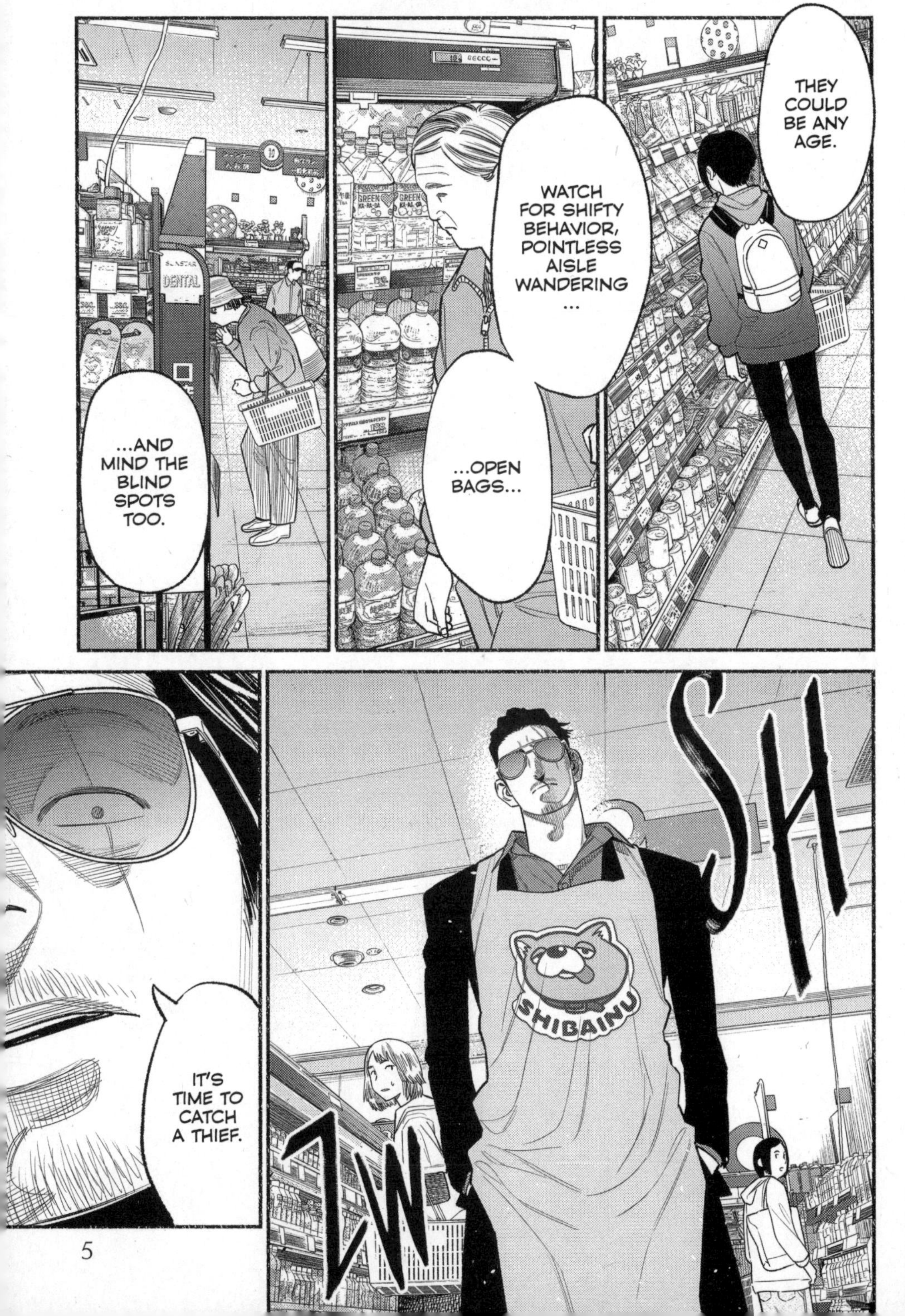
THEY COULD BE ANY AGE.
WATCH FOR SHIFTY BEHAVIOR, POINTLESS AISLE WANDERING ...
...OPEN BAGS...
...AND MIND THE BLIND SPOTS TOO.
SH
SHIBAINU
IT'S TIME TO CATCH A THIEF.

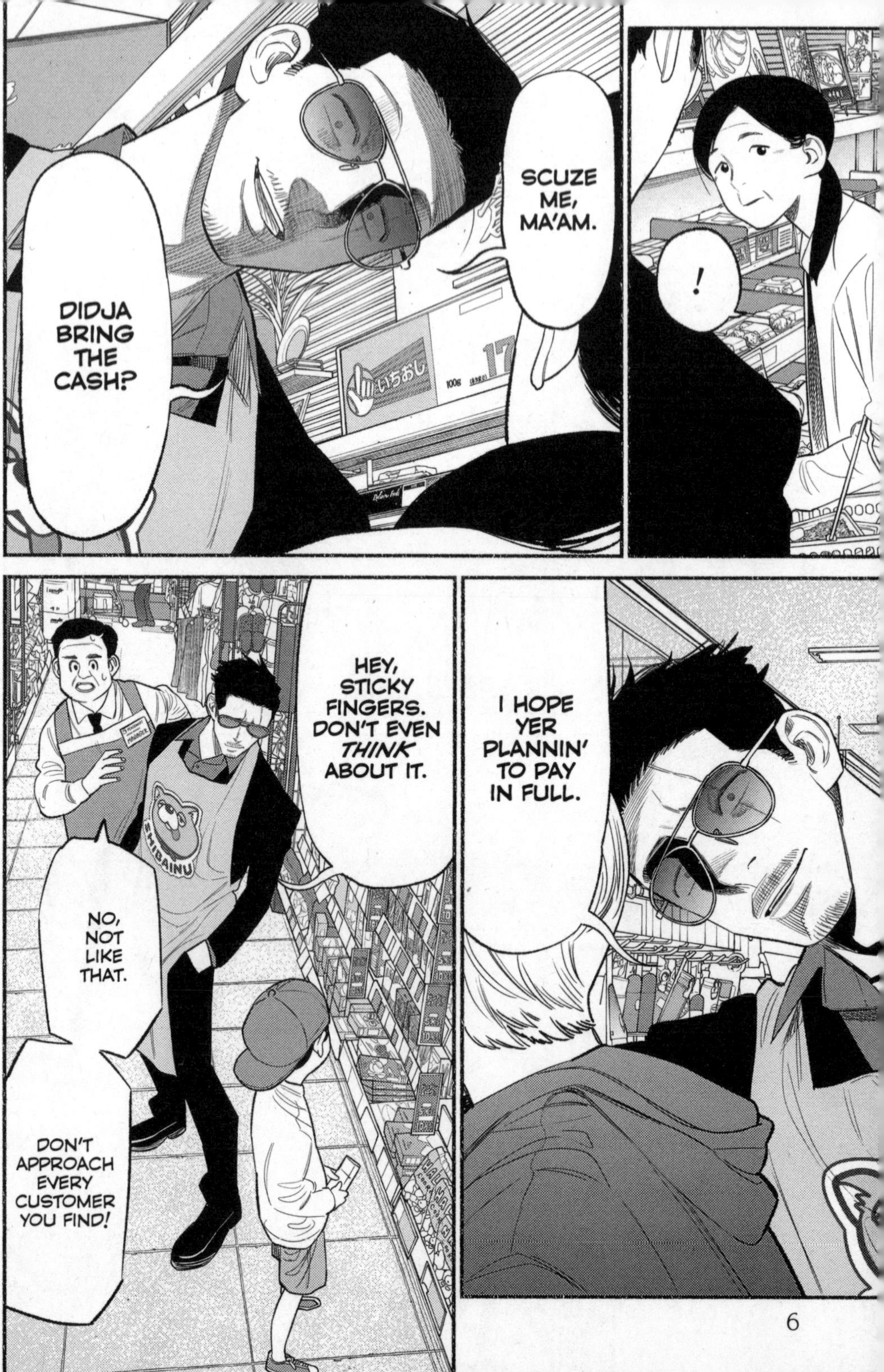
!
SCUZE ME, MA'AM.
いちおし
DIDJA BRING THE CASH?
I HOPE YER PLANNIN' TO PAY IN FULL.
HEY, STICKY FINGERS. DON'T EVEN *THINK* ABOUT IT.
NO, NOT LIKE THAT.
DON'T APPROACH EVERY CUSTOMER YOU FIND!

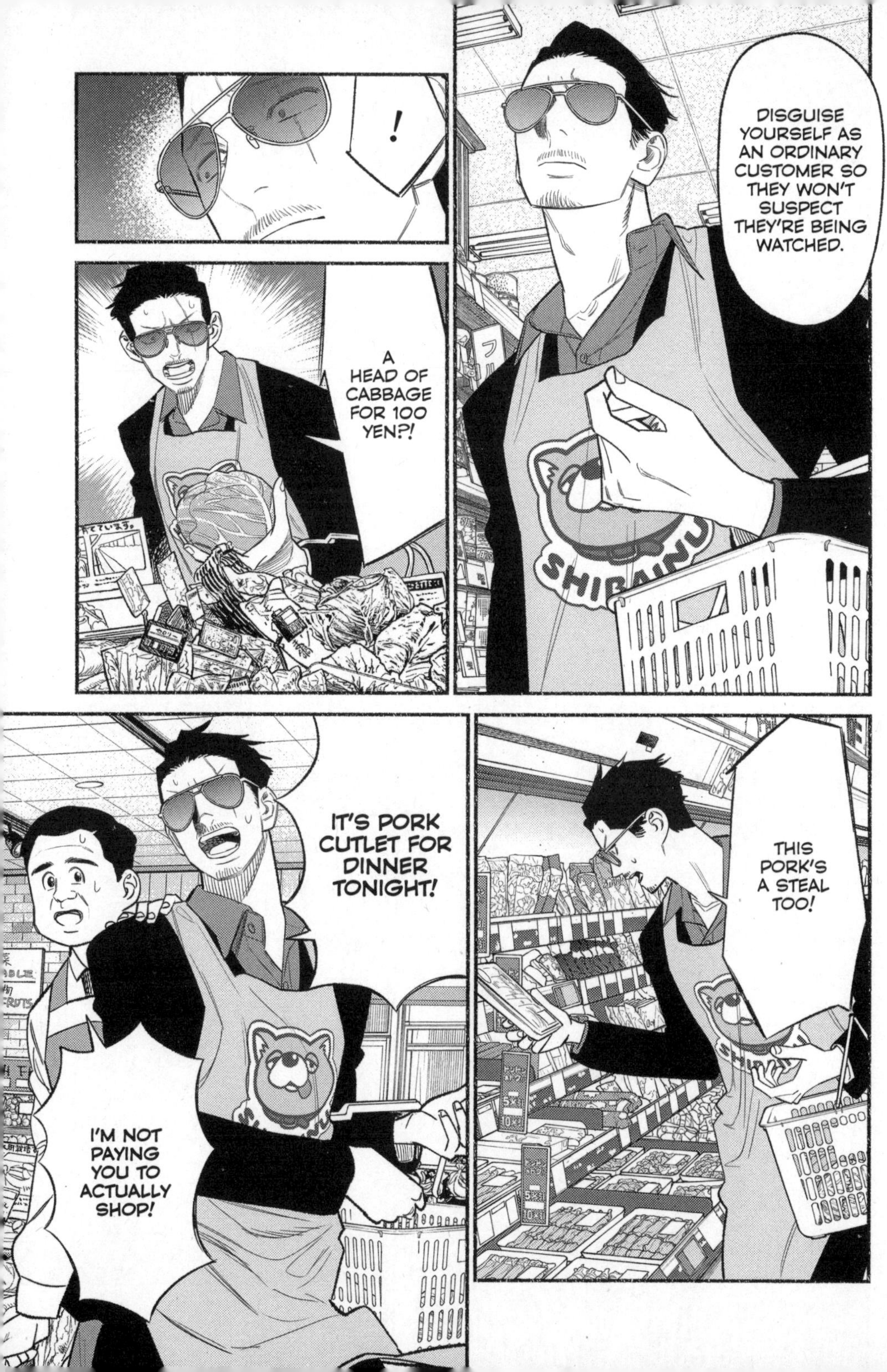

DISGUISE YOURSELF AS AN ORDINARY CUSTOMER SO THEY WON'T SUSPECT THEY'RE BEING WATCHED.
!
A HEAD OF CABBAGE FOR 100 YEN?!
THIS PORK'S A STEAL TOO!
IT'S PORK CUTLET FOR DINNER TONIGHT!
I'M NOT PAYING YOU TO ACTUALLY SHOP!

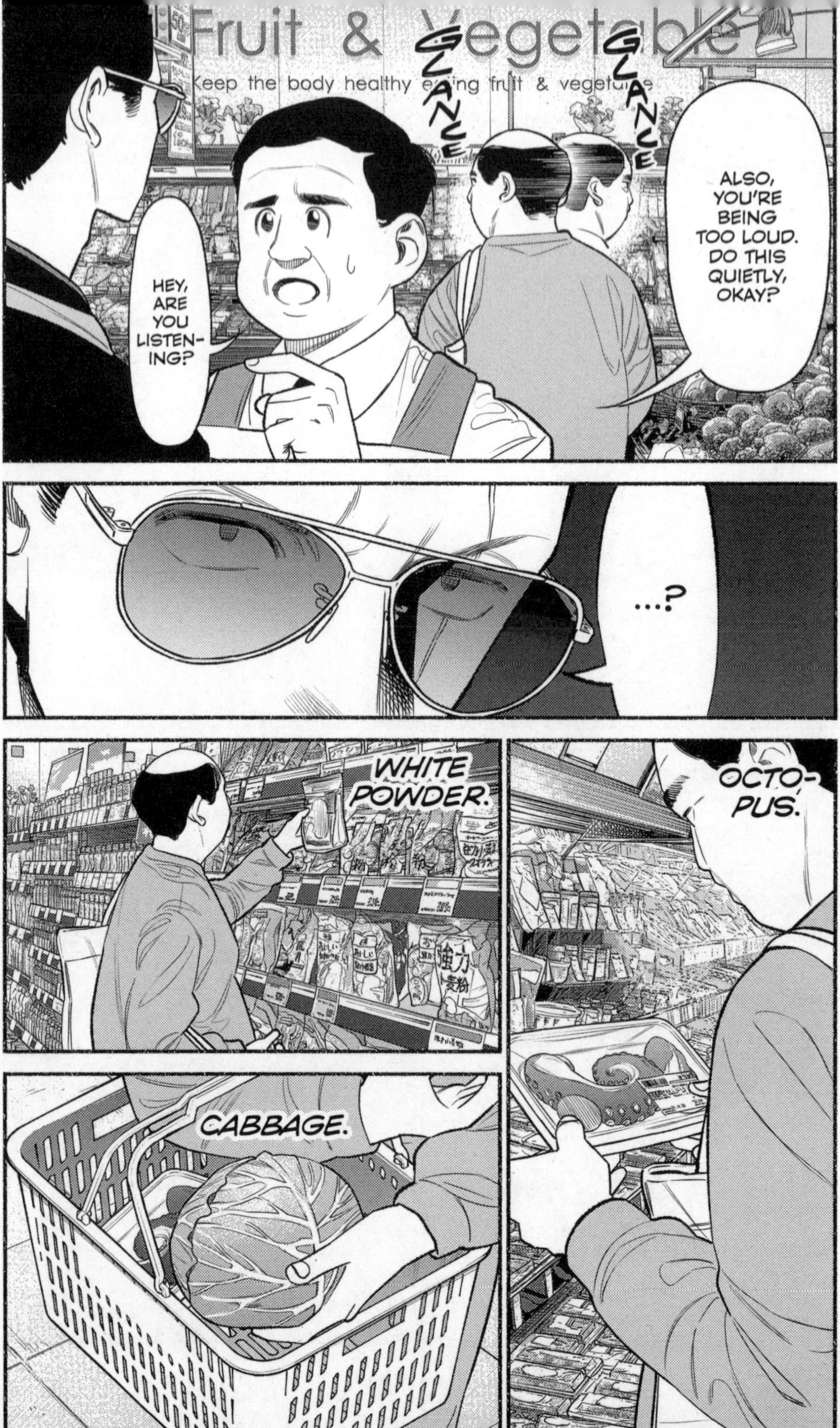
Fruit &
GLANCE
GLANCE
ALSO, YOU'RE BEING TOO LOUD. DO THIS QUIETLY, OKAY?
HEY, ARE YOU LISTENING?
...?
OCTO-PUS.
WHITE POWDER.
CABBAGE.

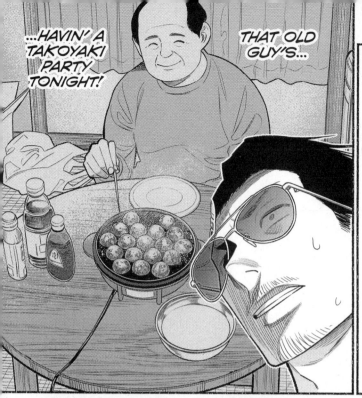

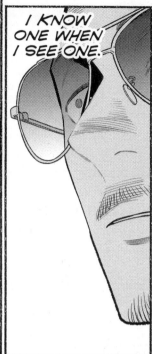

I KNOW ONE WHEN I SEE ONE.
THAT OLD GUY'S...
...HAVIN' A TAKOYAKI PARTY TONIGHT!
HUH?
HIS BASKET'S EMPTY ALL OF A SUDDEN.
HIS BAG...
WAS IT THAT FULL BEFORE?

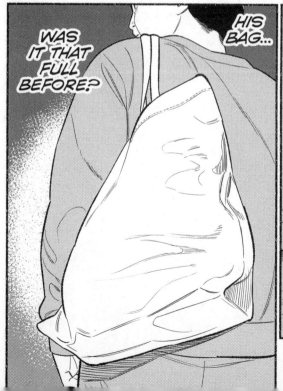

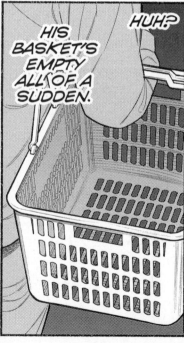

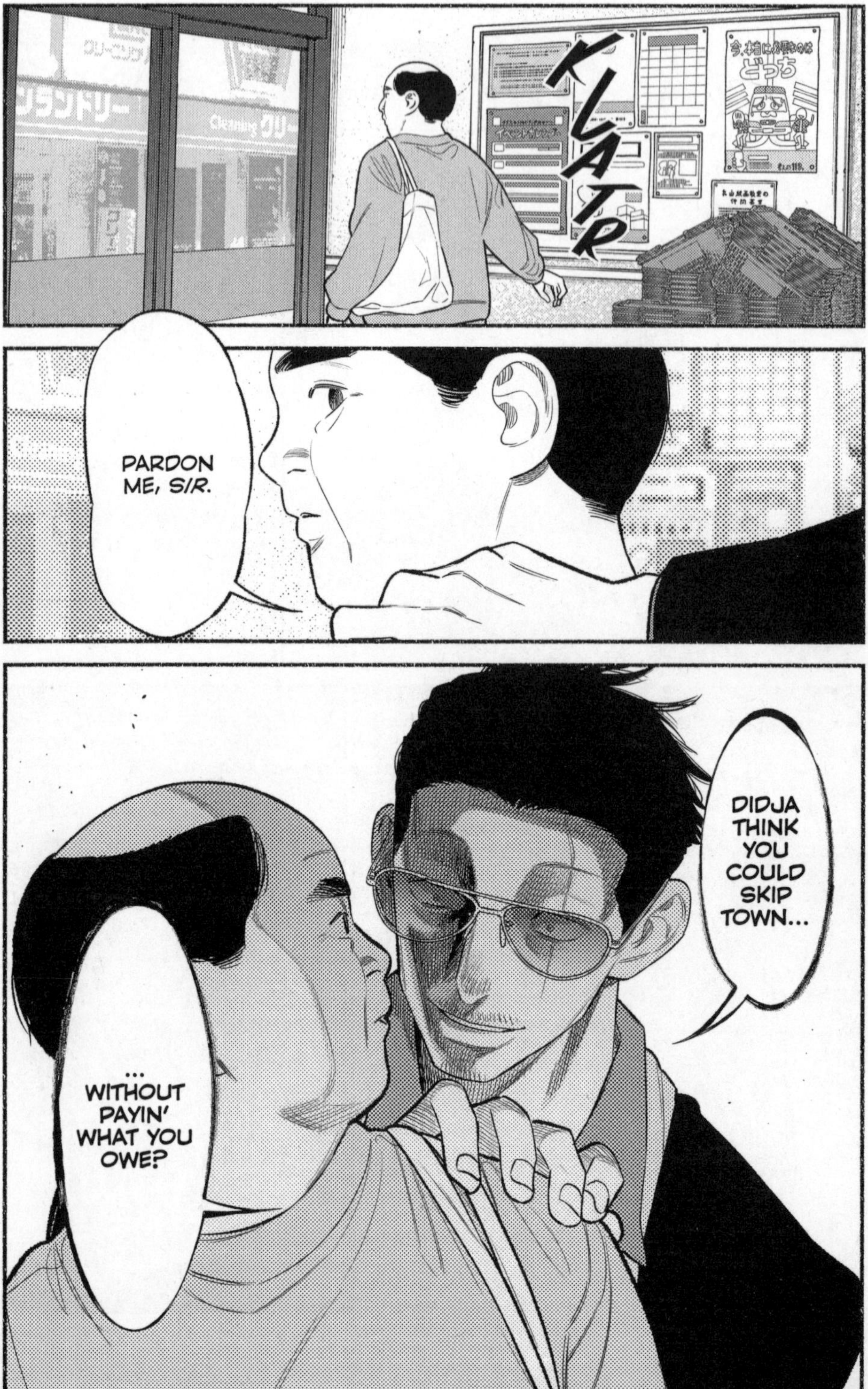
KLATR
PARDON ME, SIR.
DIDJA THINK YOU COULD SKIP TOWN...
...WITHOUT PAYIN' WHAT YOU OWE?

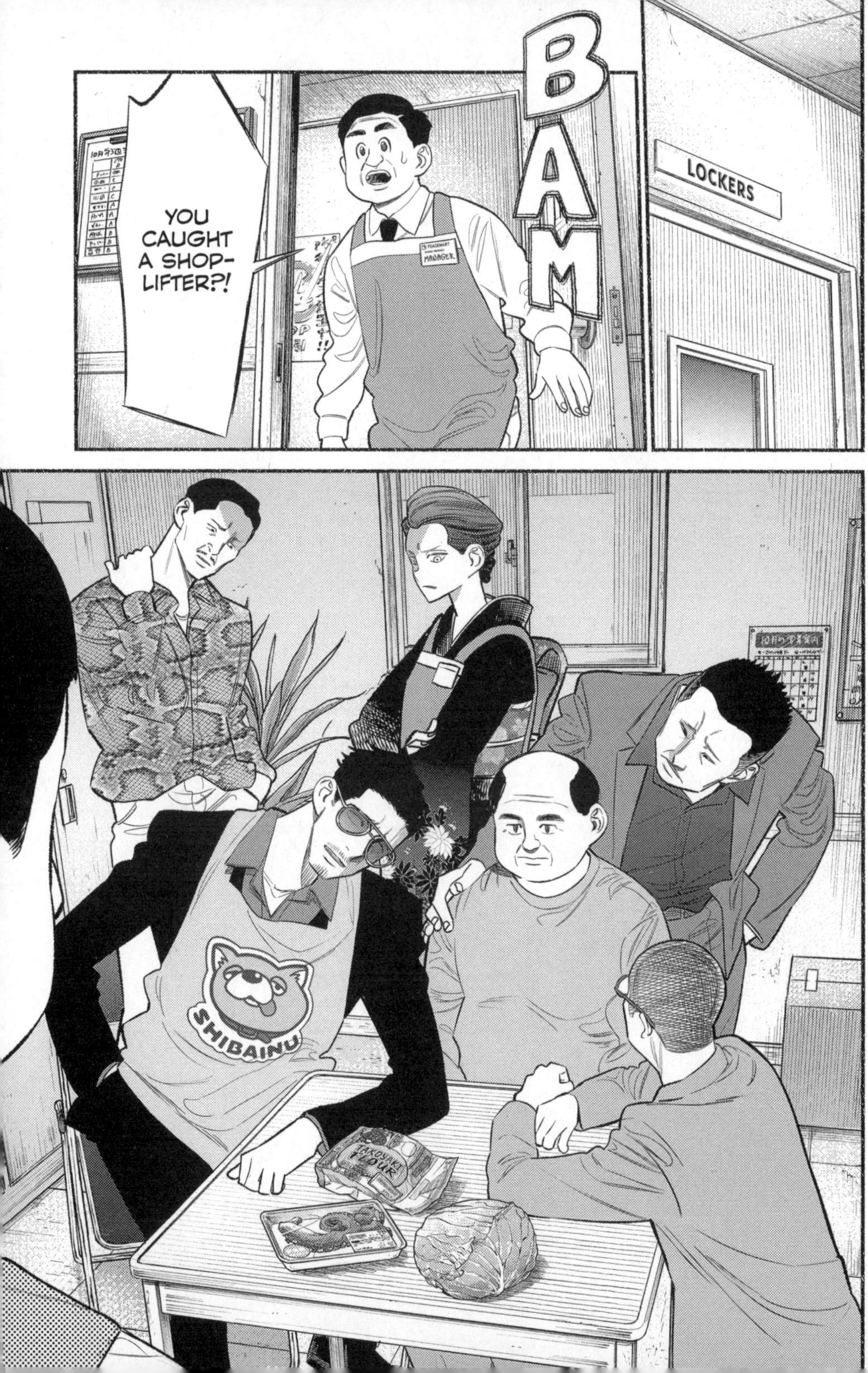
LOCKERS
BAM
YOU CAUGHT A SHOP-LIFTER?!
PEACEMART
MANAGER
SHIBAINU
TAKOYAKI FLOUR

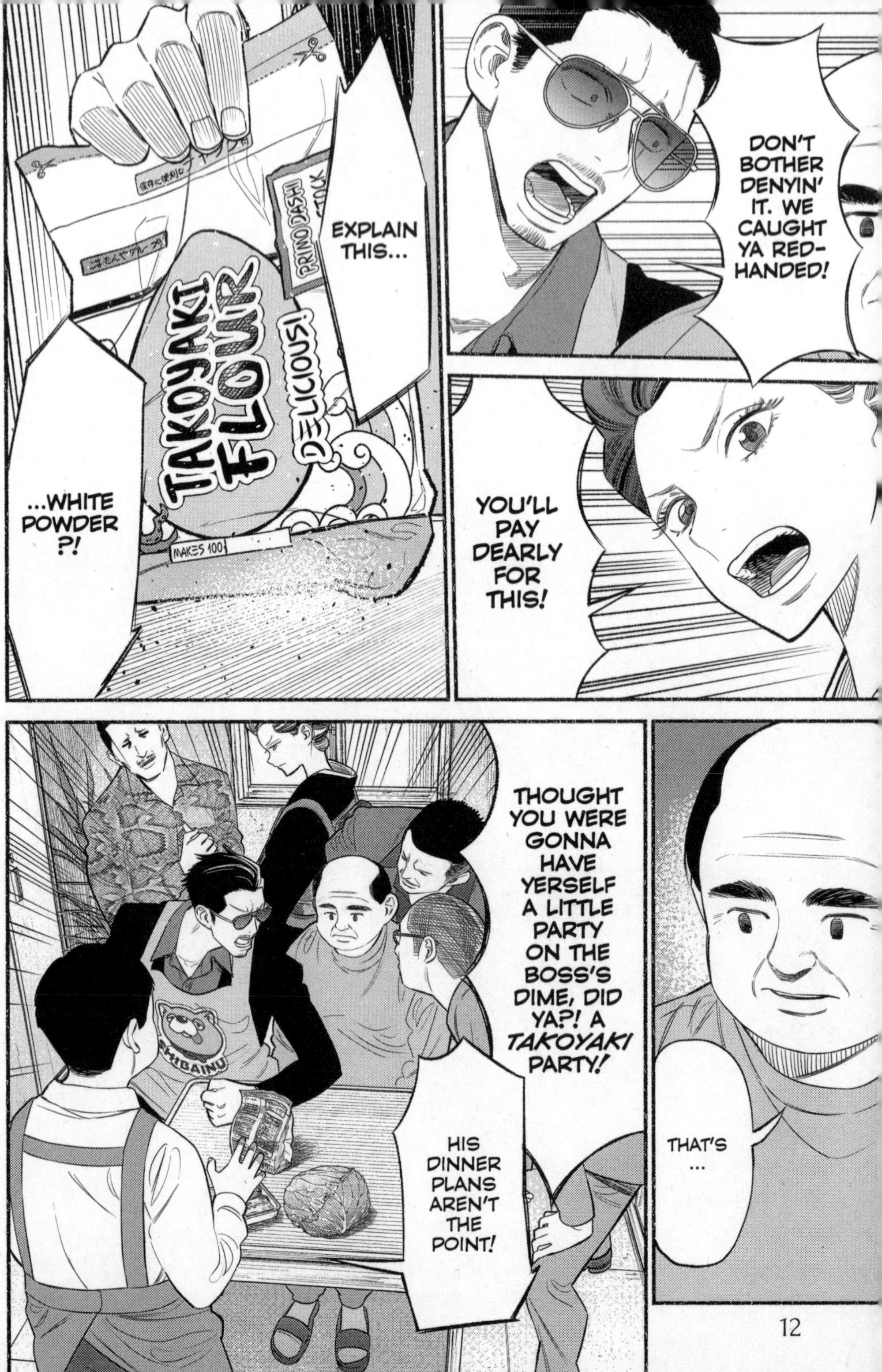
DON'T BOTHER DENYIN' IT. WE CAUGHT YA RED-HANDED!
YOU'LL PAY DEARLY FOR THIS!
EXPLAIN THIS...
PRIMO DASHI STOCK
TAKOYAKI FLOUR
DELICIOUS!
MAKES 100
...WHITE POWDER?!
THAT'S ...
THOUGHT YOU WERE GONNA HAVE YERSELF A LITTLE PARTY ON THE BOSS'S DIME, DID YA?! A *TAKOYAKI* PARTY!
SHIBAINU
HIS DINNER PLANS AREN'T THE POINT!

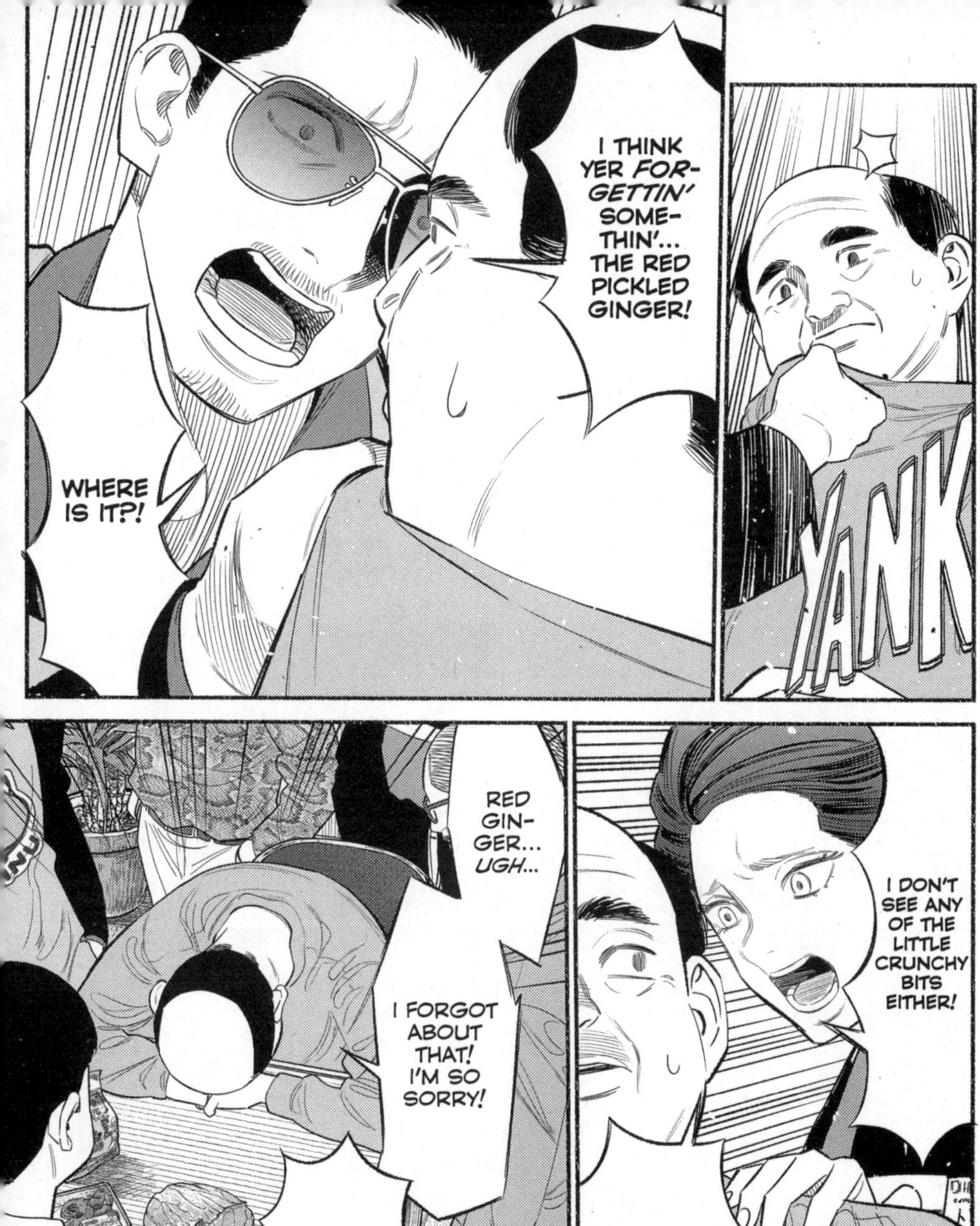
YANK
I THINK YER *FORGETTIN'* SOMETHIN'... THE RED PICKLED GINGER!
WHERE IS IT?!
I DON'T SEE ANY OF THE LITTLE CRUNCHY BITS EITHER!
ARE YOU MOCKING TAKOYAKI?!
RED GINGER... *UGH*...
I FORGOT ABOUT THAT! I'M SO SORRY!
LOOK, CAN WE JUST MOVE ON FROM THE TAKOYAKI?!

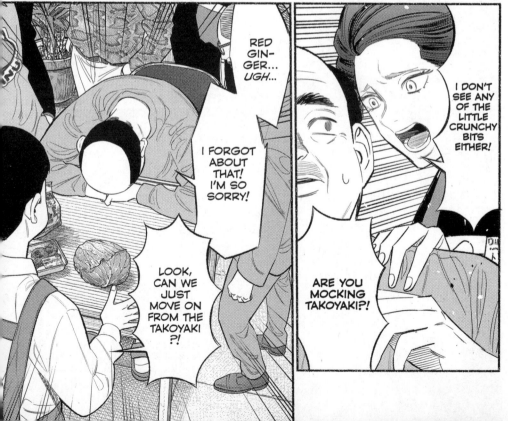

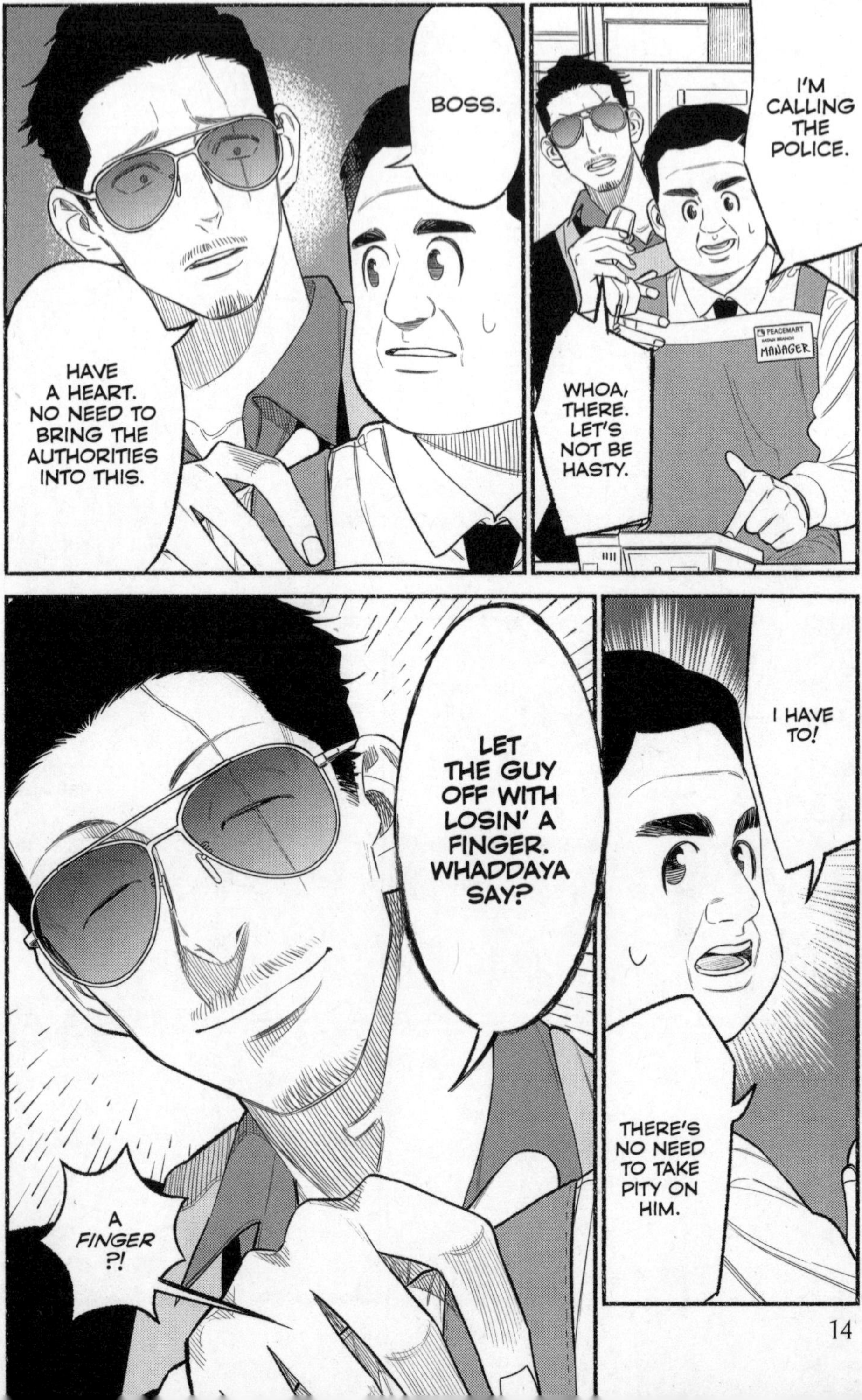
I'M CALLING THE POLICE.
PEACEMART
MANAGER
WHOA, THERE. LET'S NOT BE HASTY.
BOSS.
HAVE A HEART. NO NEED TO BRING THE AUTHORITIES INTO THIS.
I HAVE TO!
THERE'S NO NEED TO TAKE PITY ON HIM.
LET THE GUY OFF WITH LOSIN' A FINGER. WHADDAYA SAY?
A FINGER?!

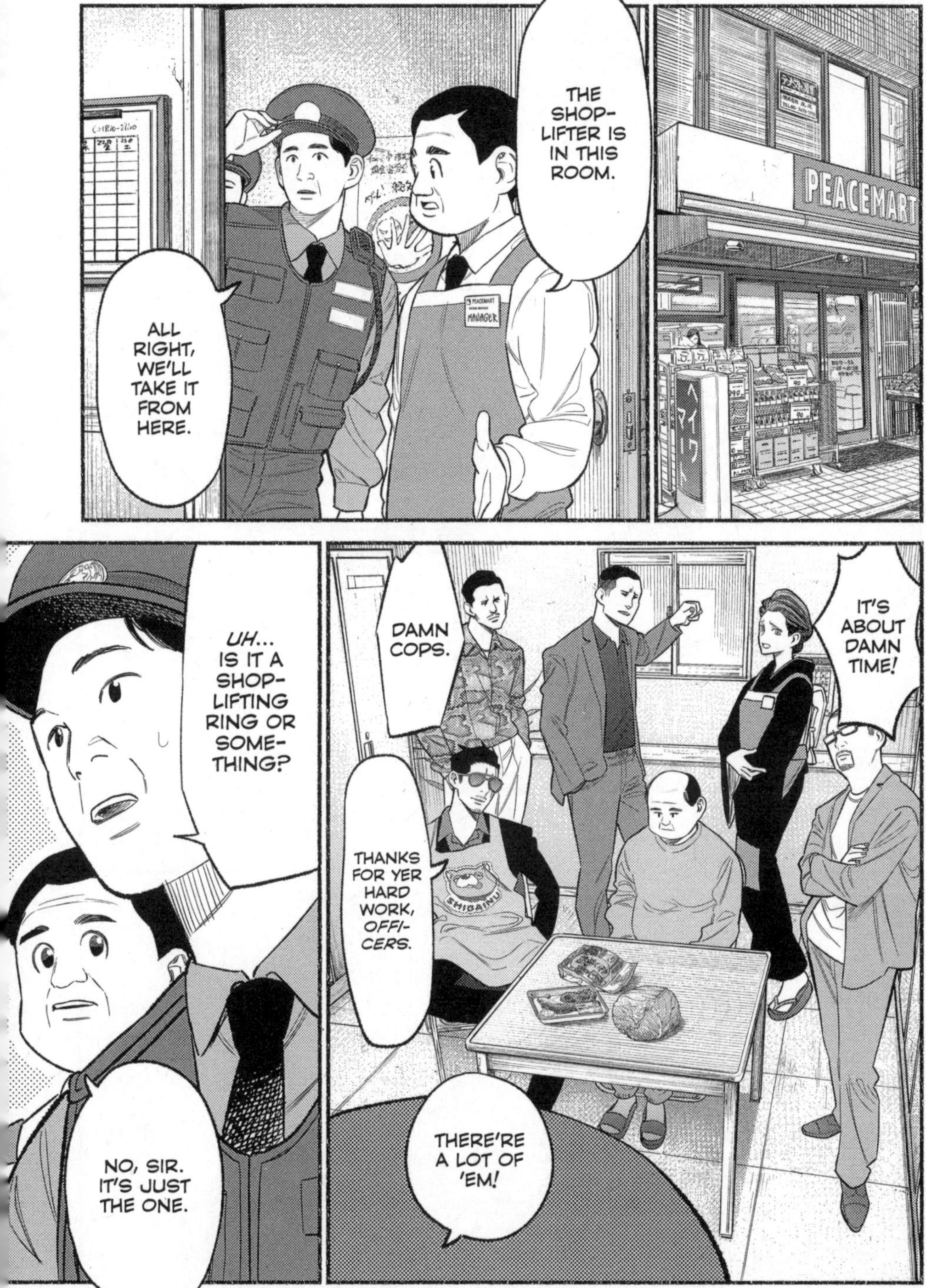
PEACEMART
THE SHOP-LIFTER IS IN THIS ROOM.
MANAGER
ALL RIGHT, WE'LL TAKE IT FROM HERE.
IT'S ABOUT DAMN TIME!
DAMN COPS.
SHIBAINU
THANKS FOR YER HARD WORK, OFFICERS.
THERE'RE A LOT OF 'EM!
UH... IS IT A SHOP-LIFTING RING OR SOME-THING?
NO, SIR. IT'S JUST THE ONE.

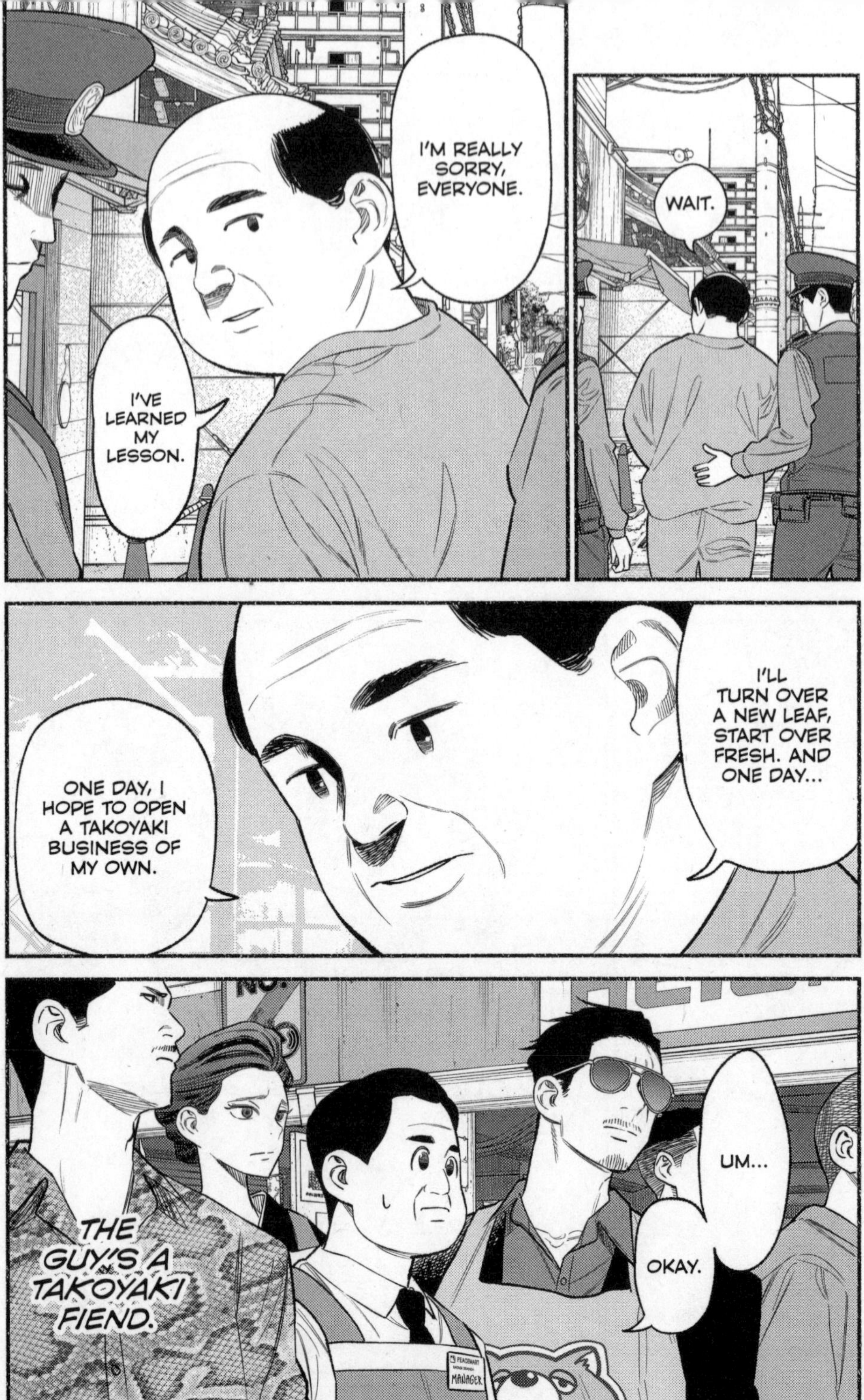
WAIT.
I'M REALLY SORRY, EVERYONE.
I'VE LEARNED MY LESSON.
I'LL TURN OVER A NEW LEAF, START OVER FRESH. AND ONE DAY...
ONE DAY, I HOPE TO OPEN A TAKOYAKI BUSINESS OF MY OWN.
UM...
OKAY.
THE GUY'S A TAKOYAKI FIEND.

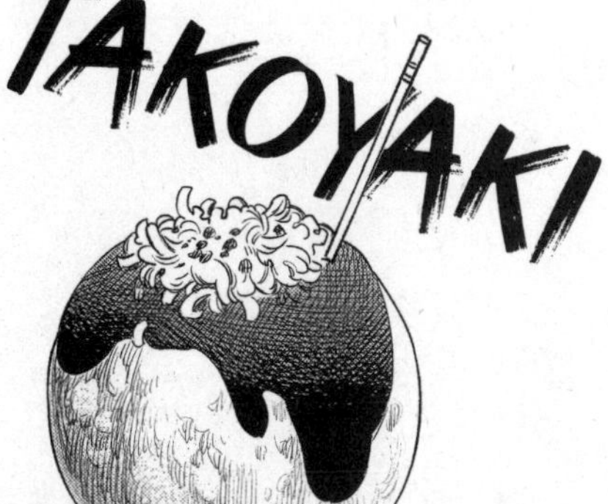
TAKOYAKI

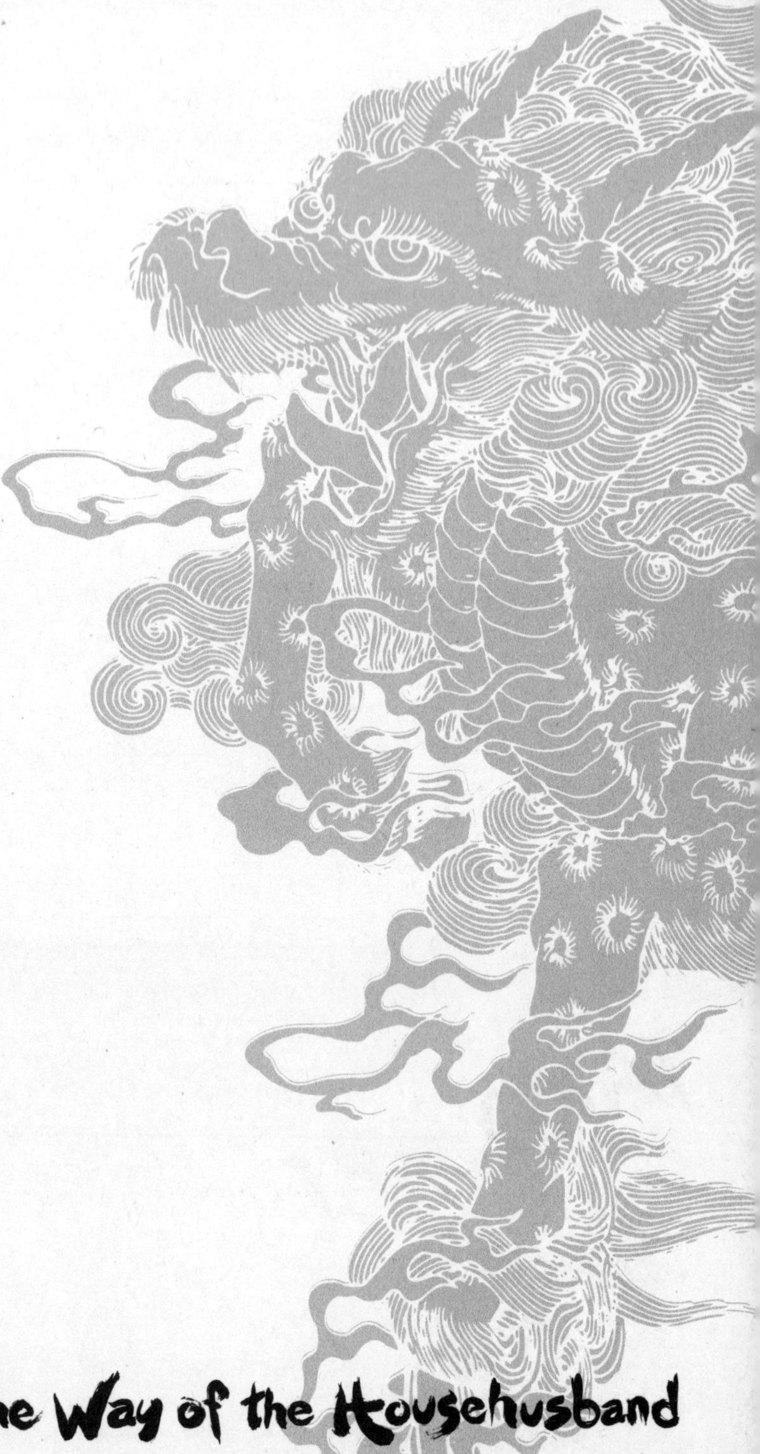

The Way of the Househusband

CHAPTER 83

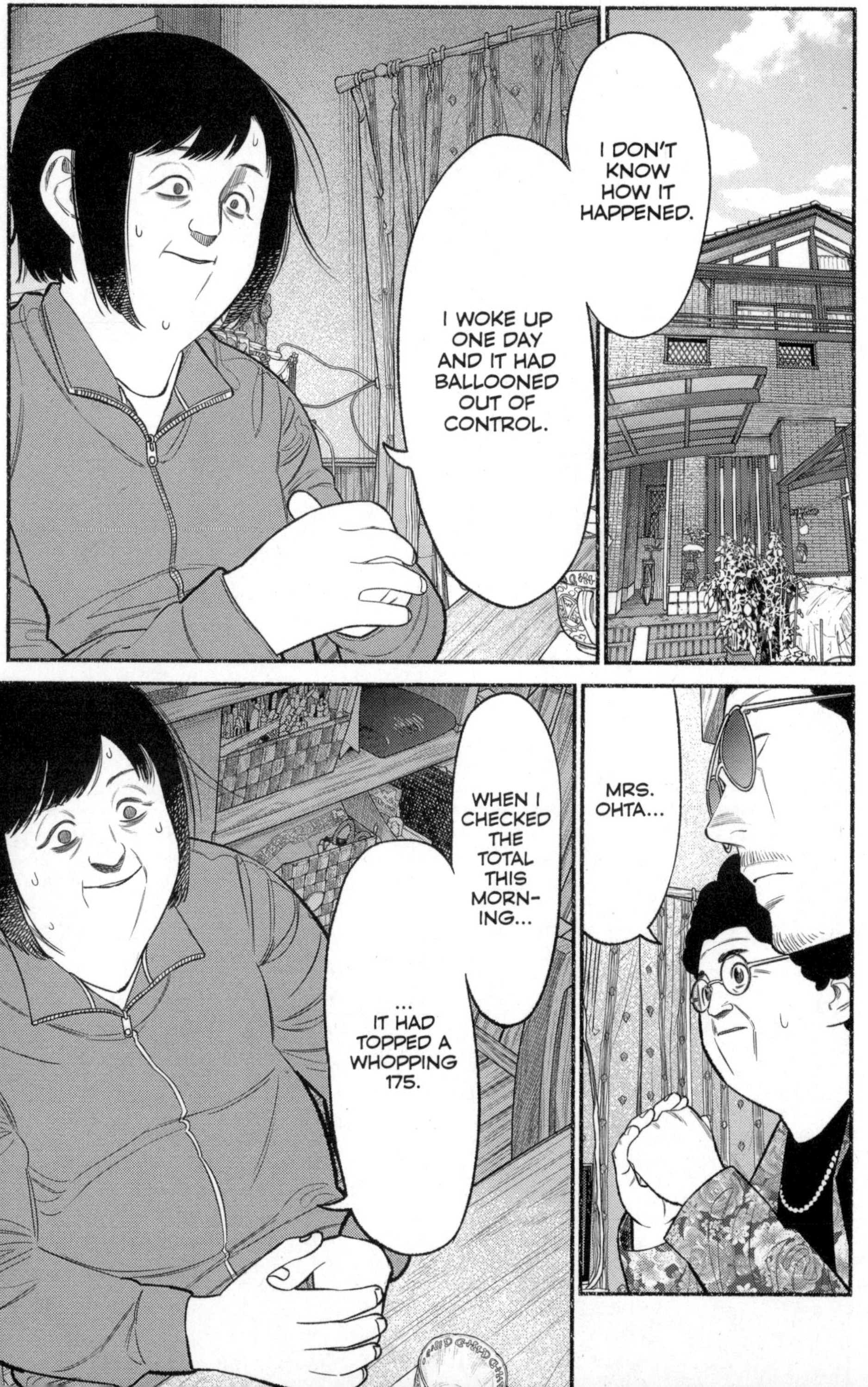
I DON'T KNOW HOW IT HAPPENED.
I WOKE UP ONE DAY AND IT HAD BALLOONED OUT OF CONTROL.
MRS. OHTA...
WHEN I CHECKED THE TOTAL THIS MORN-ING...
... IT HAD TOPPED A WHOPPING 175.

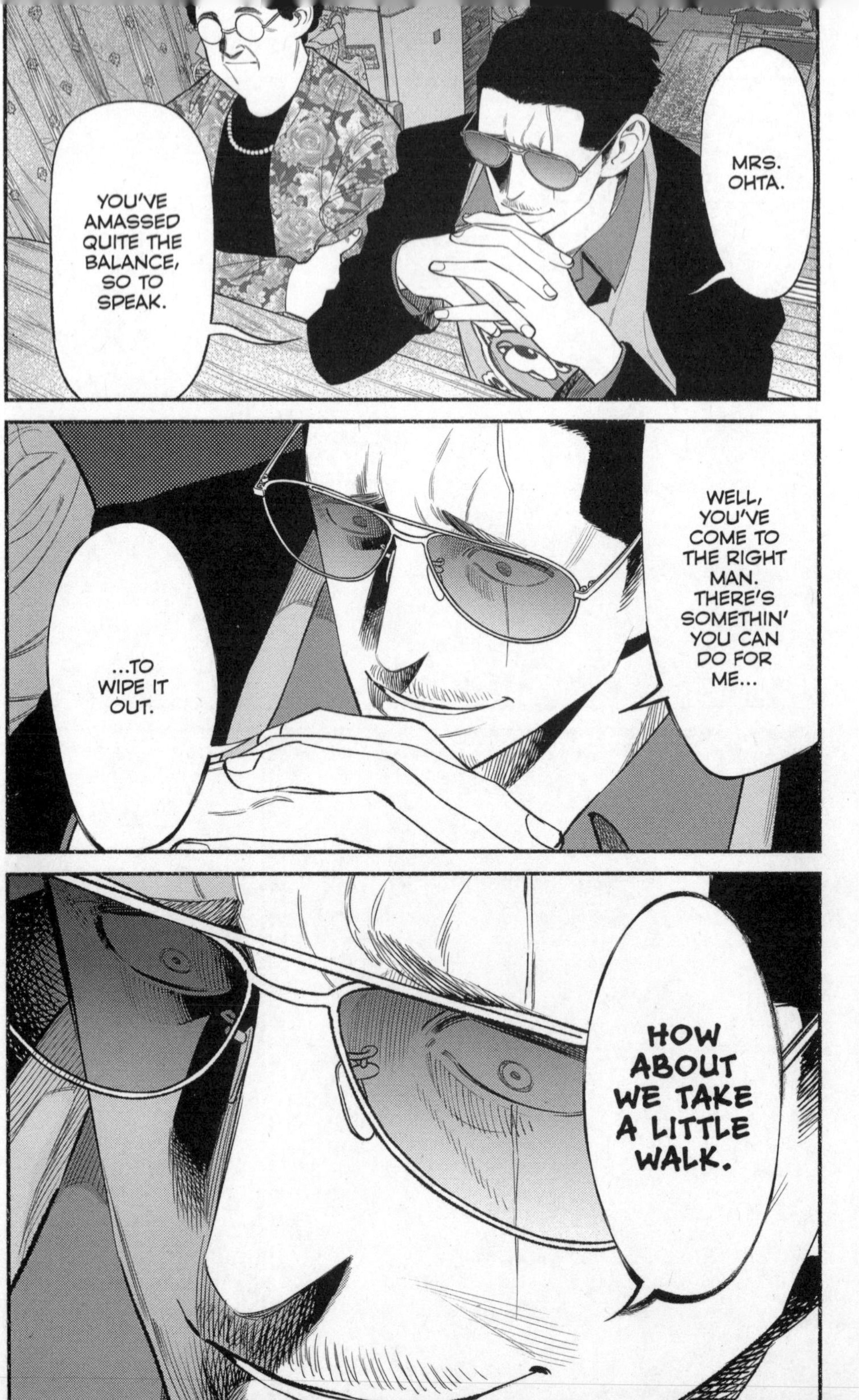
MRS. OHTA.
YOU'VE AMASSED QUITE THE BALANCE, SO TO SPEAK.
WELL, YOU'VE COME TO THE RIGHT MAN. THERE'S SOMETHIN' YOU CAN DO FOR ME...
...TO WIPE IT OUT.
HOW ABOUT WE TAKE A LITTLE WALK.

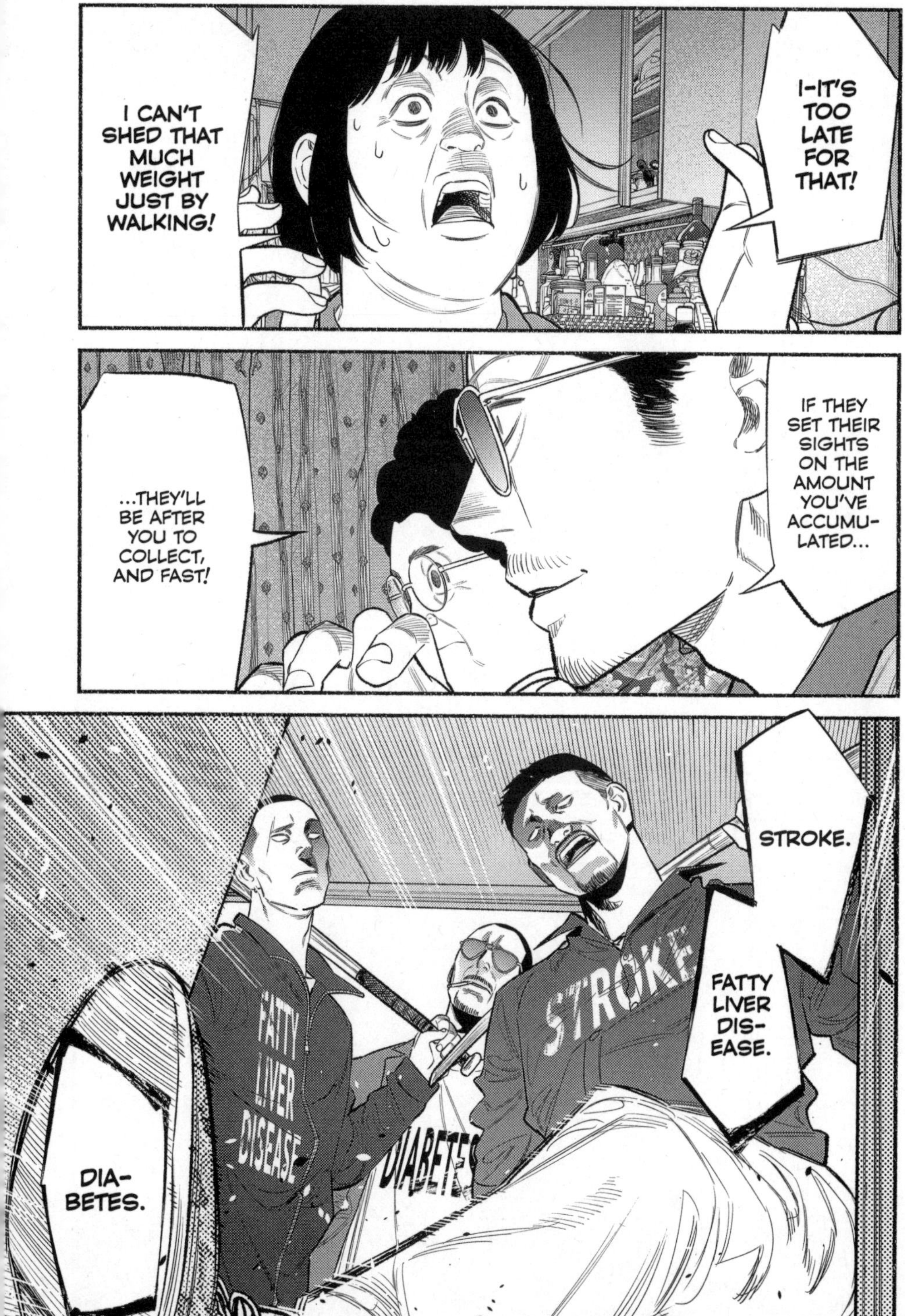
I-IT'S TOO LATE FOR THAT!
I CAN'T SHED THAT MUCH WEIGHT JUST BY WALKING!
IF THEY SET THEIR SIGHTS ON THE AMOUNT YOU'VE ACCUMU-LATED...
...THEY'LL BE AFTER YOU TO COLLECT, AND FAST!
STROKE.
STROKE
FATTY LIVER DIS-EASE.
FATTY LIVER DISEASE
DIA-BETES.

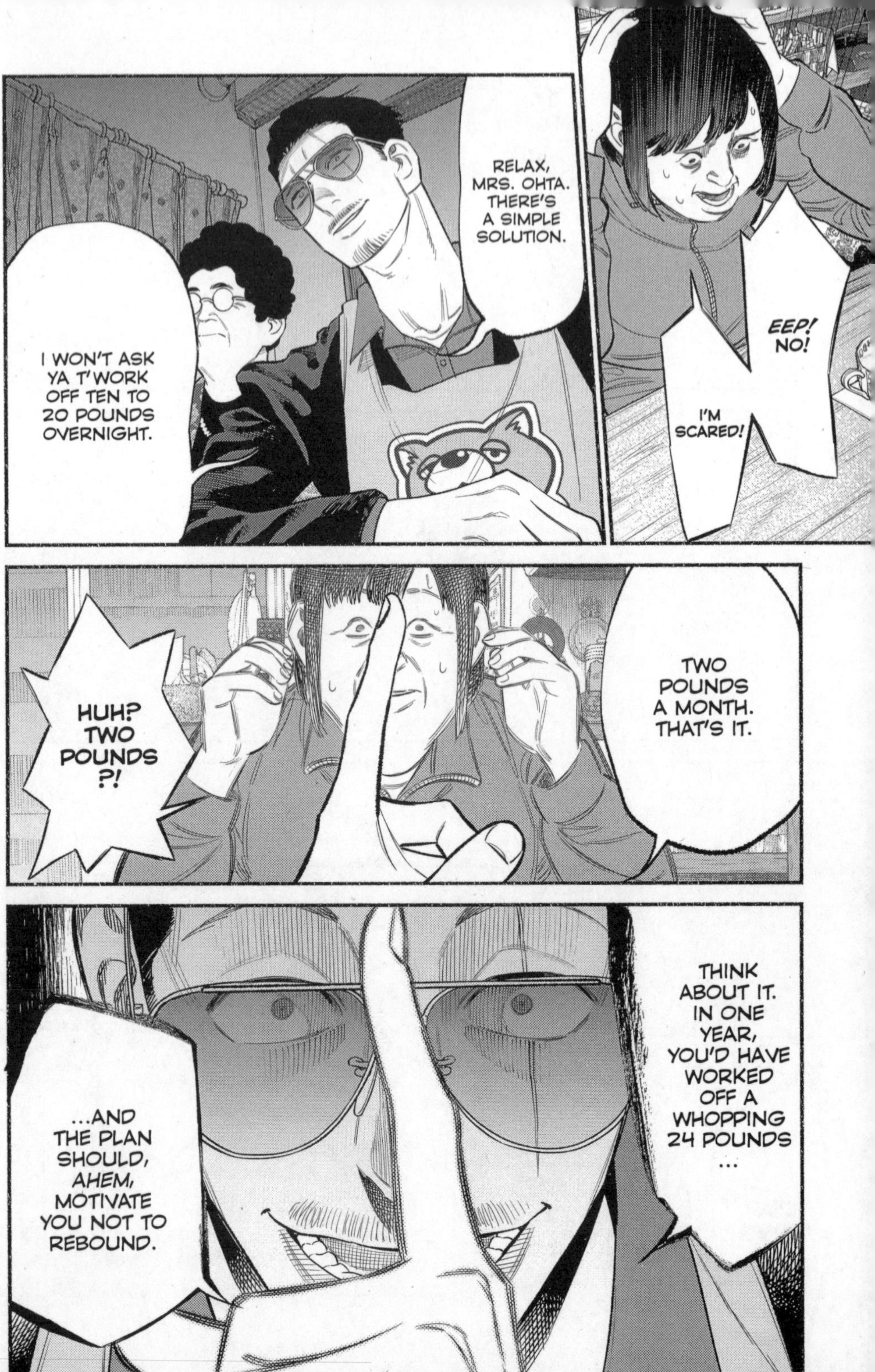
EEP! NO!
I'M SCARED!
RELAX, MRS. OHTA. THERE'S A SIMPLE SOLUTION.
I WON'T ASK YA T'WORK OFF TEN TO 20 POUNDS OVERNIGHT.
TWO POUNDS A MONTH. THAT'S IT.
HUH? TWO POUNDS?!
THINK ABOUT IT. IN ONE YEAR, YOU'D HAVE WORKED OFF A WHOPPING 24 POUNDS...
...AND THE PLAN SHOULD, AHEM, MOTIVATE YOU NOT TO REBOUND.

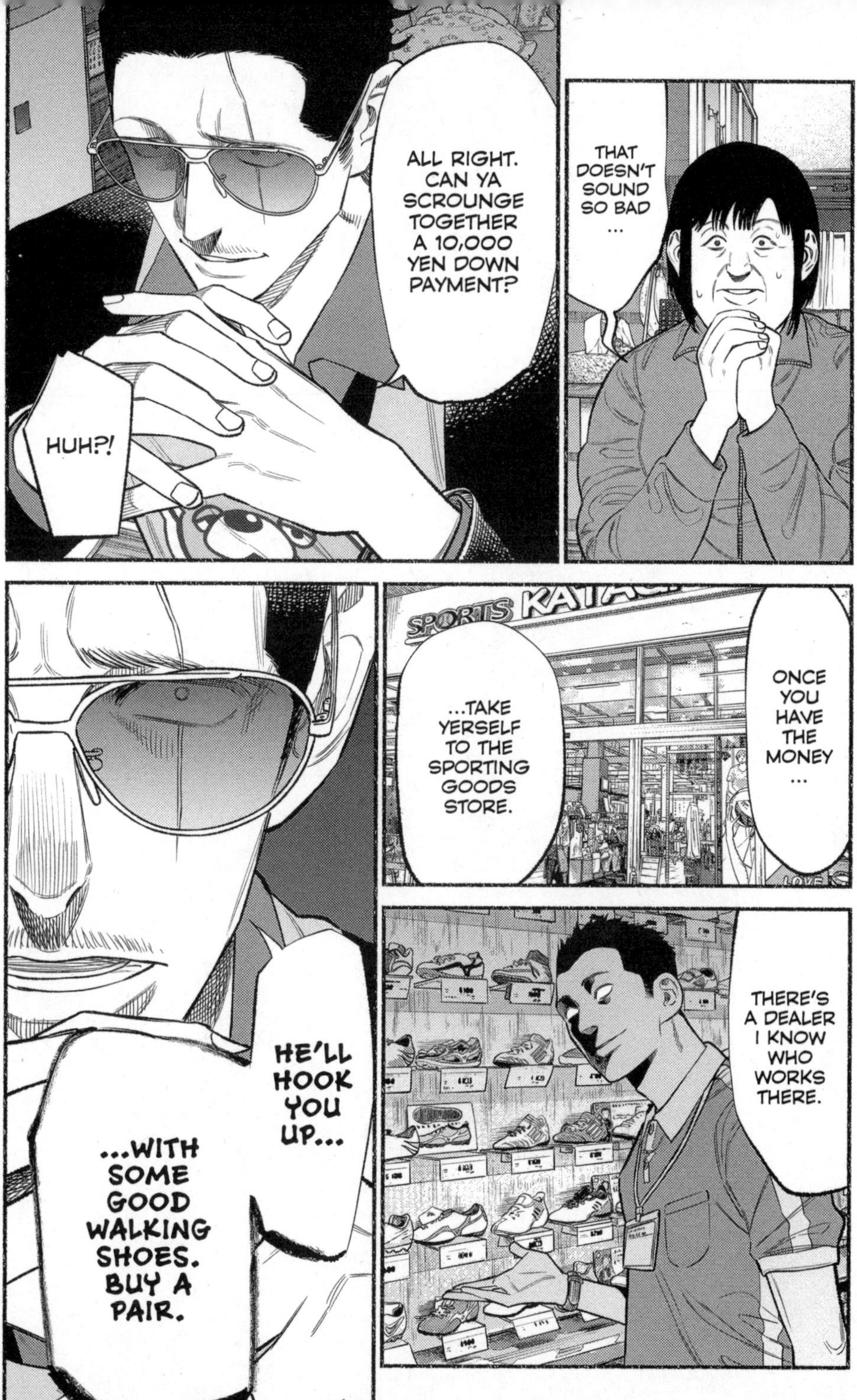
THAT DOESN'T SOUND SO BAD ...
ALL RIGHT. CAN YA SCROUNGE TOGETHER A 10,000 YEN DOWN PAYMENT?
HUH?!
ONCE YOU HAVE THE MONEY ...
...TAKE YERSELF TO THE SPORTING GOODS STORE.
THERE'S A DEALER I KNOW WHO WORKS THERE.
HE'LL HOOK YOU UP...
...WITH SOME GOOD WALKING SHOES. BUY A PAIR.

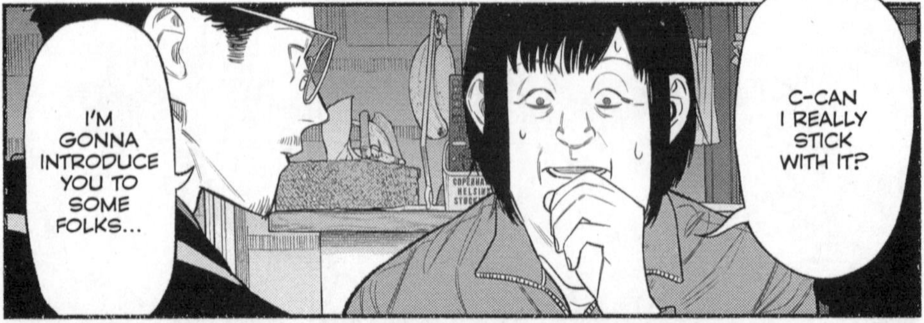
C-CAN I REALLY STICK WITH IT?
I'M GONNA INTRODUCE YOU TO SOME FOLKS...

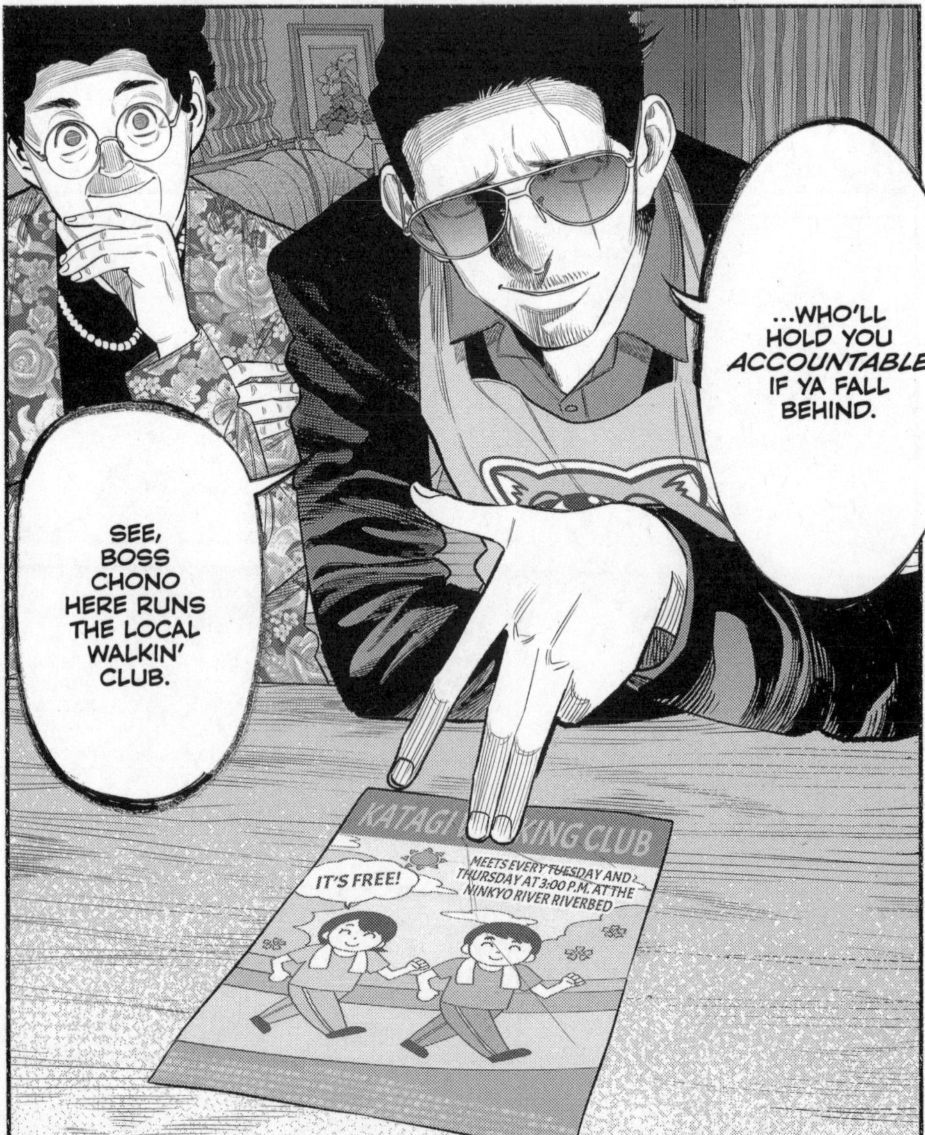
...WHO'LL HOLD YOU *ACCOUNTABLE* IF YA FALL BEHIND.
SEE, BOSS CHONO HERE RUNS THE LOCAL WALKIN' CLUB.
MEETS EVERY TUESDAY AND THURSDAY AT 3:00 P.M. AT THE NINKYO RIVER RIVERBED
IT'S FREE!

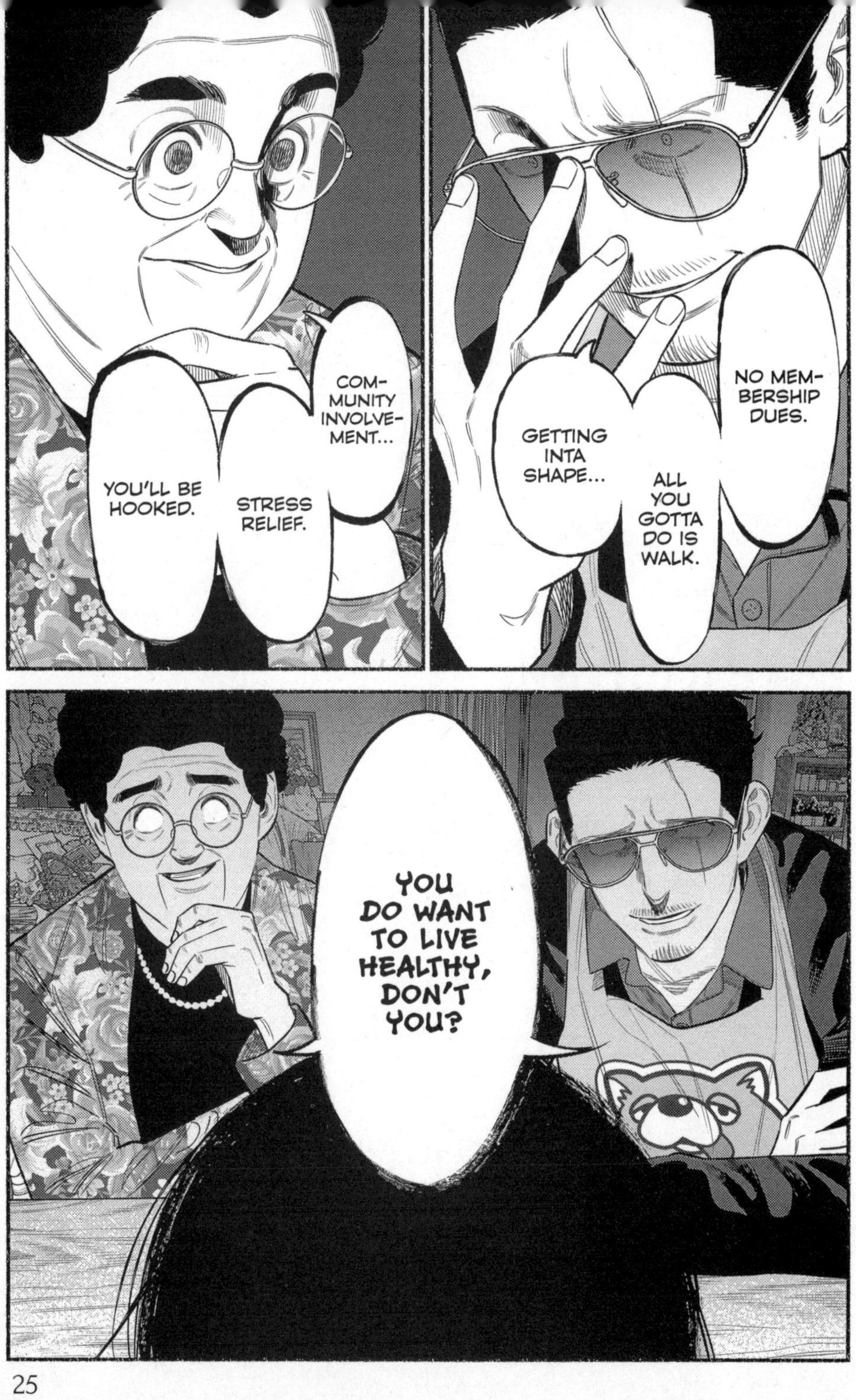
NO MEM-BERSHIP DUES.
ALL YOU GOTTA DO IS WALK.
GETTING INTA SHAPE...
COM-MUNITY INVOLVE-MENT...
STRESS RELIEF.
YOU'LL BE HOOKED.
YOU DO WANT TO LIVE HEALTHY, DON'T YOU?

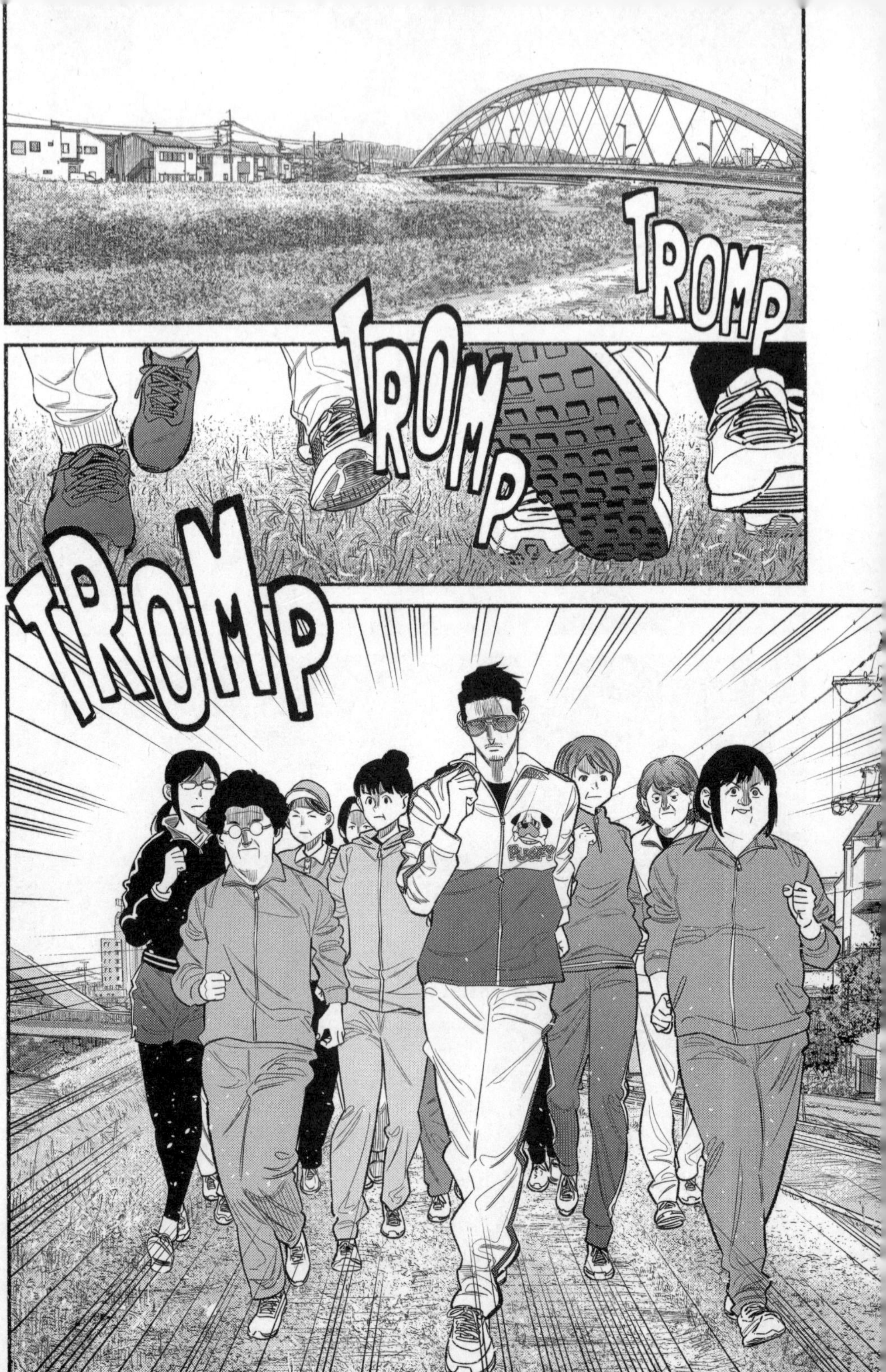
TROMP
TROMP
TROMP
TROMP

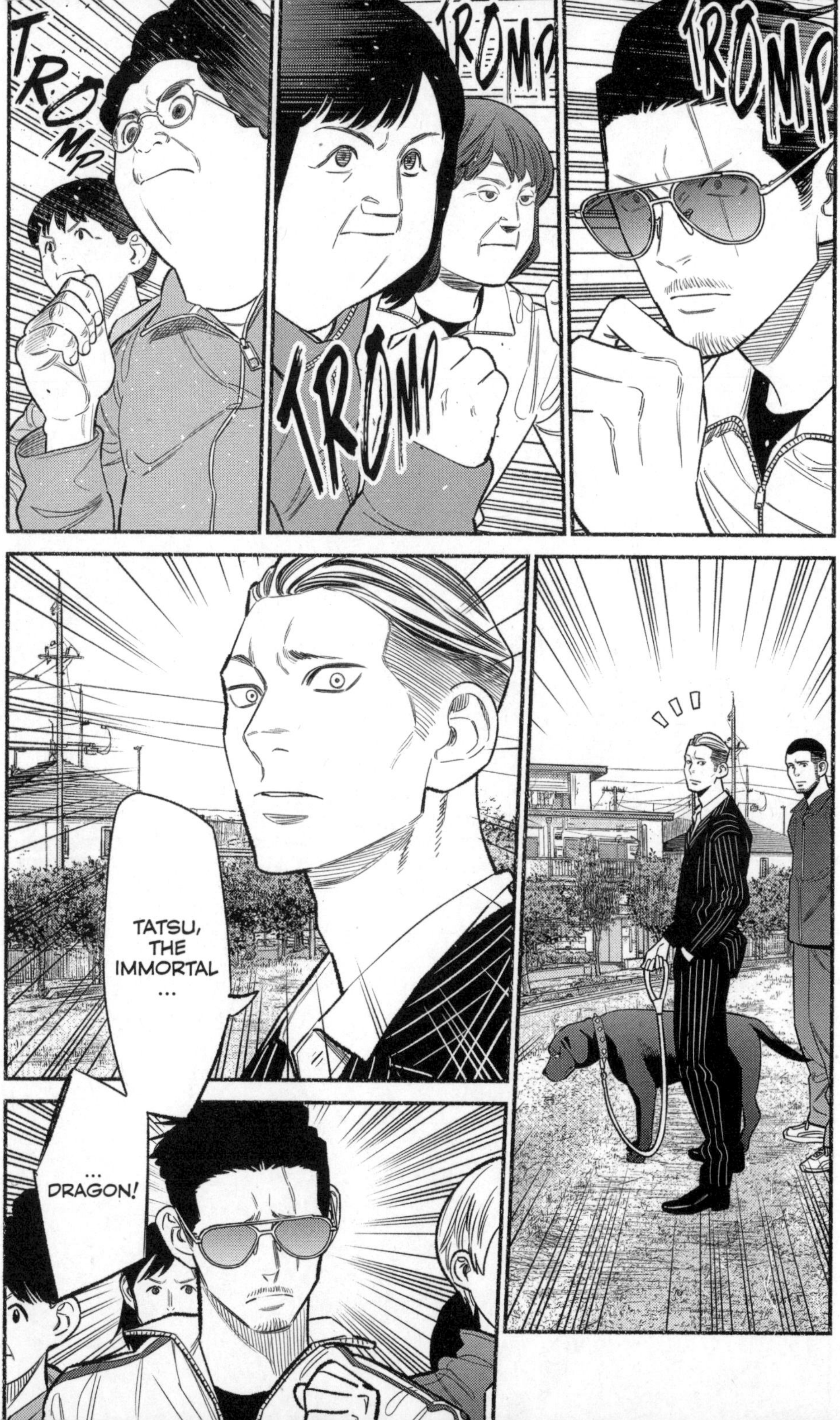
TROMP
TROMP
TROMP
TROMP
TATSU, THE IMMORTAL ...
... DRAGON!

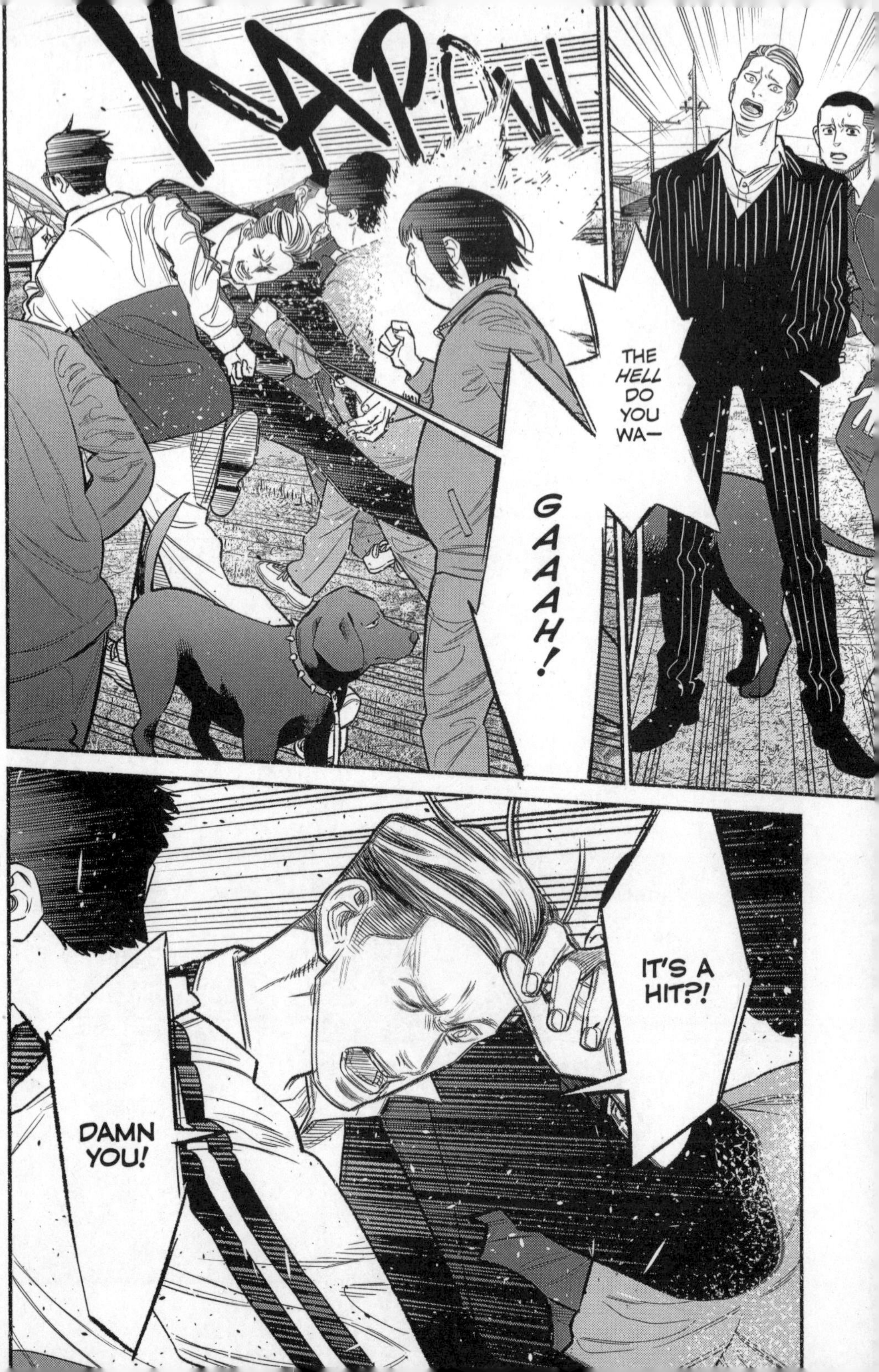
KAPOW
THE HELL DO YOU WA—
GAAAAH!
IT'S A HIT?!
DAMN YOU!

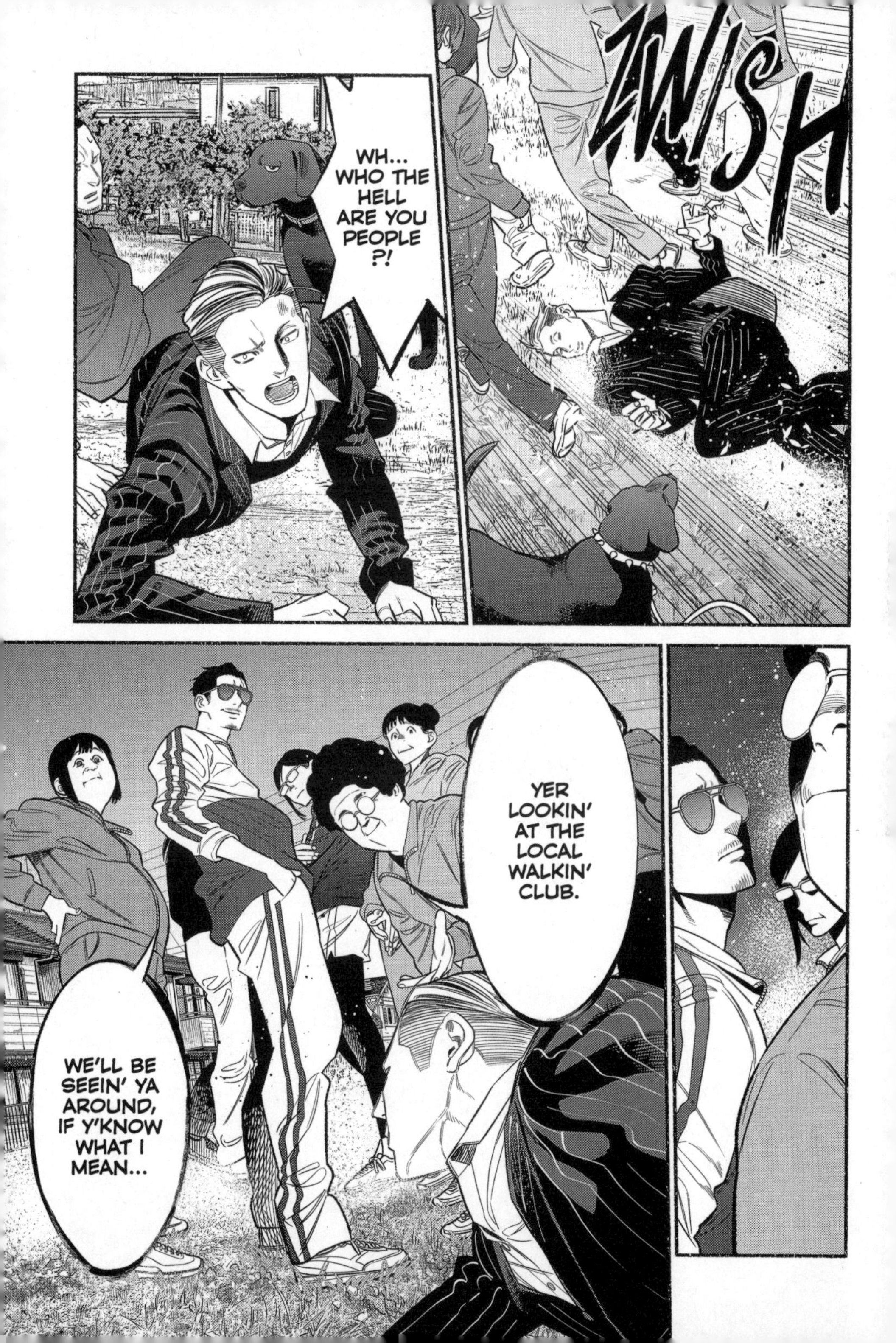
ZWISH
WH... WHO THE HELL ARE YOU PEOPLE ?!
YER LOOKIN' AT THE LOCAL WALKIN' CLUB.
WE'LL BE SEEIN' YA AROUND, IF Y'KNOW WHAT I MEAN...

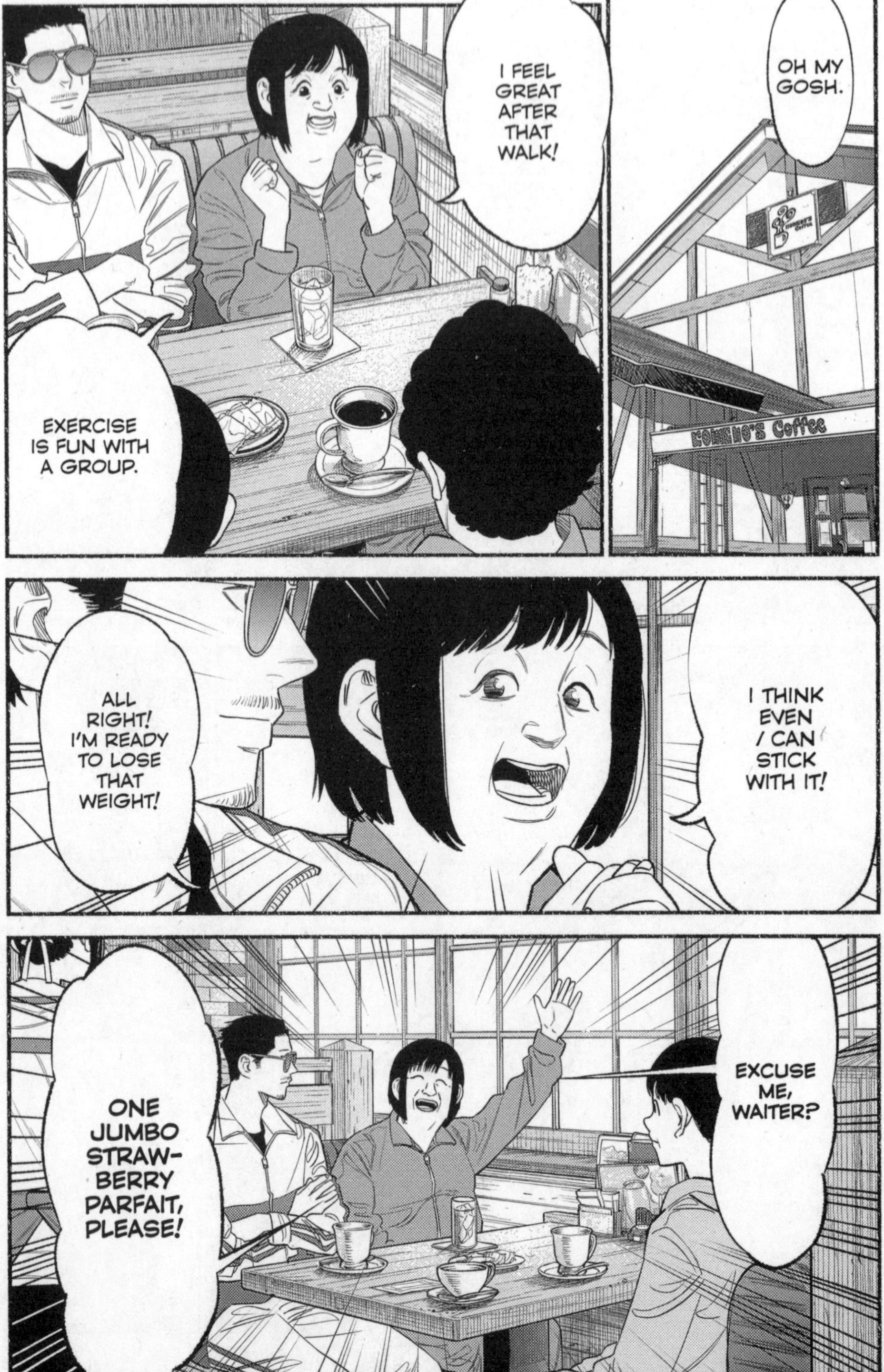
OH MY GOSH.
I FEEL GREAT AFTER THAT WALK!
EXERCISE IS FUN WITH A GROUP.
I THINK EVEN I CAN STICK WITH IT!
ALL RIGHT! I'M READY TO LOSE THAT WEIGHT!
EXCUSE ME, WAITER?
ONE JUMBO STRAW-BERRY PARFAIT, PLEASE!

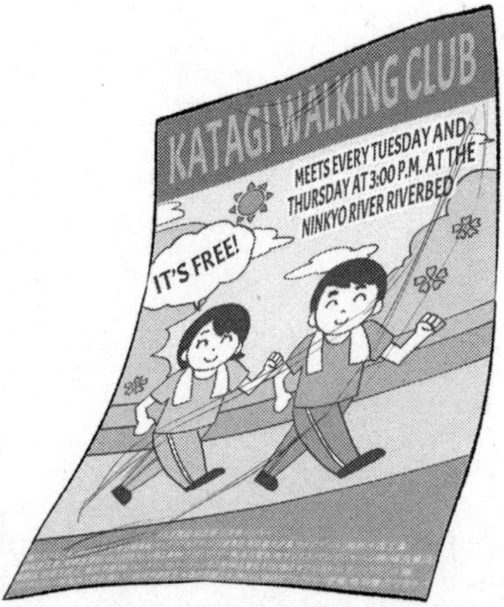
KATAGI WALKING CLUB
MEETS EVERY TUESDAY AND THURSDAY AT 3:00 P.M. AT THE NINKYO RIVER RIVERBED
IT'S FREE!

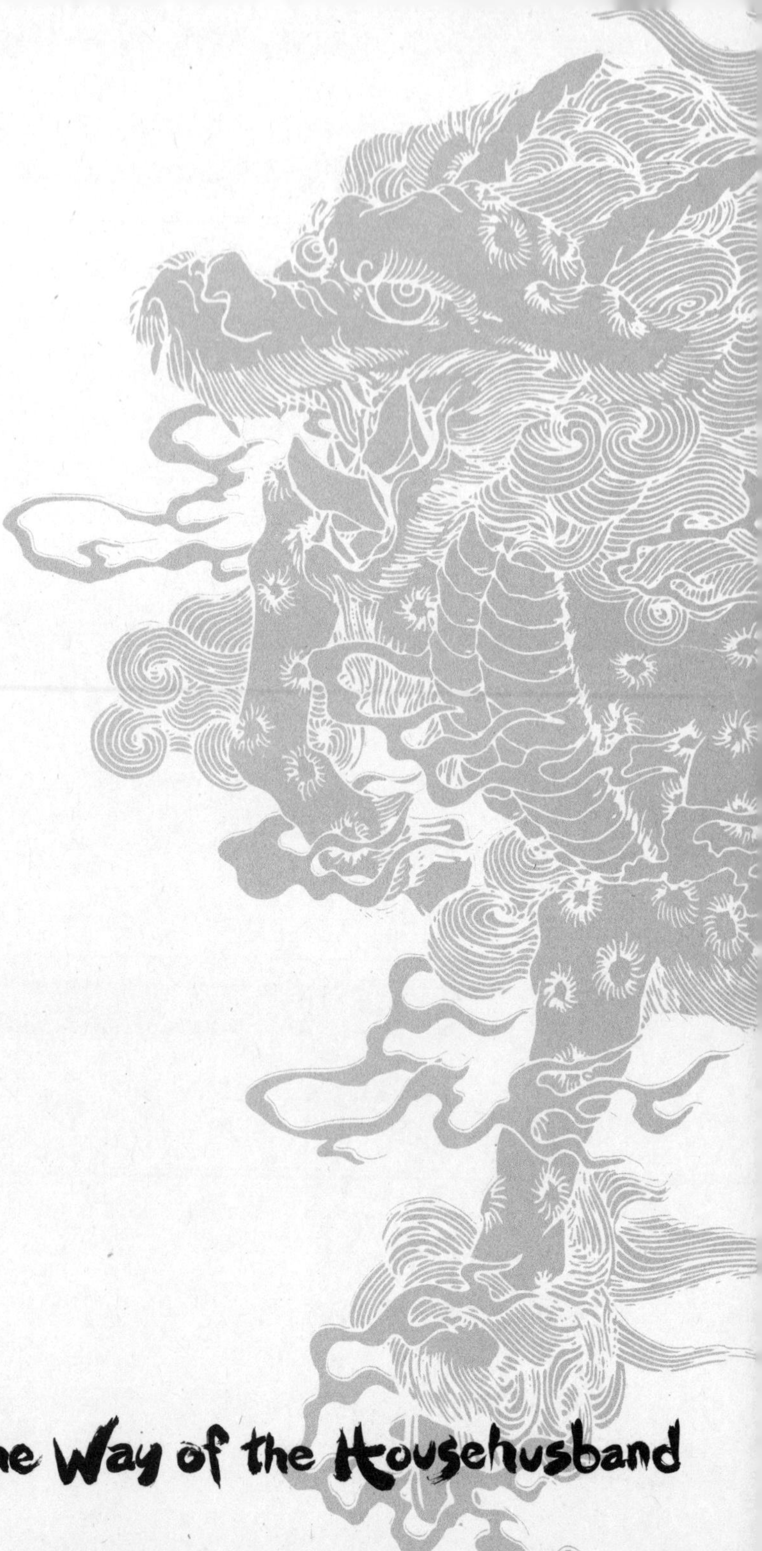

The Way of the Househusband

CHAPTER 84

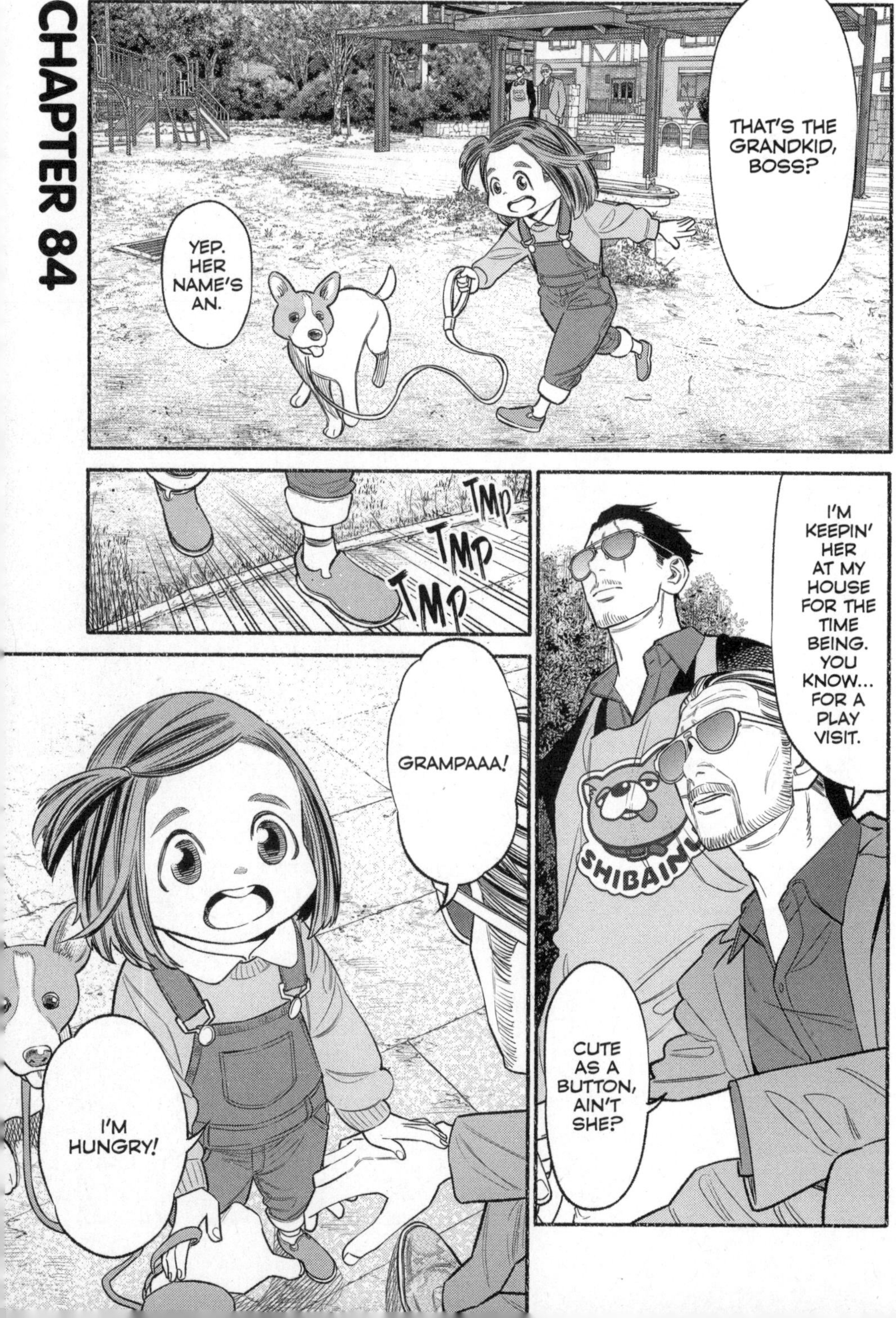
THAT'S THE GRANDKID, BOSS?
YEP. HER NAME'S AN.
I'M KEEPIN' HER AT MY HOUSE FOR THE TIME BEING. YOU KNOW... FOR A PLAY VISIT.
CUTE AS A BUTTON, AIN'T SHE?
TMP TMP TMP
GRAMPAAA!
I'M HUNGRY!

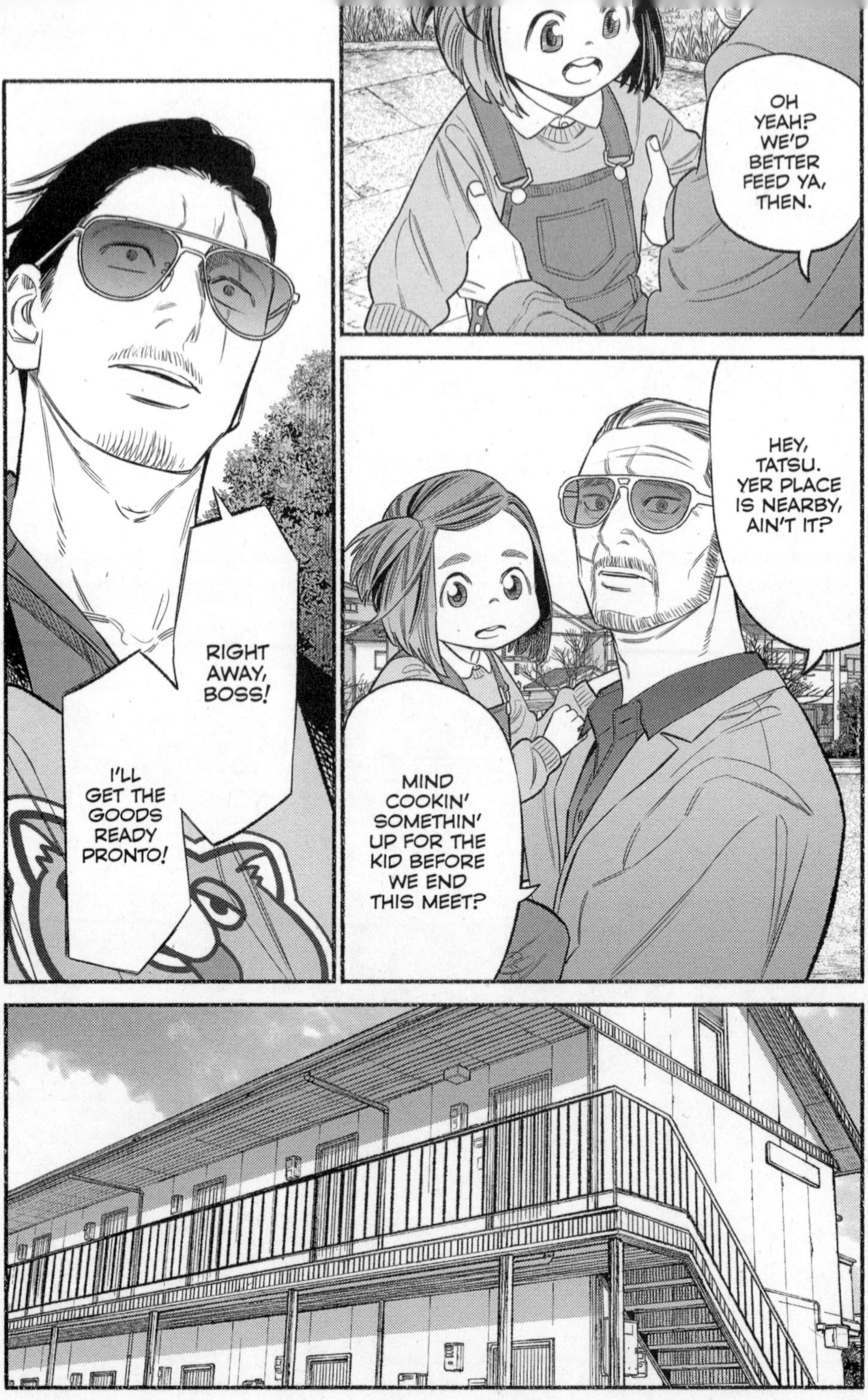
OH YEAH? WE'D BETTER FEED YA, THEN.
HEY, TATSU. YER PLACE IS NEARBY, AIN'T IT?
MIND COOKIN' SOMETHIN' UP FOR THE KID BEFORE WE END THIS MEET?
RIGHT AWAY, BOSS!
I'LL GET THE GOODS READY PRONTO!

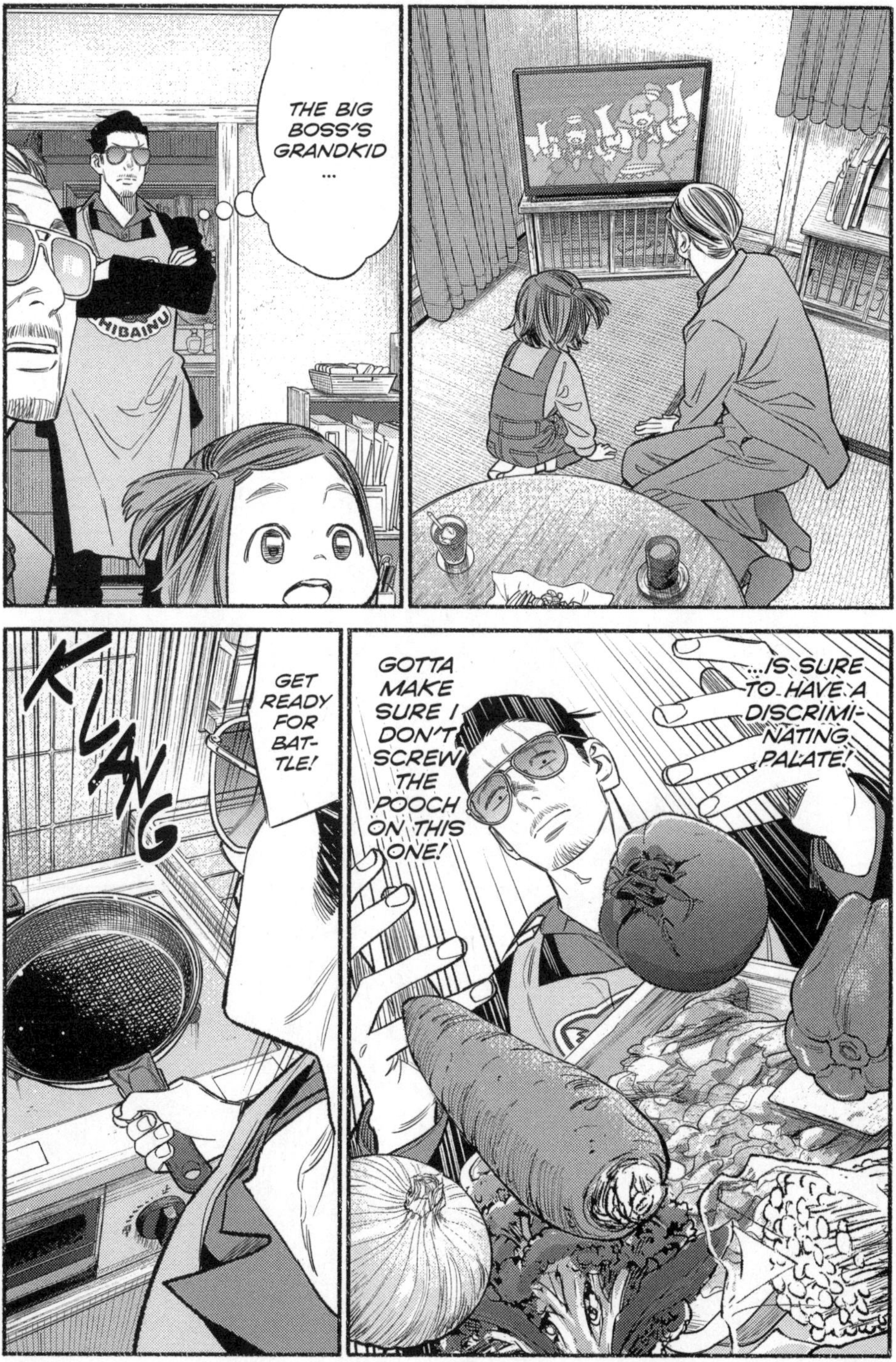
THE BIG BOSS'S GRANDKID ...
...IS SURE TO HAVE A DISCRIMINATING PALATE!
GOTTA MAKE SURE I DON'T SCREW THE POOCH ON THIS ONE!
GET READY FOR BATTLE!
KLANG

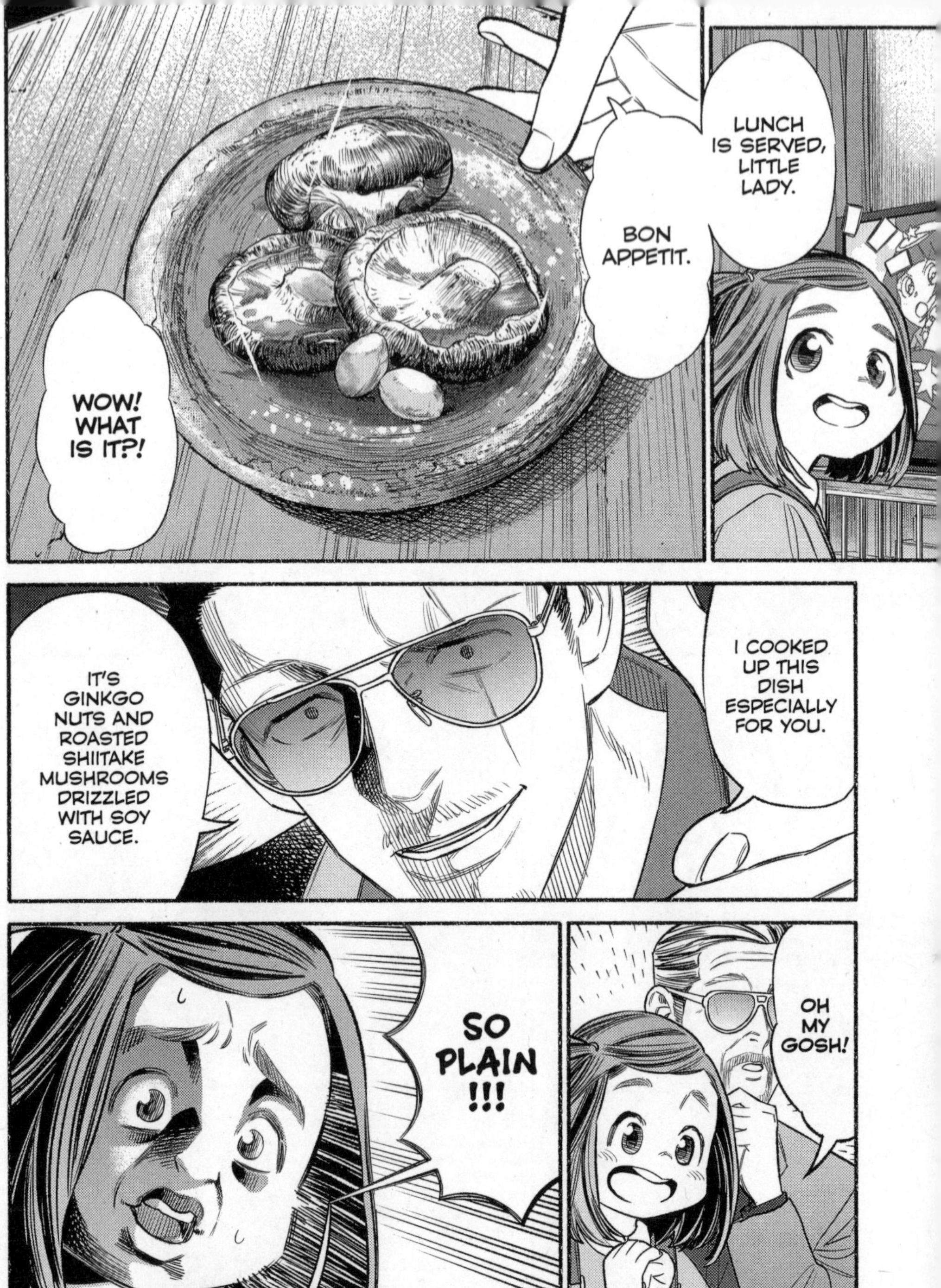

LUNCH IS SERVED, LITTLE LADY.
BON APPETIT.
WOW! WHAT IS IT?!
I COOKED UP THIS DISH ESPECIALLY FOR YOU.
IT'S GINKGO NUTS AND ROASTED SHIITAKE MUSHROOMS DRIZZLED WITH SOY SAUCE.
OH MY GOSH!
SO PLAIN !!!

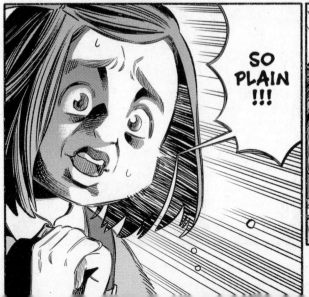

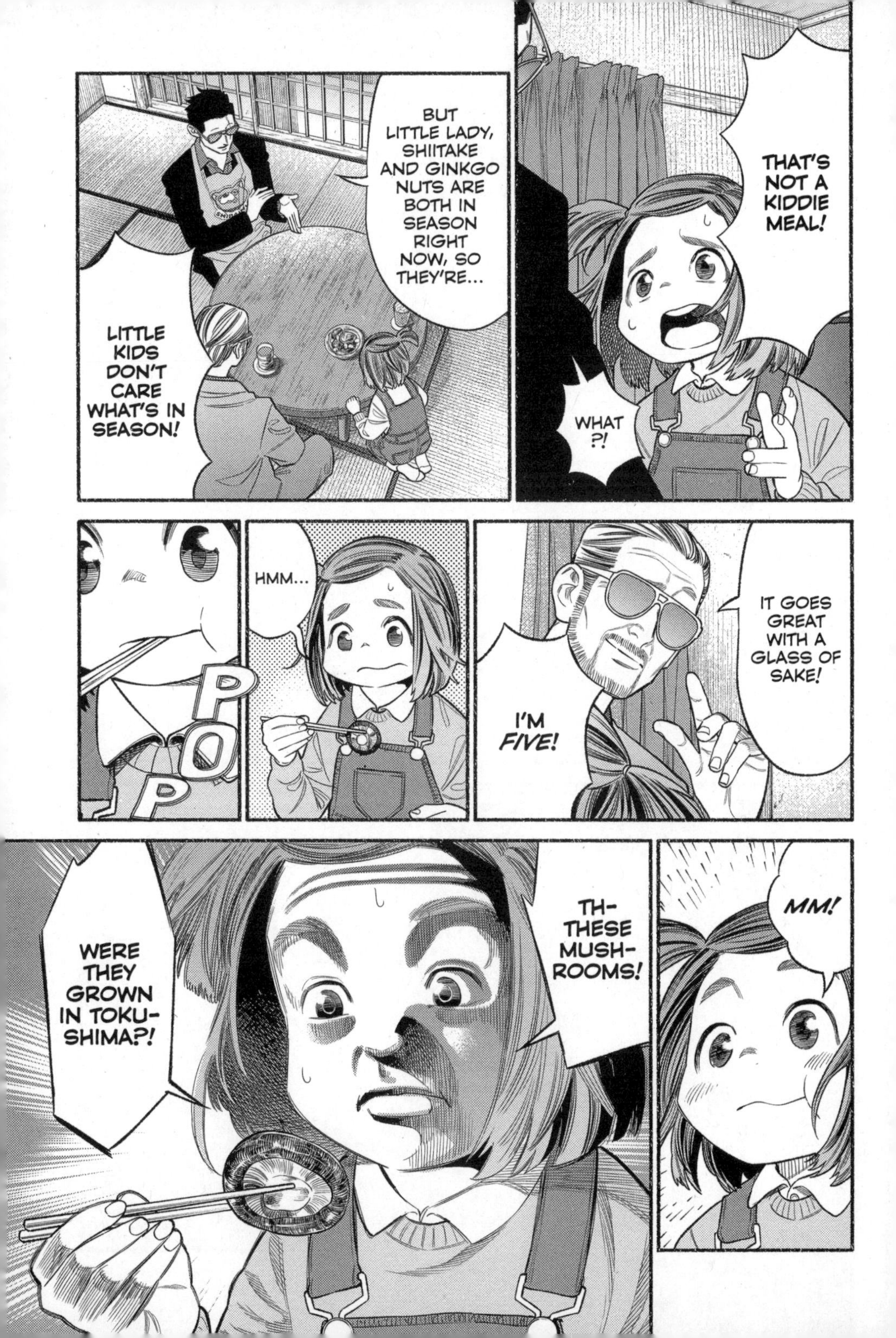
THAT'S NOT A KIDDIE MEAL!
WHAT?!
BUT LITTLE LADY, SHIITAKE AND GINKGO NUTS ARE BOTH IN SEASON RIGHT NOW, SO THEY'RE...
LITTLE KIDS DON'T CARE WHAT'S IN SEASON!
IT GOES GREAT WITH A GLASS OF SAKE!
I'M *FIVE*!
HMM...
POP
MM!
TH-THESE MUSH-ROOMS!
WERE THEY GROWN IN TOKU-SHIMA?!

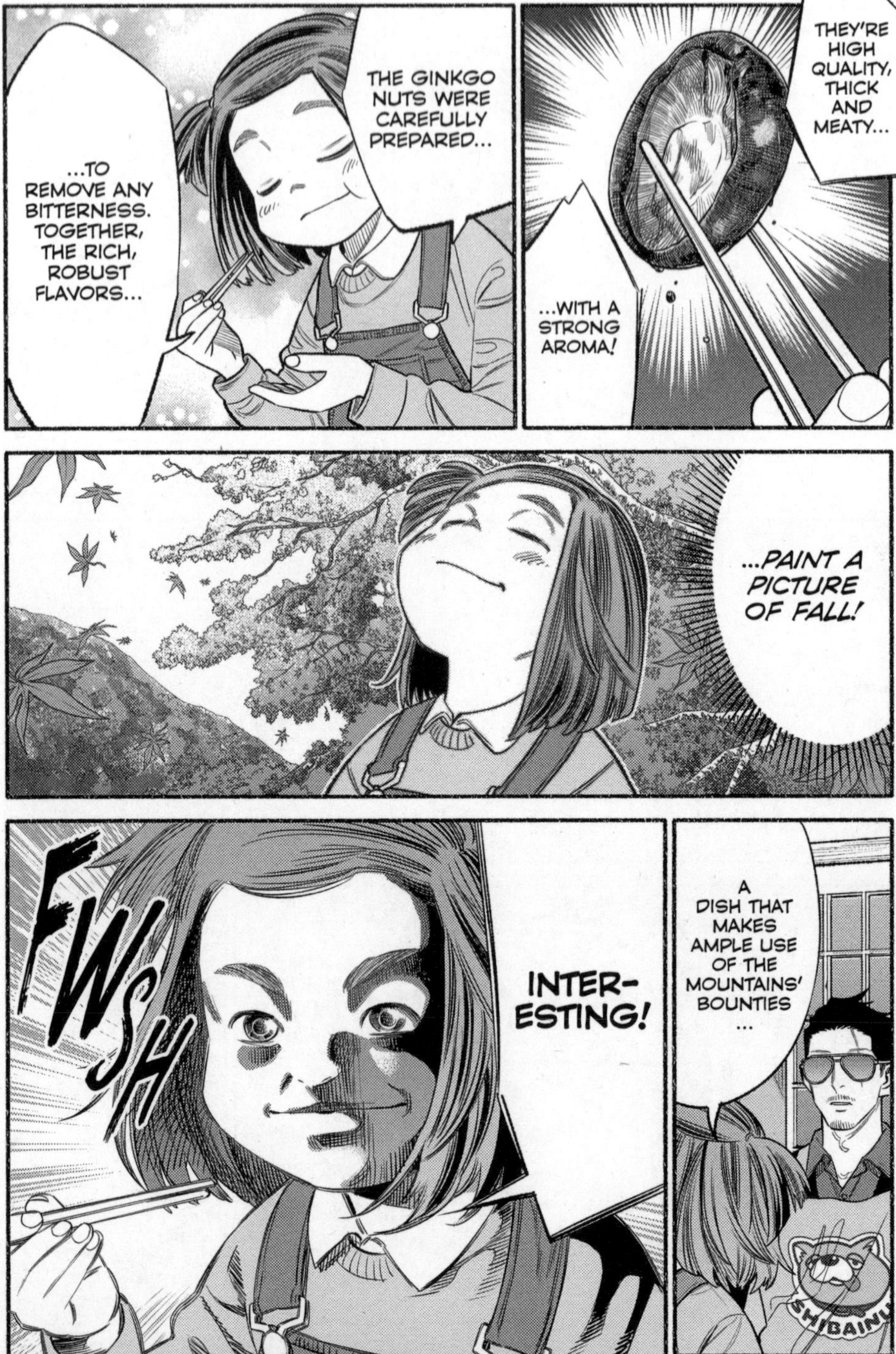
THEY'RE HIGH QUALITY, THICK AND MEATY...
...WITH A STRONG AROMA!
THE GINKGO NUTS WERE CAREFULLY PREPARED...
...TO REMOVE ANY BITTERNESS. TOGETHER, THE RICH, ROBUST FLAVORS...
...PAINT A PICTURE OF FALL!
A DISH THAT MAKES AMPLE USE OF THE MOUNTAINS' BOUNTIES ...
SHIBAINU
FWSH
INTER-ESTING!

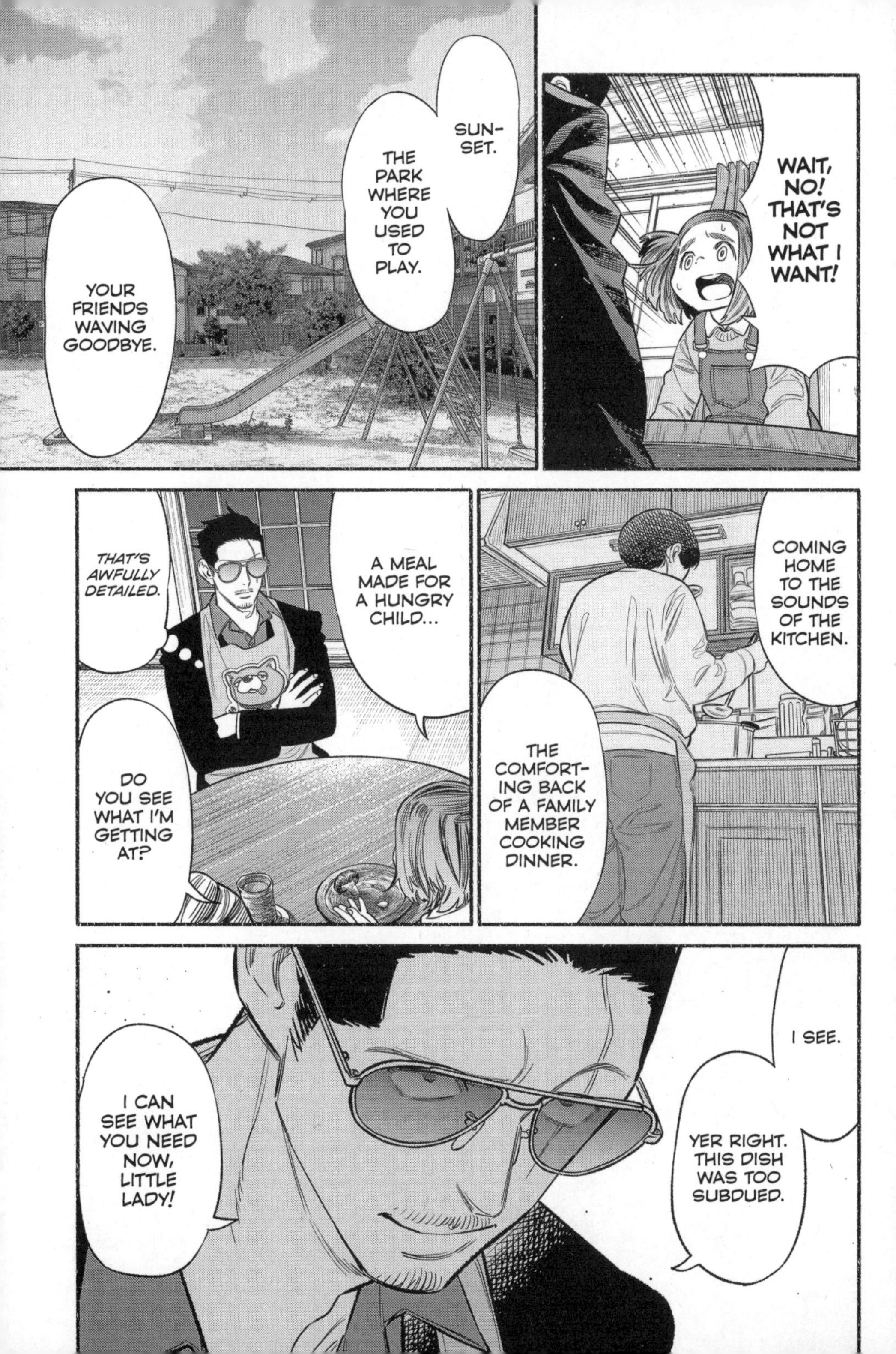
WAIT, NO! THAT'S NOT WHAT I WANT!
SUN-SET.
THE PARK WHERE YOU USED TO PLAY.
YOUR FRIENDS WAVING GOODBYE.
COMING HOME TO THE SOUNDS OF THE KITCHEN.
THE COMFORT-ING BACK OF A FAMILY MEMBER COOKING DINNER.
A MEAL MADE FOR A HUNGRY CHILD...
THAT'S AWFULLY DETAILED.
DO YOU SEE WHAT I'M GETTING AT?
I SEE.
YER RIGHT. THIS DISH WAS TOO SUBDUED.
I CAN SEE WHAT YOU NEED NOW, LITTLE LADY!

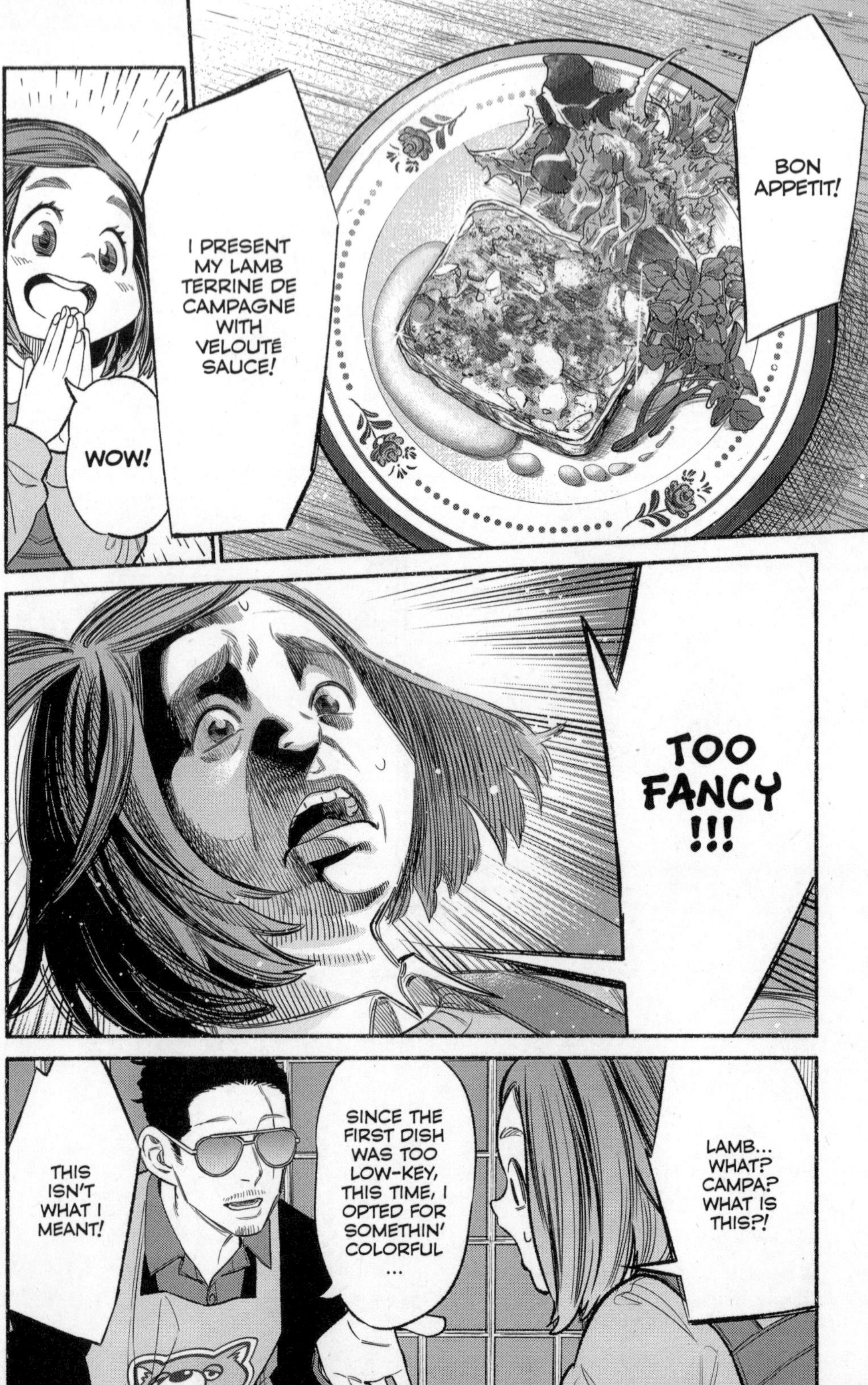
BON APPETIT!
I PRESENT MY LAMB TERRINE DE CAMPAGNE WITH VELOUTE SAUCE!
WOW!
TOO FANCY!!!
LAMB... WHAT? CAMPA? WHAT IS THIS?!
SINCE THE FIRST DISH WAS TOO LOW-KEY, THIS TIME, I OPTED FOR SOMETHIN' COLORFUL...
THIS ISN'T WHAT I MEANT!

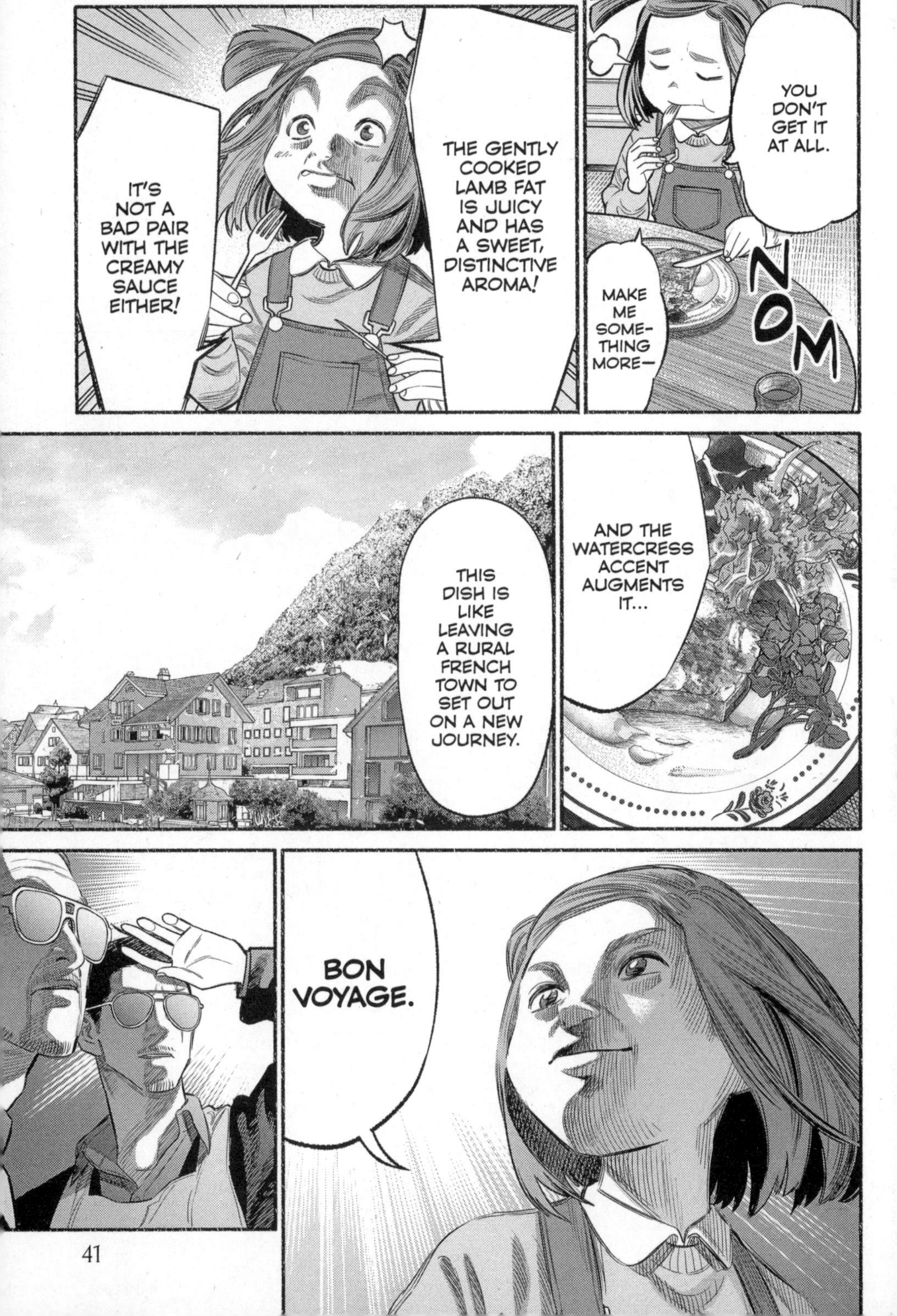
YOU DON'T GET IT AT ALL.
MAKE ME SOME-THING MORE—
NOM
THE GENTLY COOKED LAMB FAT IS JUICY AND HAS A SWEET, DISTINCTIVE AROMA!
IT'S NOT A BAD PAIR WITH THE CREAMY SAUCE EITHER!
AND THE WATERCRESS ACCENT AUGMENTS IT...
THIS DISH IS LIKE LEAVING A RURAL FRENCH TOWN TO SET OUT ON A NEW JOURNEY.
BON VOYAGE.

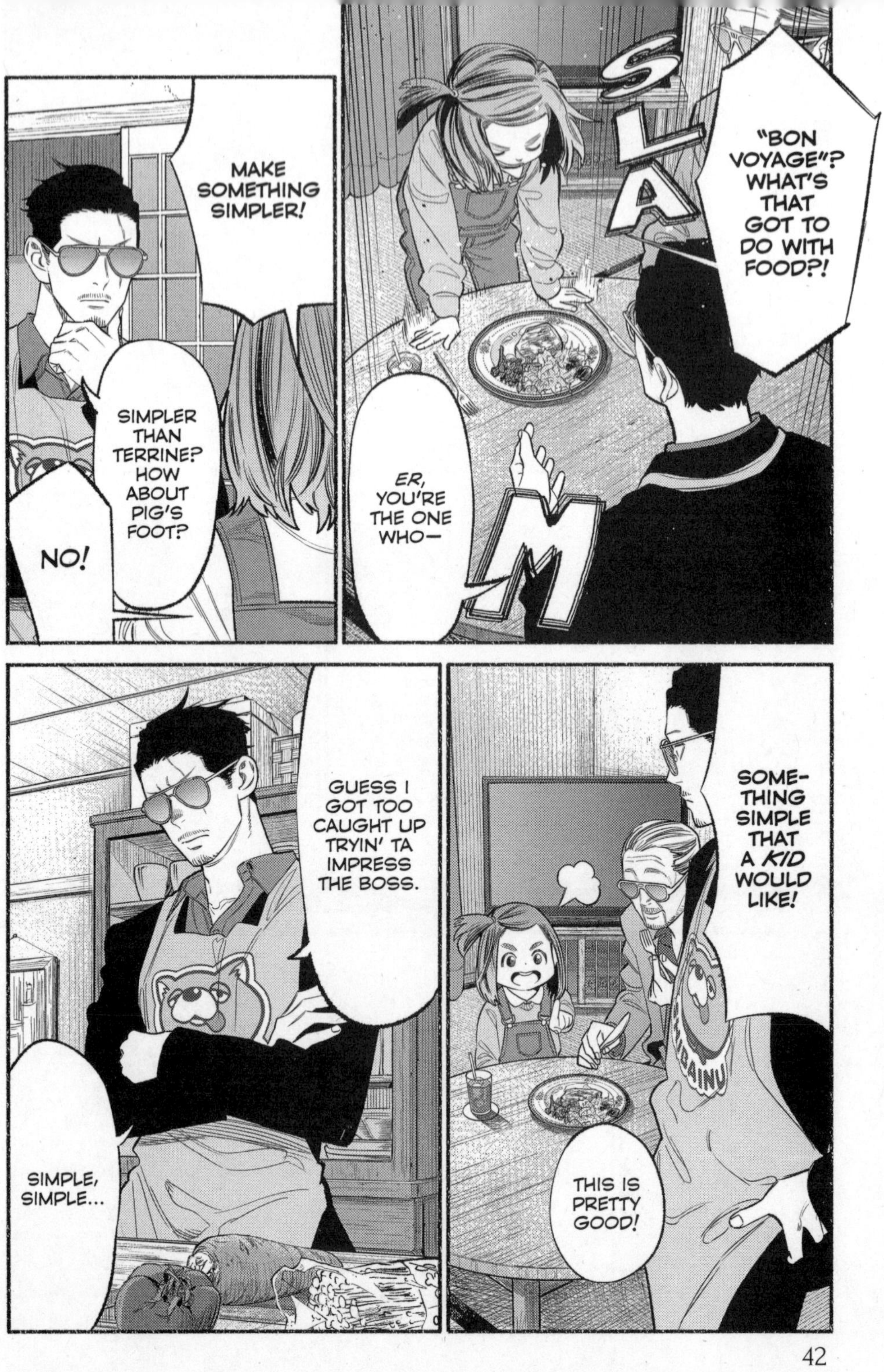
SLAM
"BON VOYAGE"? WHAT'S THAT GOT TO DO WITH FOOD?!
ER, YOU'RE THE ONE WHO—
MAKE SOMETHING SIMPLER!
SIMPLER THAN TERRINE? HOW ABOUT PIG'S FOOT?
NO!
SOME-THING SIMPLE THAT A KID WOULD LIKE!
THIS IS PRETTY GOOD!
GUESS I GOT TOO CAUGHT UP TRYIN' TA IMPRESS THE BOSS.
SIMPLE, SIMPLE...

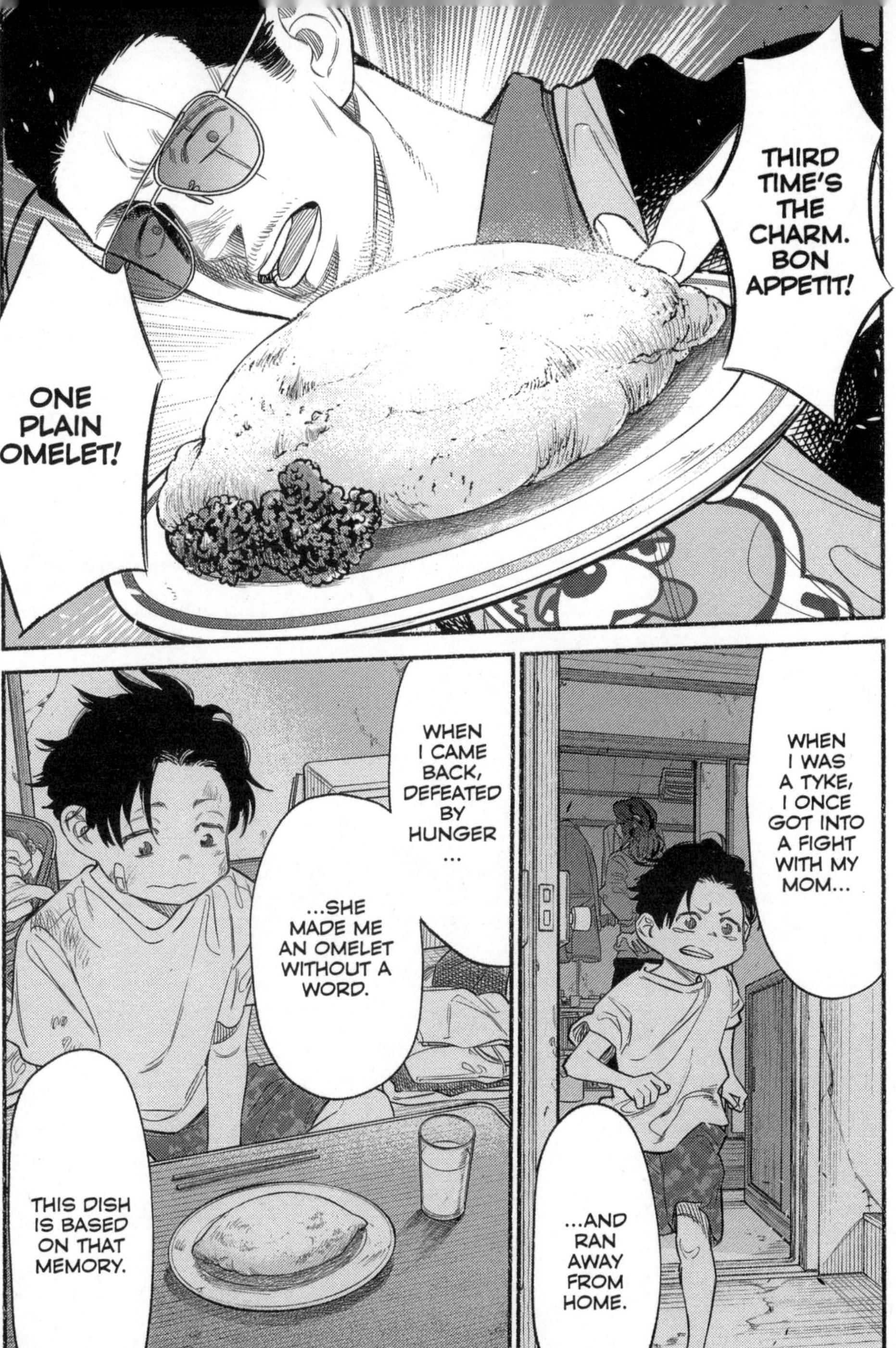
THIRD TIME'S THE CHARM. BON APPETIT!
ONE PLAIN OMELET!
WHEN I WAS A TYKE, I ONCE GOT INTO A FIGHT WITH MY MOM...
...AND RAN AWAY FROM HOME.
WHEN I CAME BACK, DEFEATED BY HUNGER ...
...SHE MADE ME AN OMELET WITHOUT A WORD.
THIS DISH IS BASED ON THAT MEMORY.

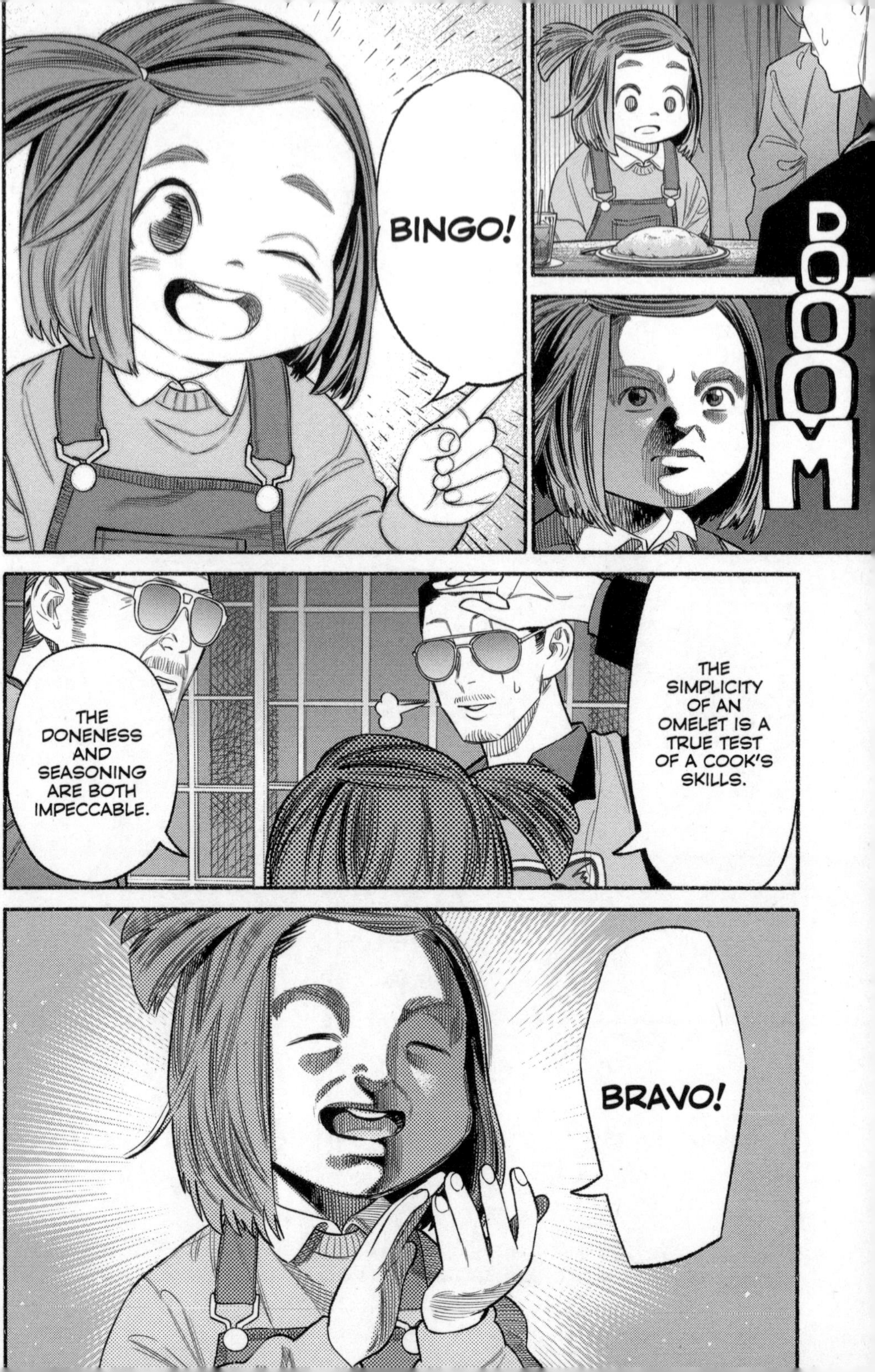
DOOOOM
BINGO!
THE SIMPLICITY OF AN OMELET IS A TRUE TEST OF A COOK'S SKILLS.
THE DONENESS AND SEASONING ARE BOTH IMPECCABLE.
BRAVO!

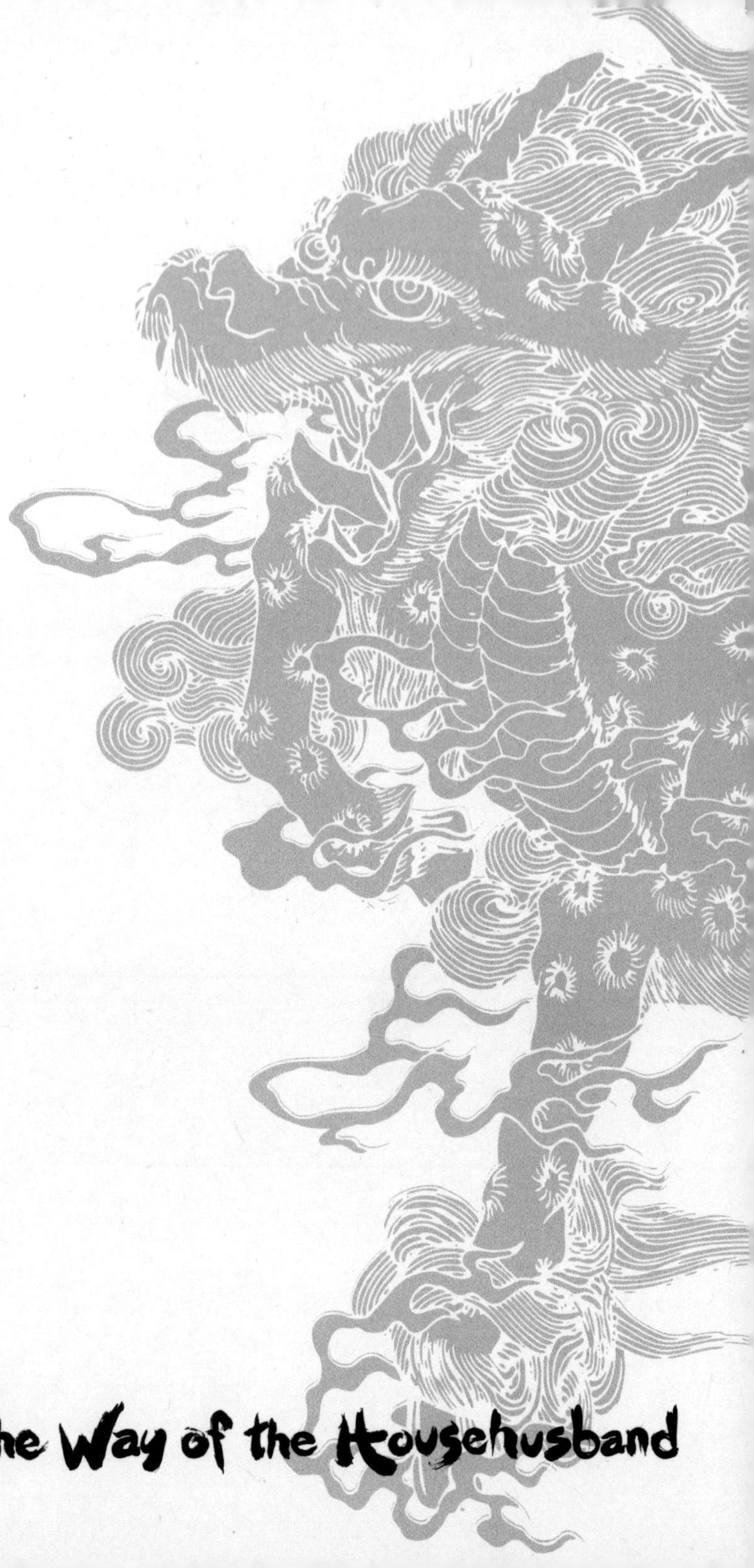

The Way of the Househusband

CHAPTER 85

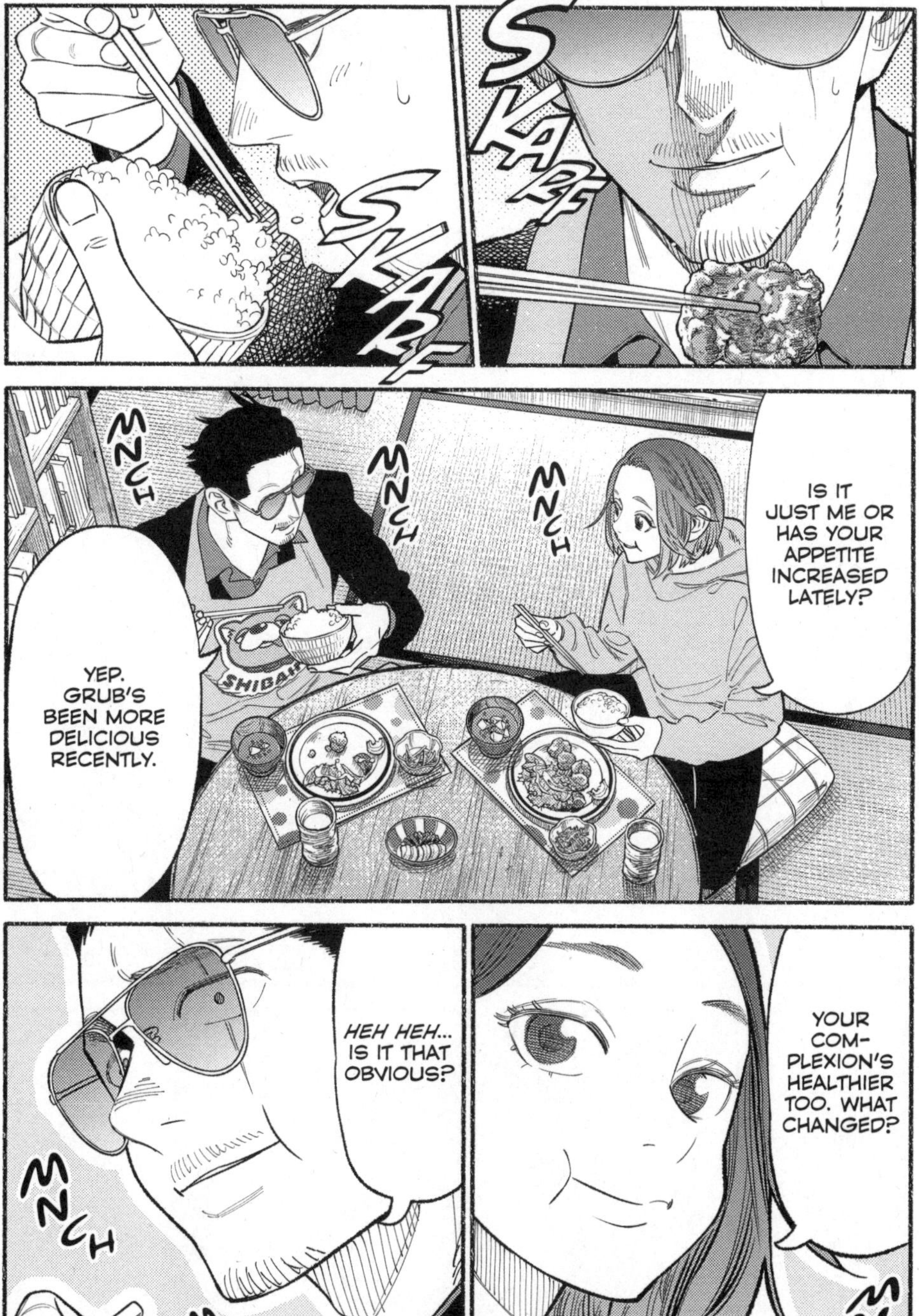
SKARF
SKARF
SKARF
SKARF
IS IT JUST ME OR HAS YOUR APPETITE INCREASED LATELY?
MNCH
MNCH
MNCH
YEP. GRUB'S BEEN MORE DELICIOUS RECENTLY.
SHIBAH
YOUR COM-PLEXION'S HEALTHIER TOO. WHAT CHANGED?
MNCH
HEH HEH... IS IT THAT OBVIOUS?
MNCH
MNCH

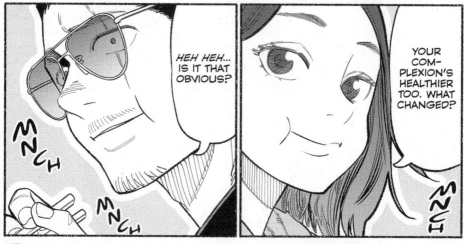

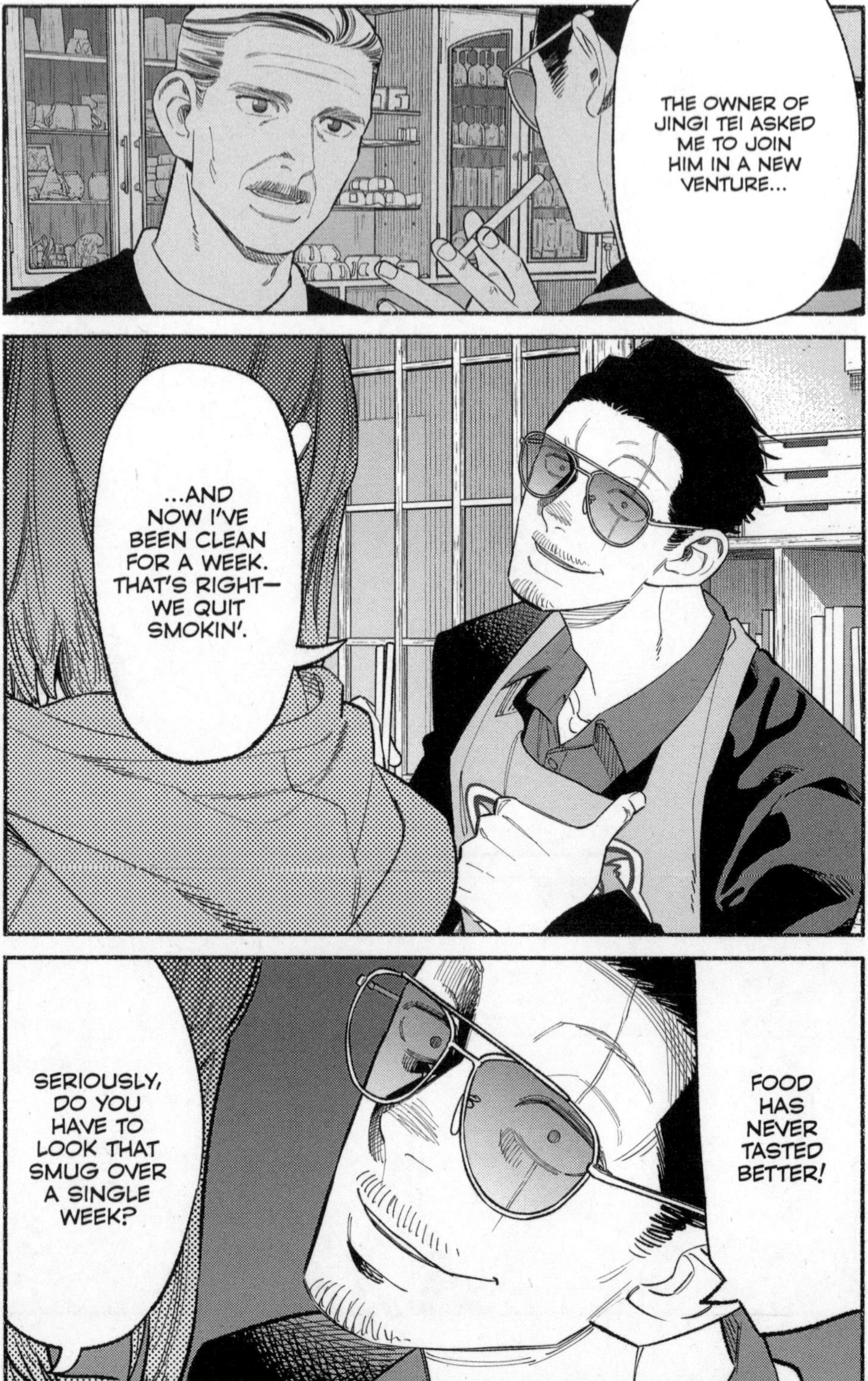
THE OWNER OF JINGI TEI ASKED ME TO JOIN HIM IN A NEW VENTURE...
...AND NOW I'VE BEEN CLEAN FOR A WEEK. THAT'S RIGHT—WE QUIT SMOKIN'.
FOOD HAS NEVER TASTED BETTER!
SERIOUSLY, DO YOU HAVE TO LOOK THAT SMUG OVER A SINGLE WEEK?

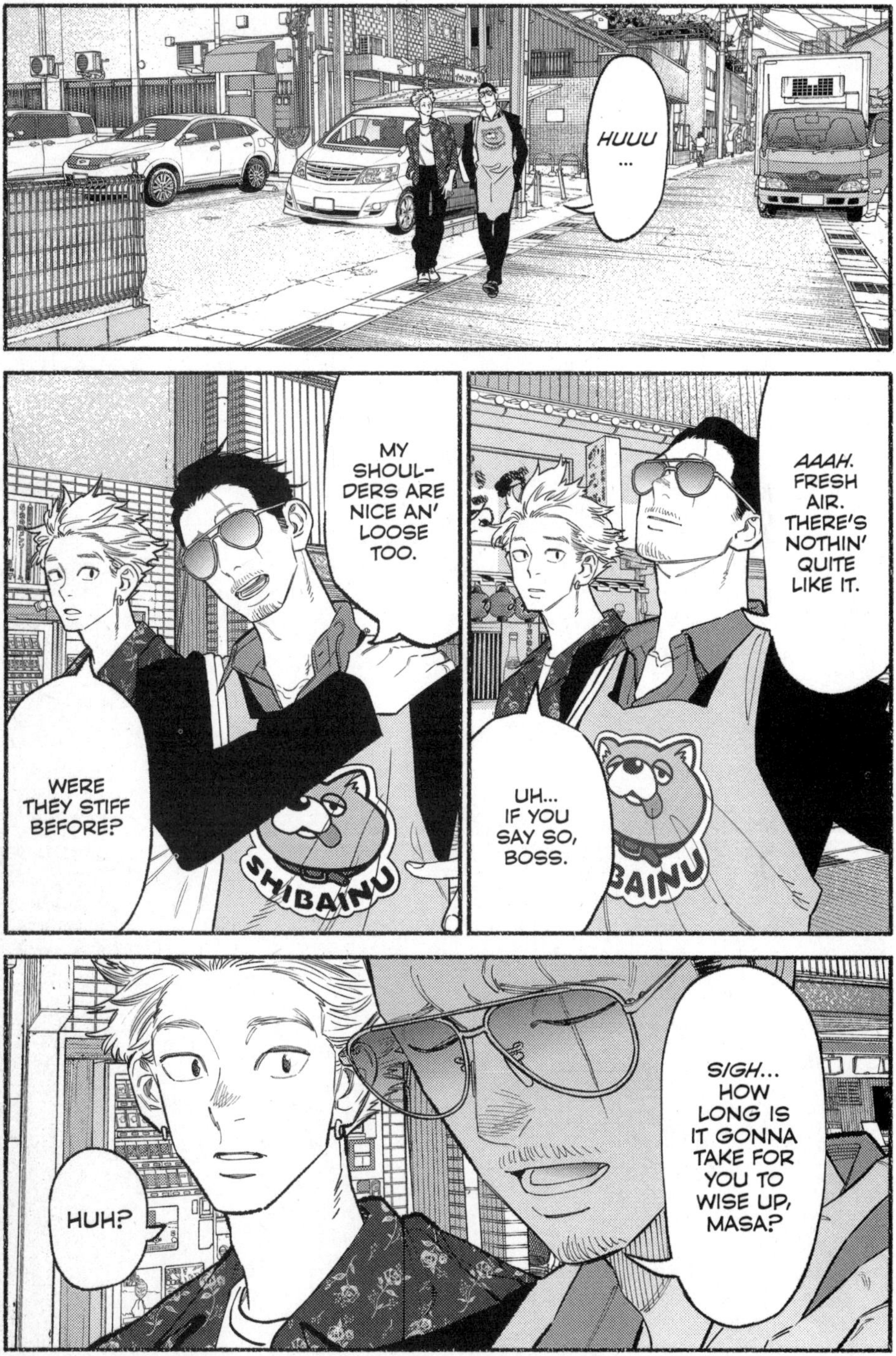
HUUU ...
AAAH. FRESH AIR. THERE'S NOTHIN' QUITE LIKE IT.
UH... IF YOU SAY SO, BOSS.
BAINU
MY SHOUL-DERS ARE NICE AN' LOOSE TOO.
WERE THEY STIFF BEFORE?
SHIBAINU
SIGH... HOW LONG IS IT GONNA TAKE FOR YOU TO WISE UP, MASA?
HUH?

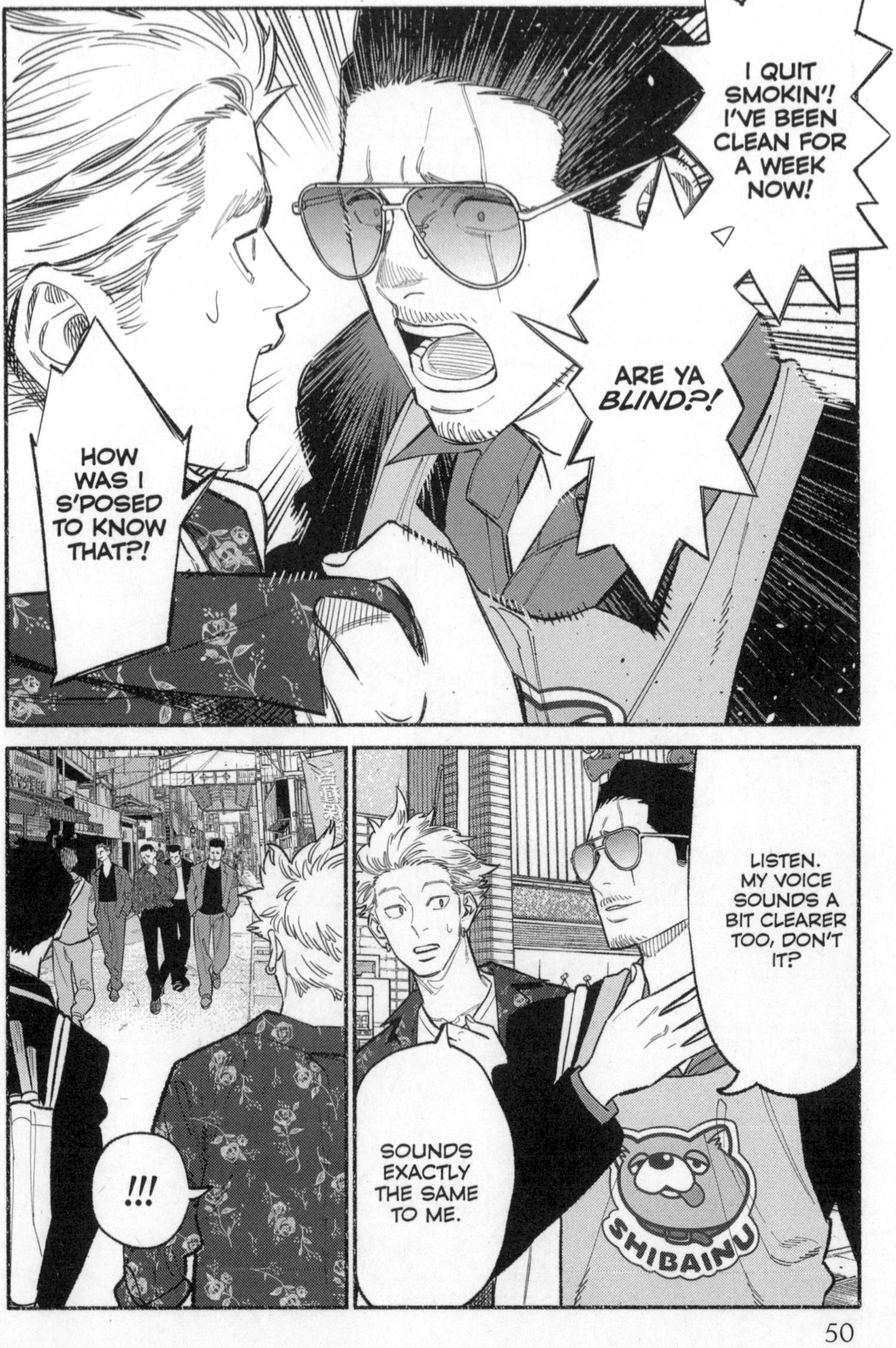
I QUIT SMOKIN'! I'VE BEEN CLEAN FOR A WEEK NOW!
ARE YA *BLIND?!*
HOW WAS I S'POSED TO KNOW THAT?!
LISTEN. MY VOICE SOUNDS A BIT CLEARER TOO, DON'T IT?
SOUNDS EXACTLY THE SAME TO ME.
SHIBAINU
!!!

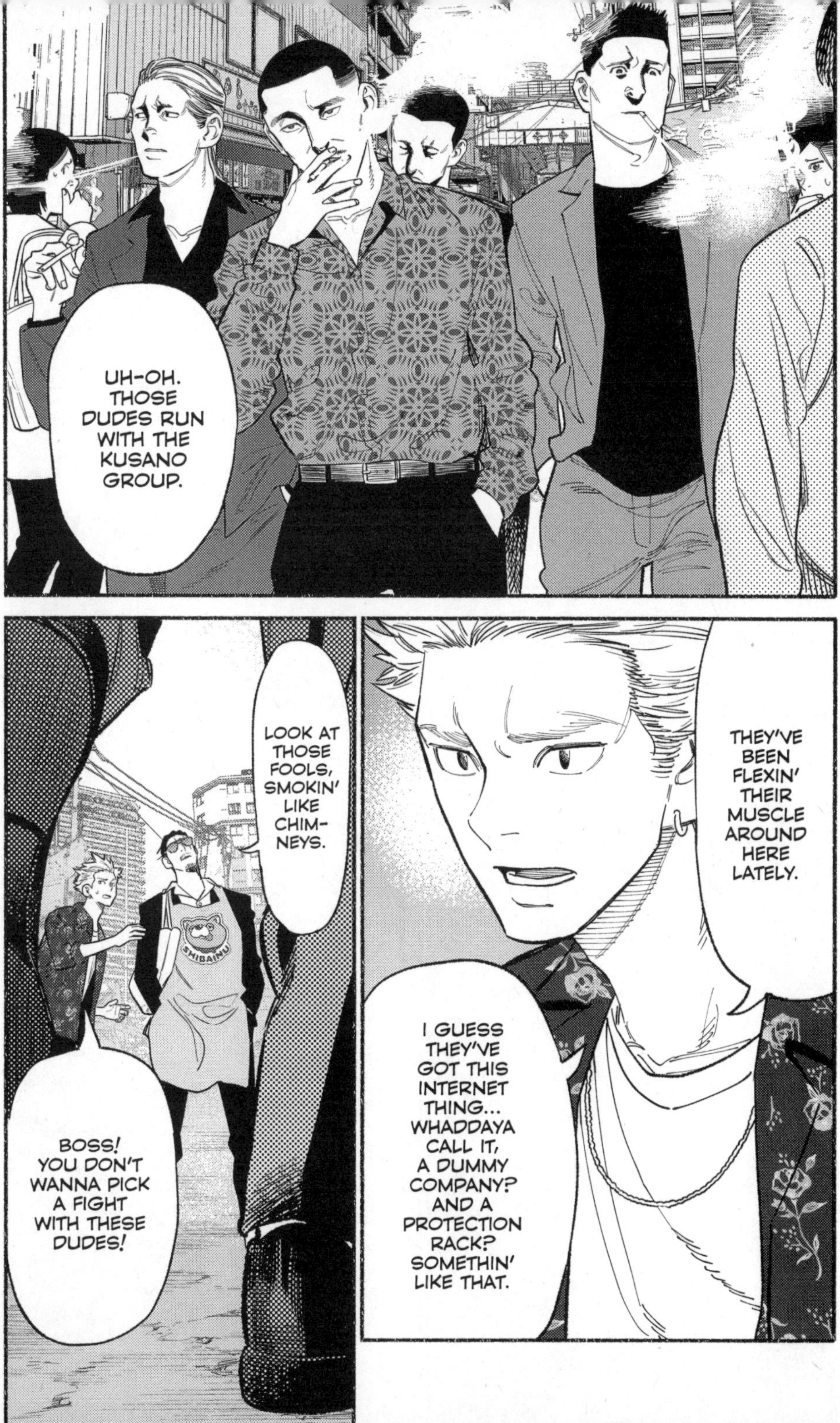
UH-OH. THOSE DUDES RUN WITH THE KUSANO GROUP.
THEY'VE BEEN FLEXIN' THEIR MUSCLE AROUND HERE LATELY.
I GUESS THEY'VE GOT THIS INTERNET THING... WHADDAYA CALL IT, A DUMMY COMPANY? AND A PROTECTION RACK? SOMETHIN' LIKE THAT.
LOOK AT THOSE FOOLS, SMOKIN' LIKE CHIM-NEYS.
SHIBAINU
BOSS! YOU DON'T WANNA PICK A FIGHT WITH THESE DUDES!

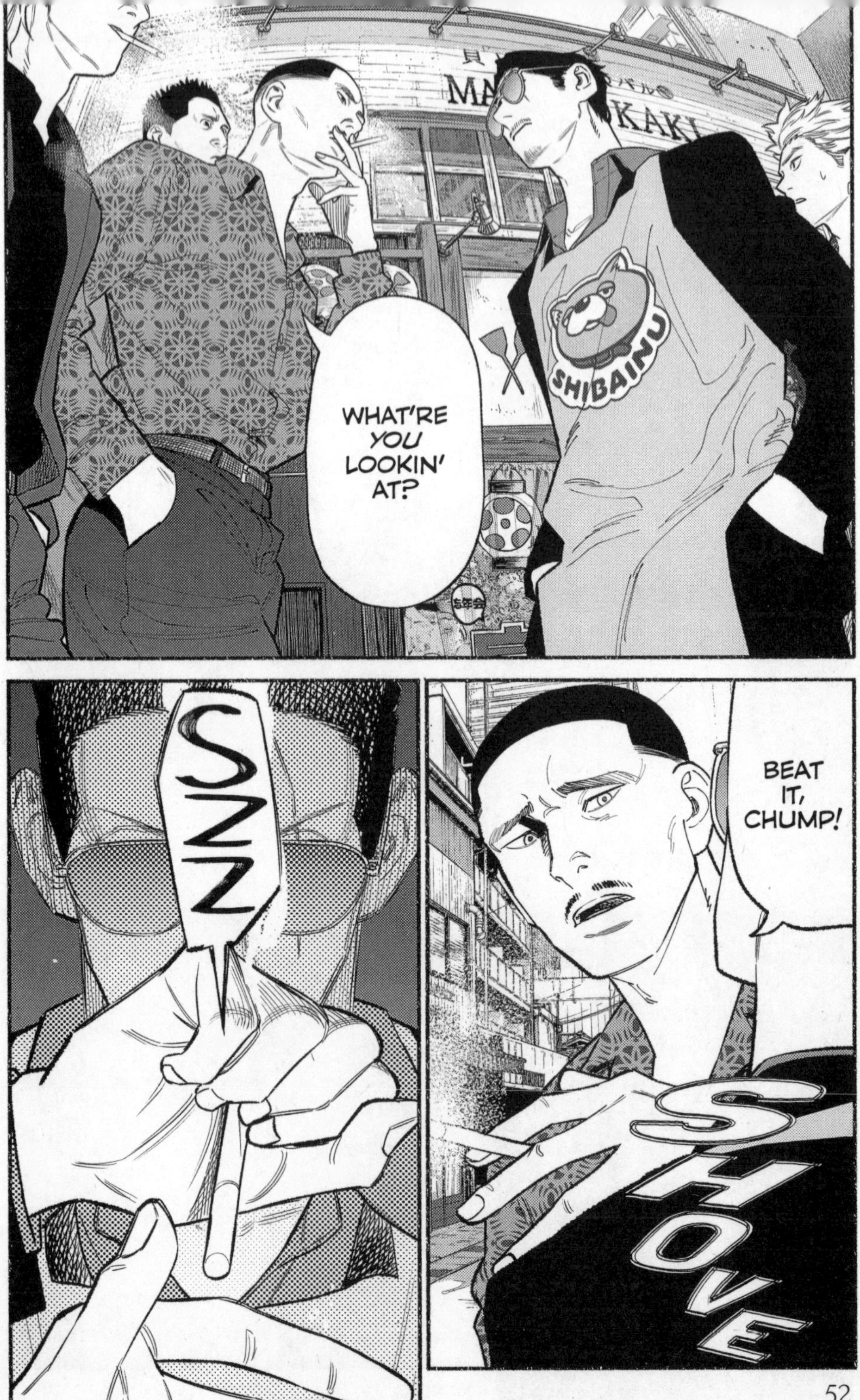
SHIBAINU
WHAT'RE *YOU* LOOKIN' AT?
BEAT IT, CHUMP!
SHOVE
SZZ

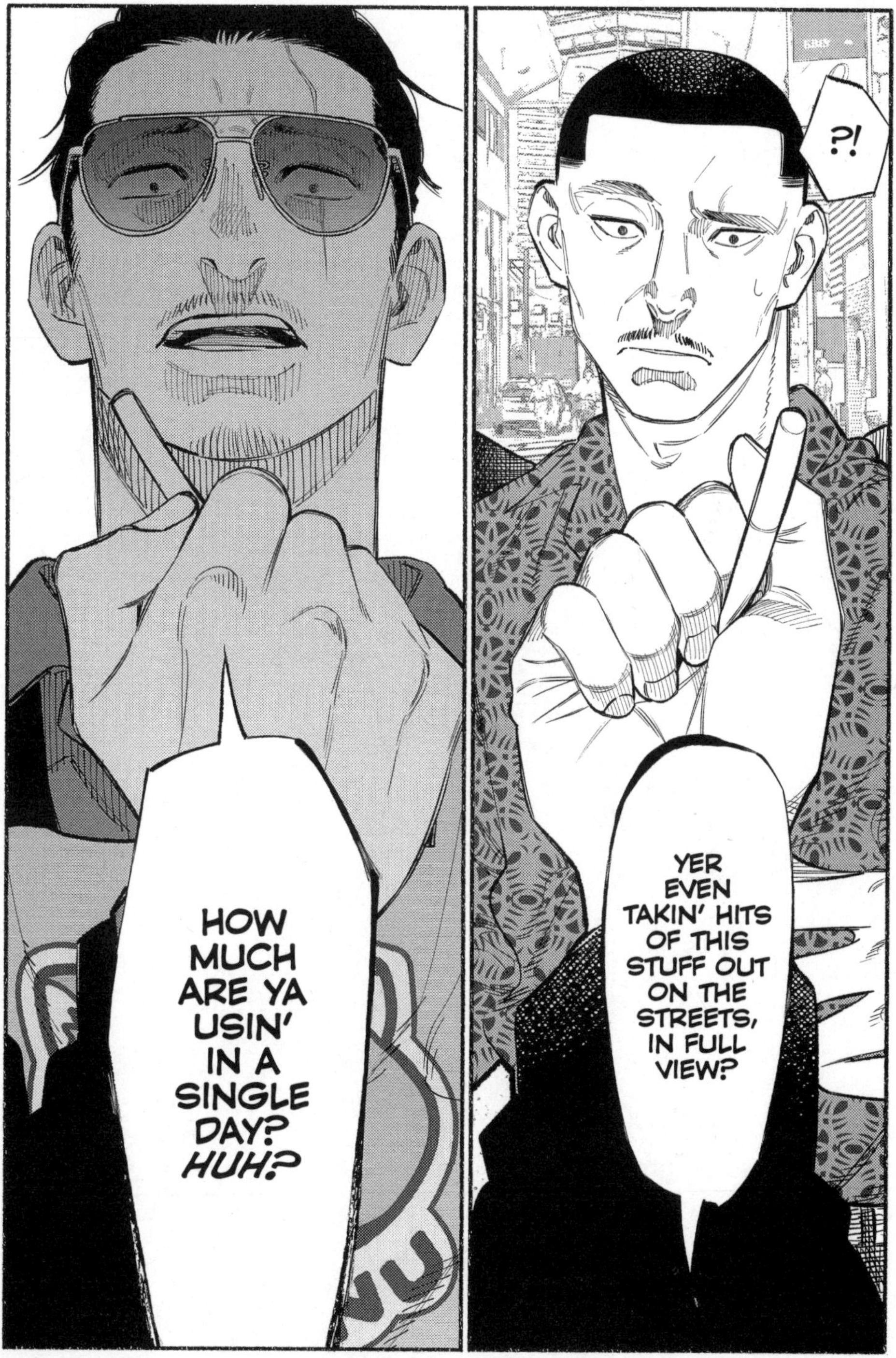
?!
YER EVEN TAKIN' HITS OF THIS STUFF OUT ON THE STREETS, IN FULL VIEW?
HOW MUCH ARE YA USIN' IN A SINGLE DAY? *HUH?*

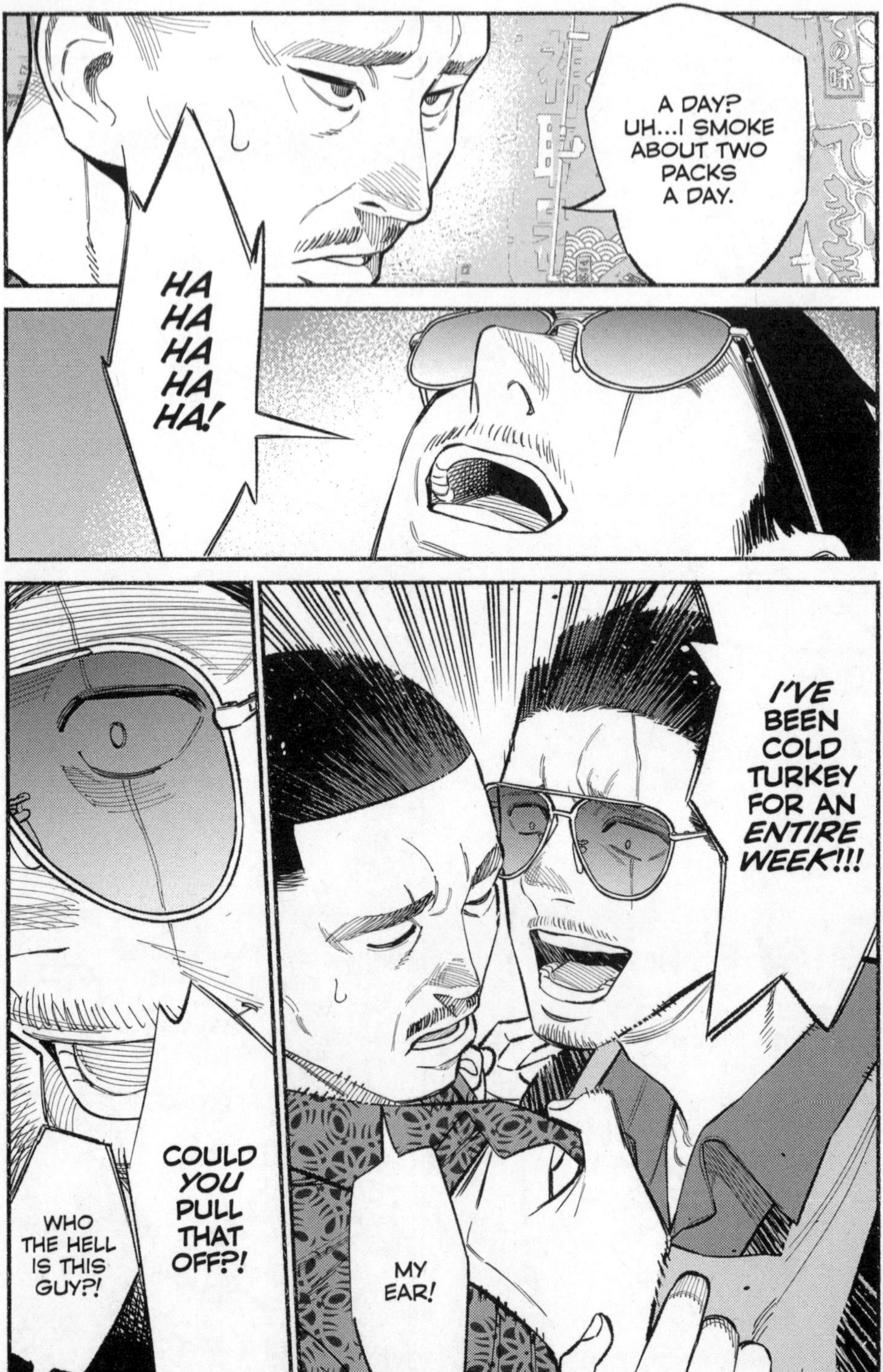
A DAY? UH...I SMOKE ABOUT TWO PACKS A DAY.
HA HA HA HA HA!
I'VE BEEN COLD TURKEY FOR AN ENTIRE WEEK!!!
MY EAR!
COULD YOU PULL THAT OFF?!
WHO THE HELL IS THIS GUY?!

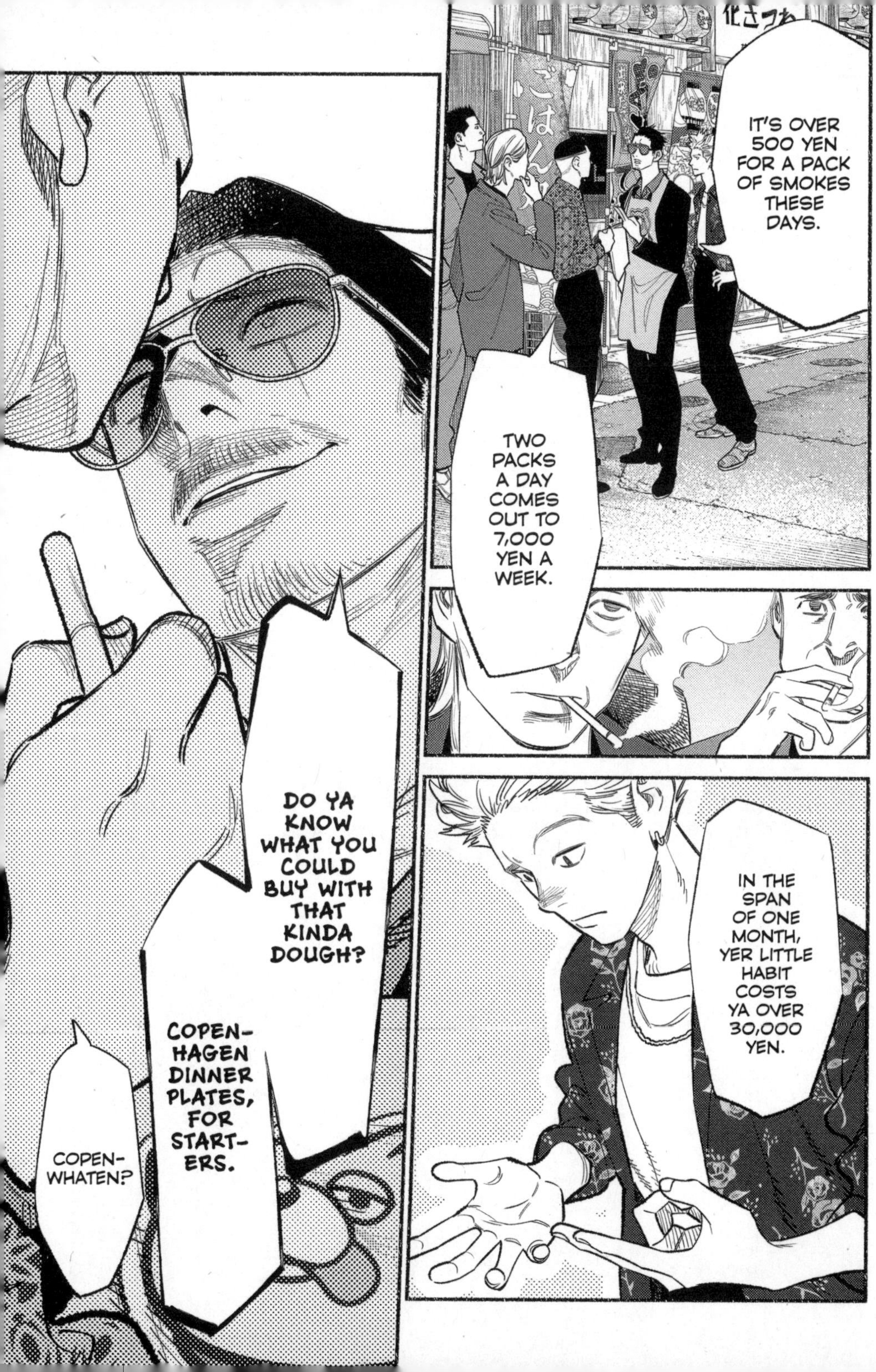
IT'S OVER 500 YEN FOR A PACK OF SMOKES THESE DAYS.
TWO PACKS A DAY COMES OUT TO 7,000 YEN A WEEK.
IN THE SPAN OF ONE MONTH, YER LITTLE HABIT COSTS YA OVER 30,000 YEN.
DO YA KNOW WHAT YOU COULD BUY WITH THAT KINDA DOUGH?
COPEN-HAGEN DINNER PLATES, FOR START-ERS.
COPEN-WHATEN?

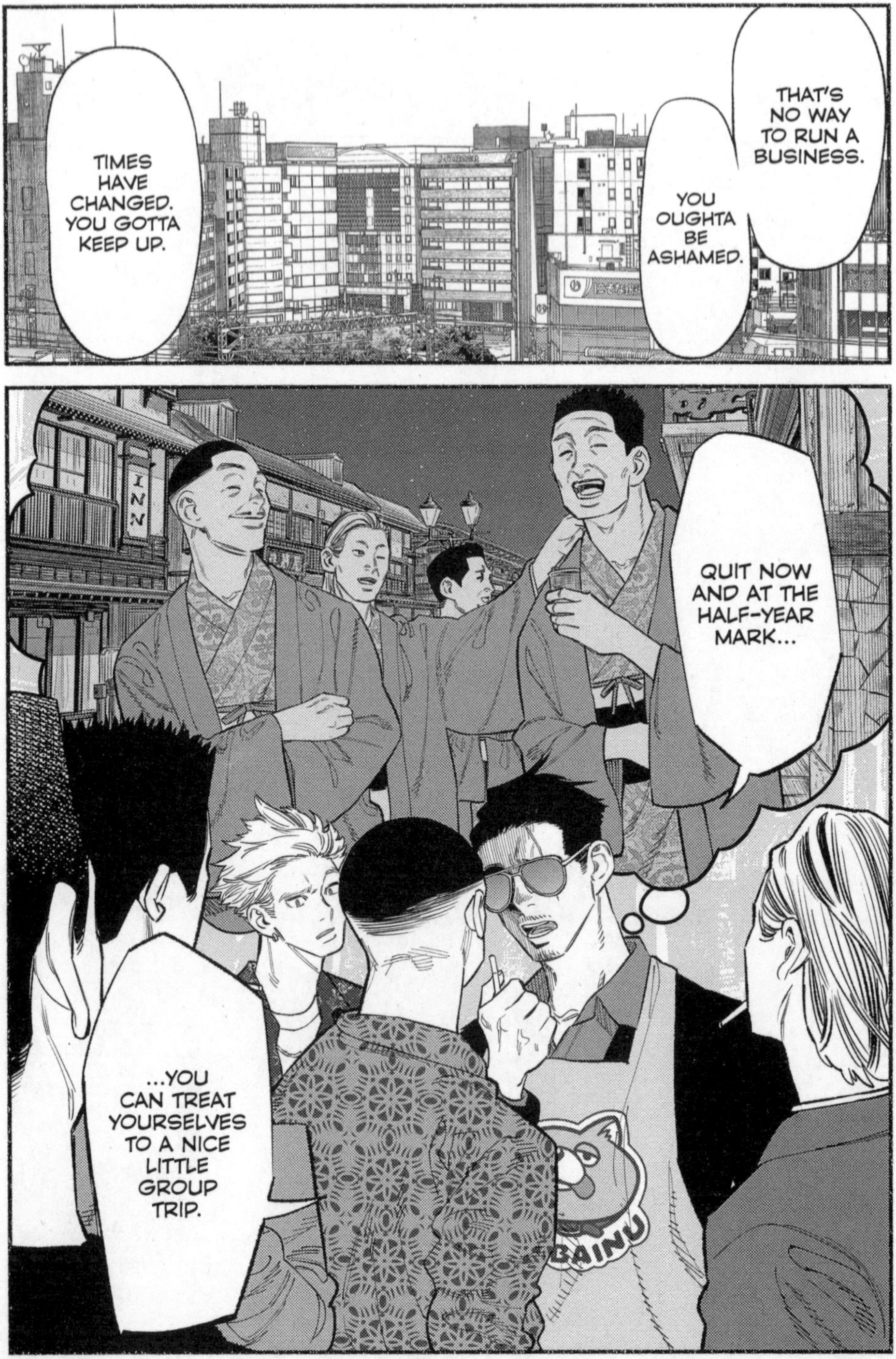
THAT'S NO WAY TO RUN A BUSINESS.
YOU OUGHTA BE ASHAMED.
TIMES HAVE CHANGED. YOU GOTTA KEEP UP.
QUIT NOW AND AT THE HALF-YEAR MARK...
INN
...YOU CAN TREAT YOURSELVES TO A NICE LITTLE GROUP TRIP.

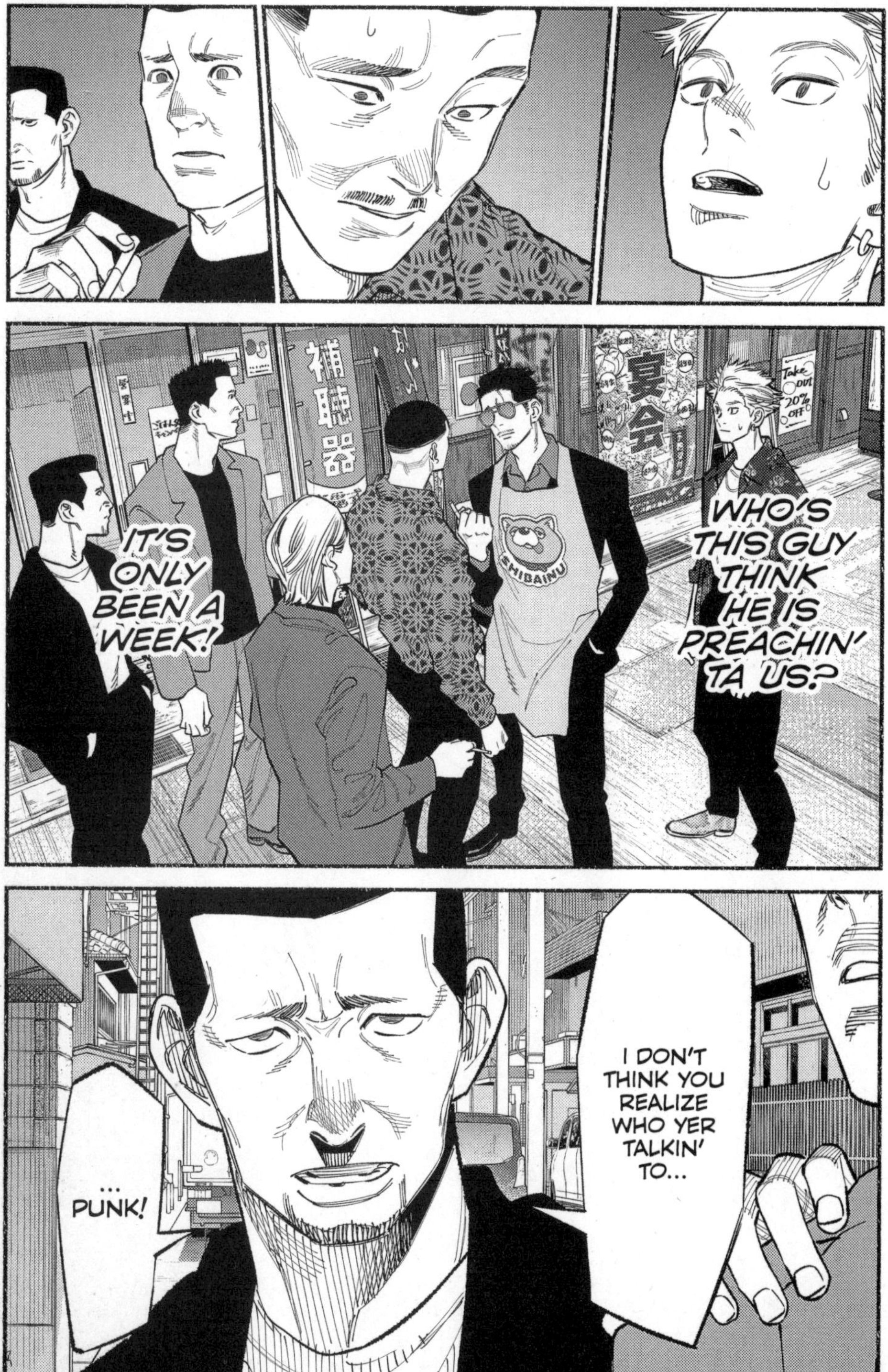
WHO'S THIS GUY THINK HE IS PREACHIN' TA US?
Take out 20% OFF
宴会
補聴器
IT'S ONLY BEEN A WEEK!
I DON'T THINK YOU REALIZE WHO YER TALKIN' TO...
... PUNK!

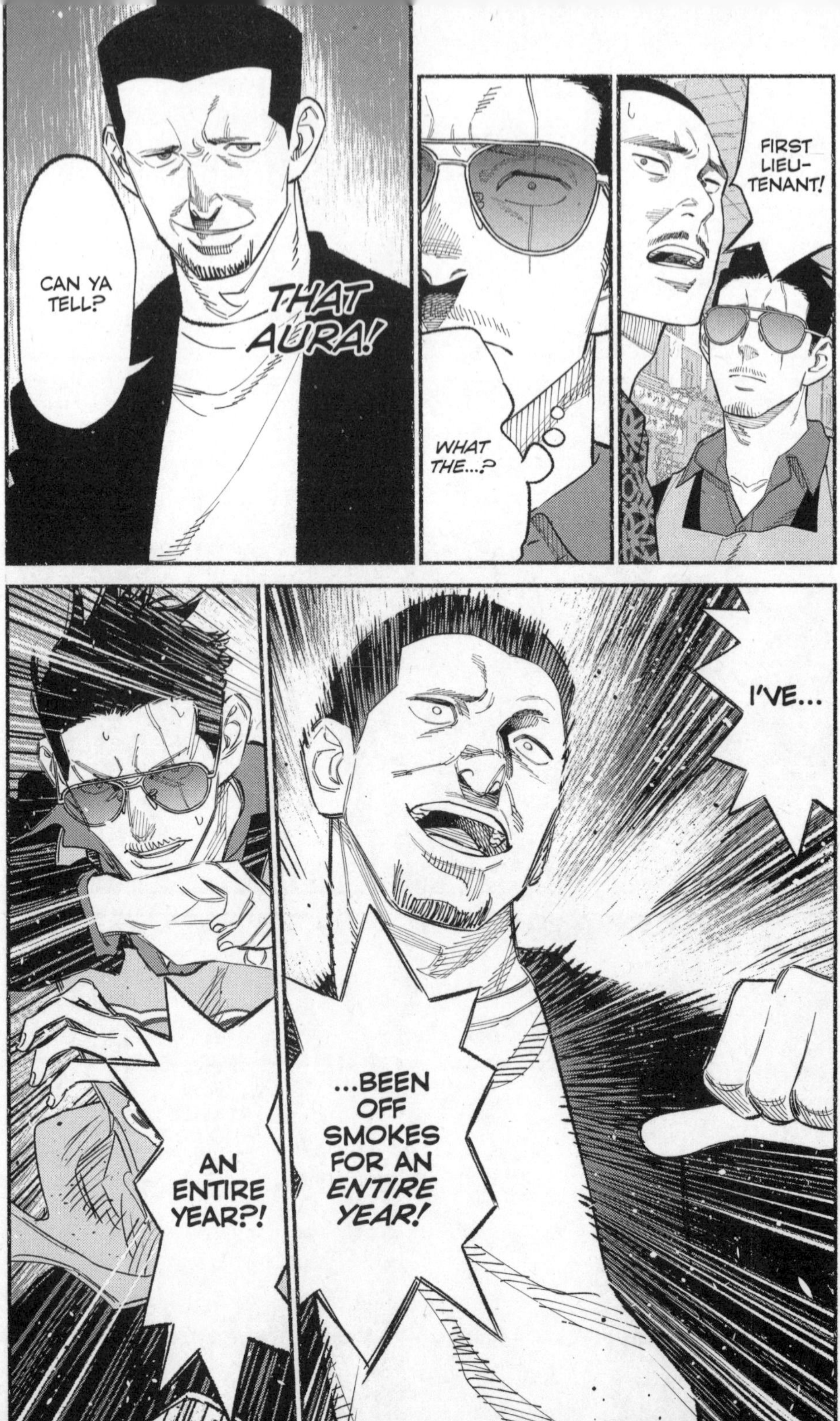
FIRST LIEU-TENANT!
WHAT THE...?
THAT AURA!
CAN YA TELL?
I'VE...
...BEEN OFF SMOKES FOR AN ENTIRE YEAR!
AN ENTIRE YEAR?!

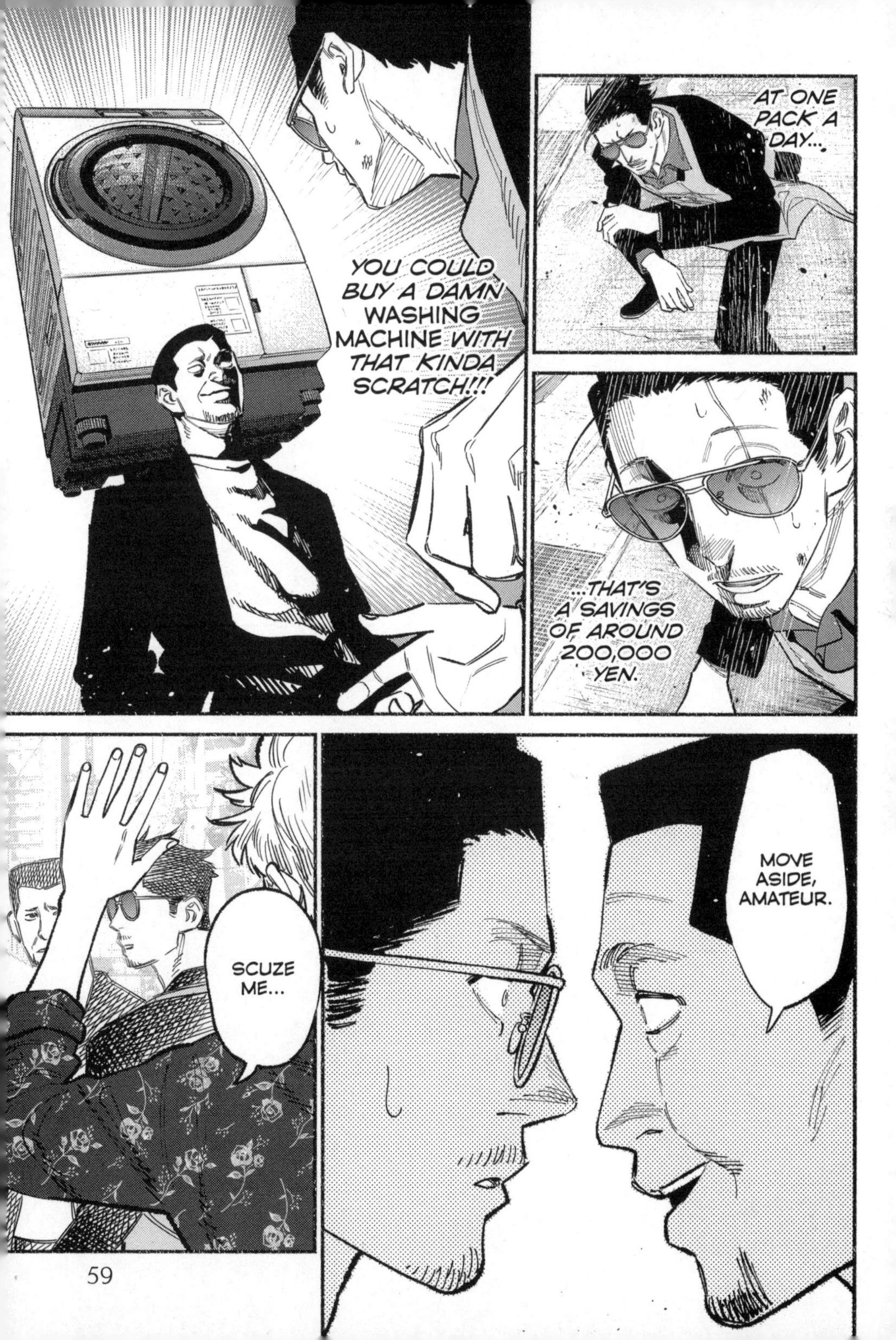
AT ONE PACK A DAY...
...THAT'S A SAVINGS OF AROUND 200,000 YEN.
YOU COULD BUY A DAMN WASHING MACHINE WITH THAT KINDA SCRATCH!!!
MOVE ASIDE, AMATEUR.
SCUZE ME...

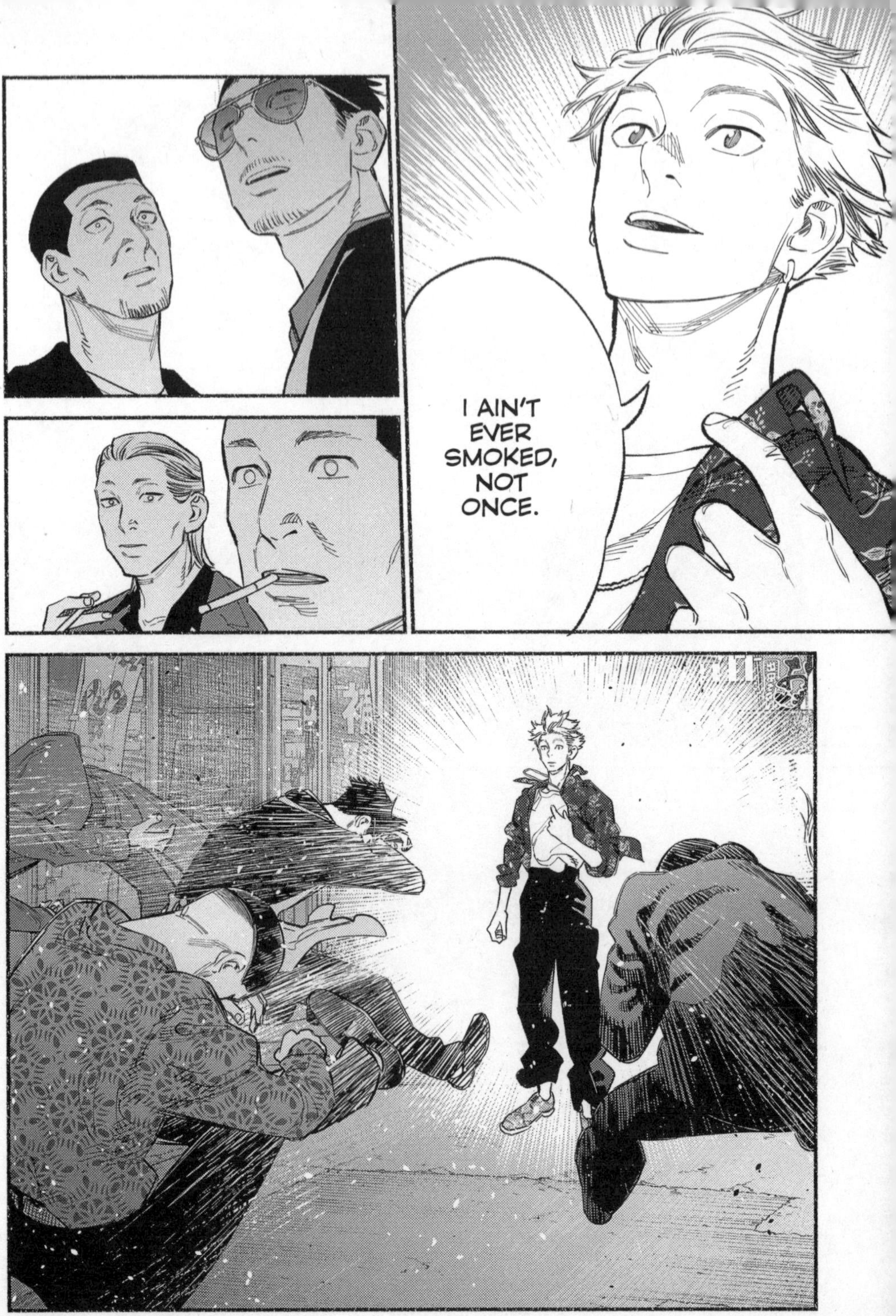
I AIN'T EVER SMOKED, NOT ONCE.

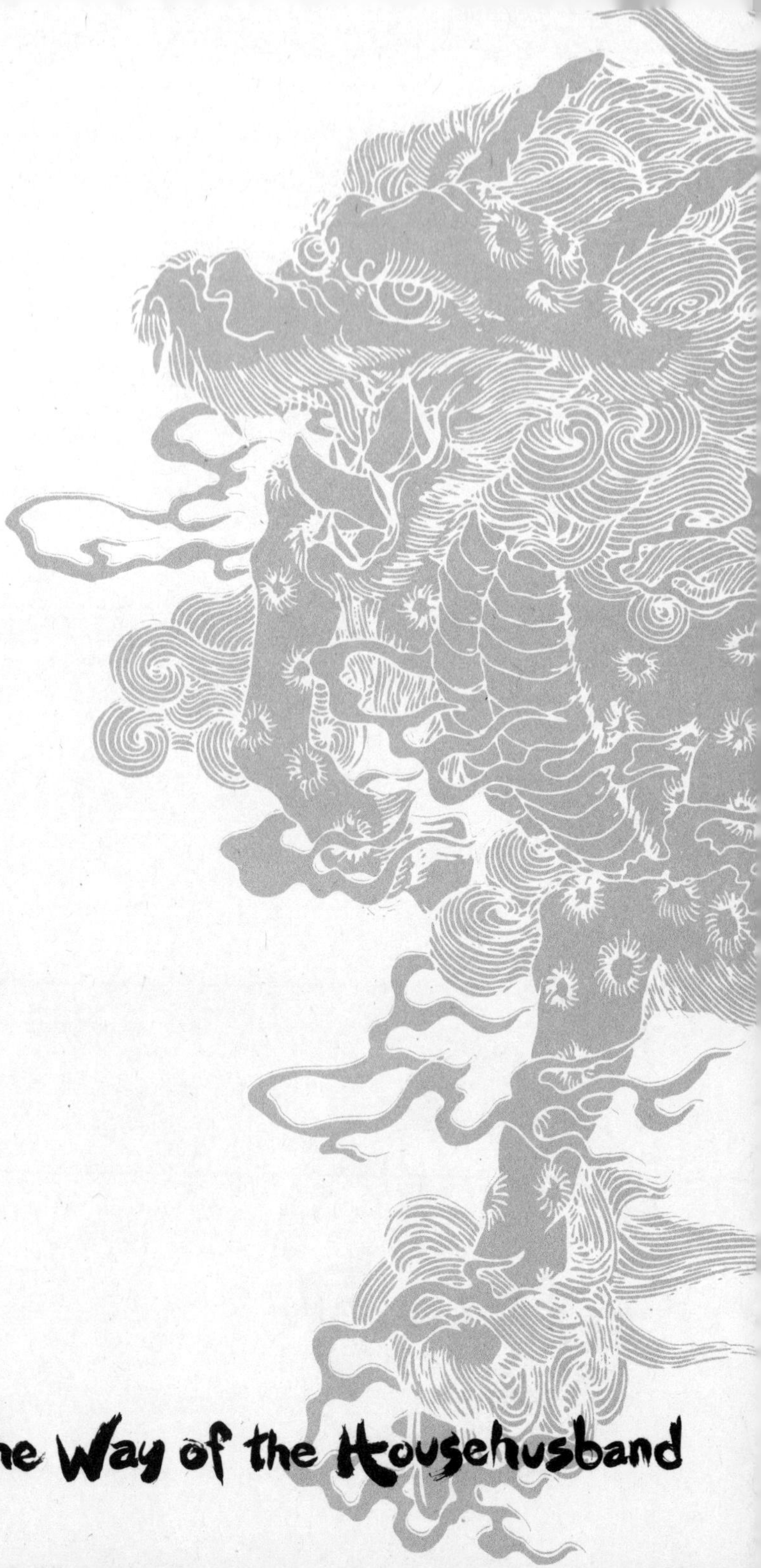

The Way of the Househusband

CHAPTER 86

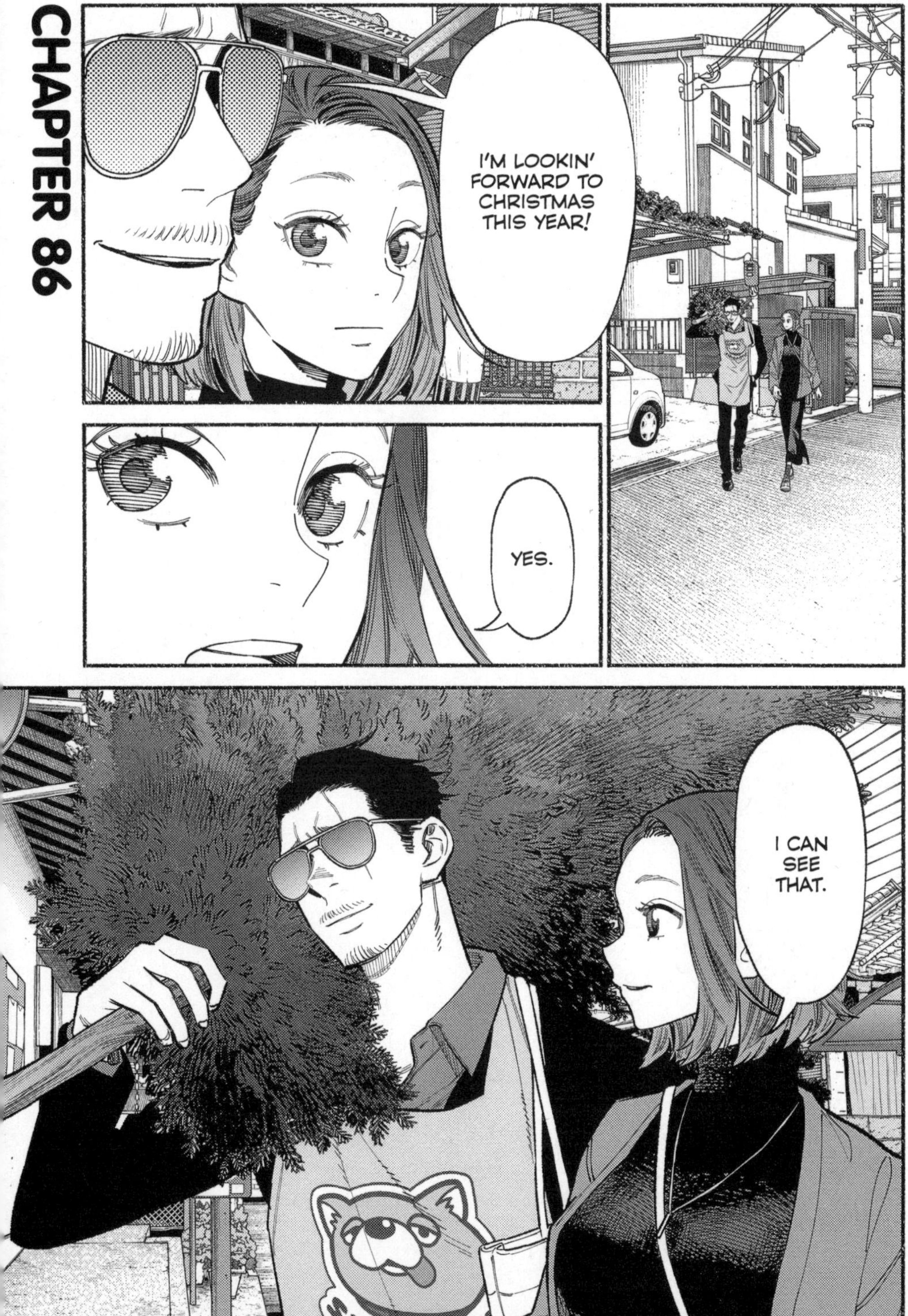
I'M LOOKIN' FORWARD TO CHRISTMAS THIS YEAR!
YES.
I CAN SEE THAT.

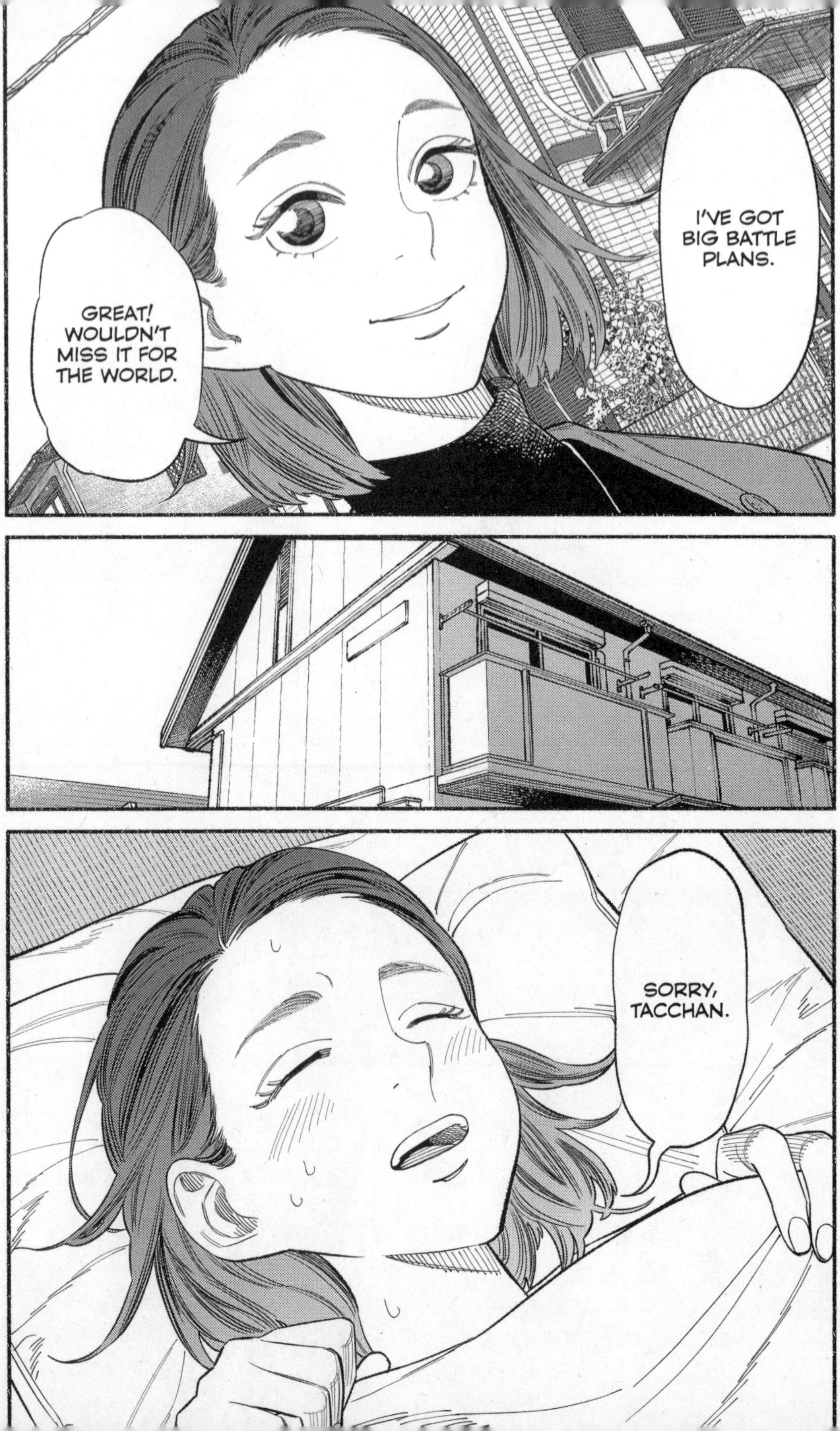
I'VE GOT BIG BATTLE PLANS.
GREAT! WOULDN'T MISS IT FOR THE WORLD.
SORRY, TACCHAN.

I MUST'VE CAUGHT A BUG.
DON'T SWEAT IT. STAY IN BED AND REST UP.
MERRY ...
... XMAS ...

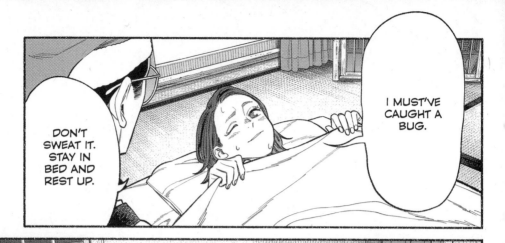

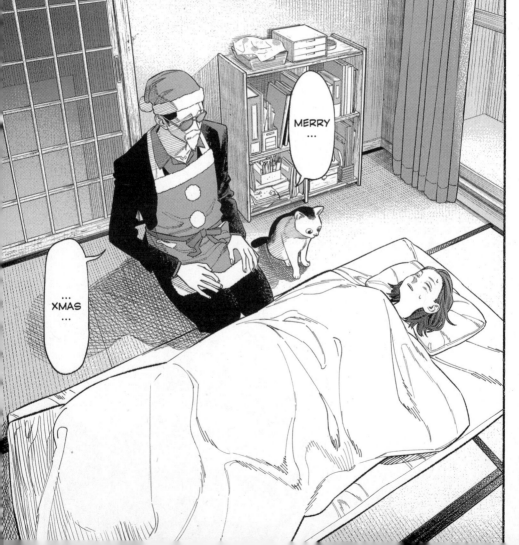

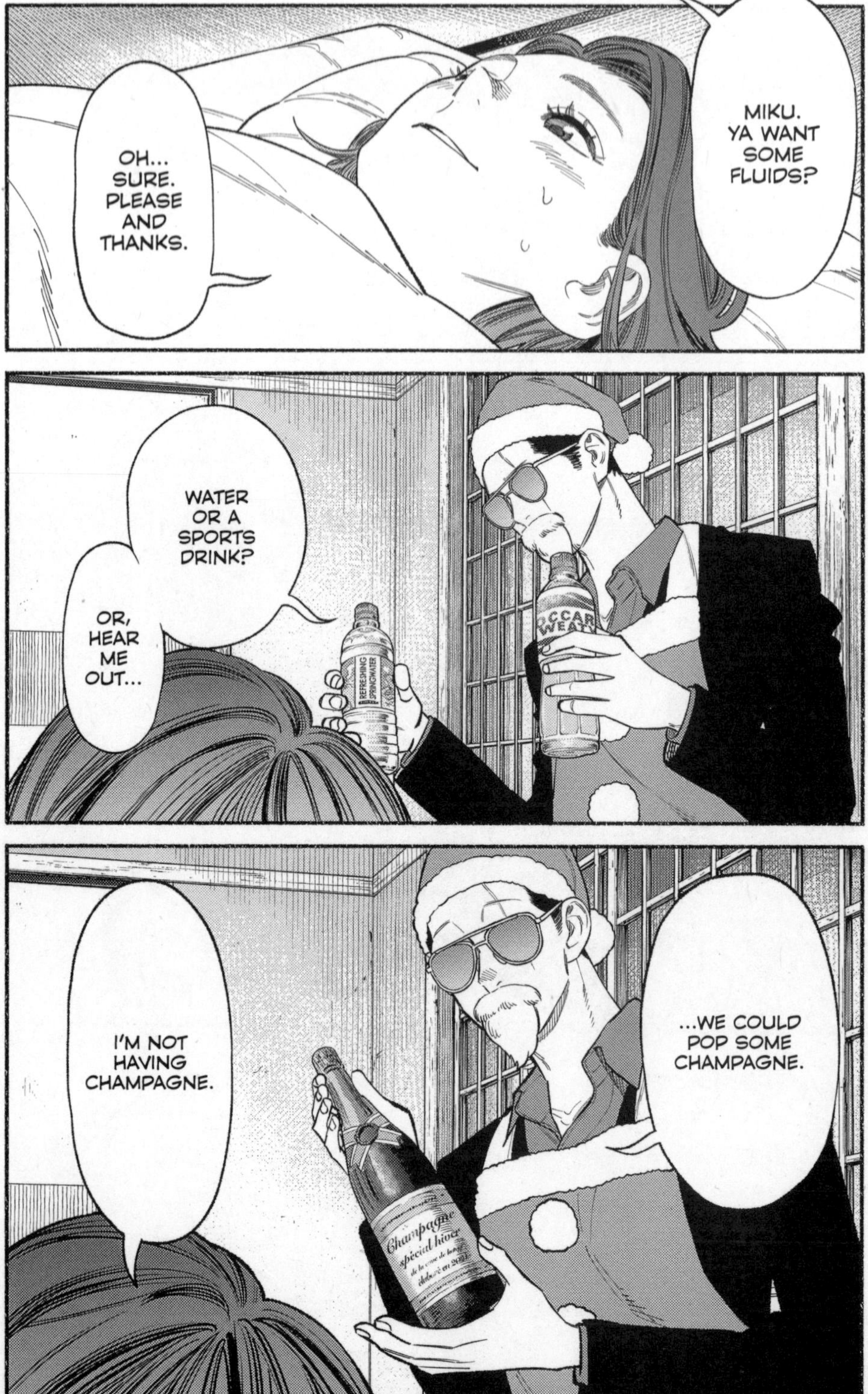
MIKU. YA WANT SOME FLUIDS?
OH... SURE. PLEASE AND THANKS.
WATER OR A SPORTS DRINK?
OR, HEAR ME OUT...
REFRESHING SPRINGWATER
...WE COULD POP SOME CHAMPAGNE.
Champagne
special hiver
I'M NOT HAVING CHAMPAGNE.

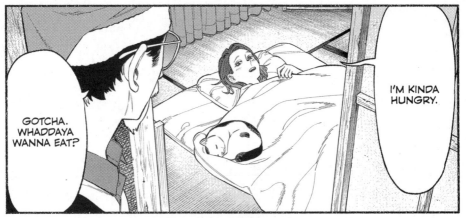

I'M KINDA HUNGRY.

GOTCHA. WHADDAYA WANNA EAT?

POR- RIDGE?

OR I COULD WHIP UP SOME UDON NOODLES.

HMM...

THERE'S ALSO CAKE!

ANYTHING BUT THAT.

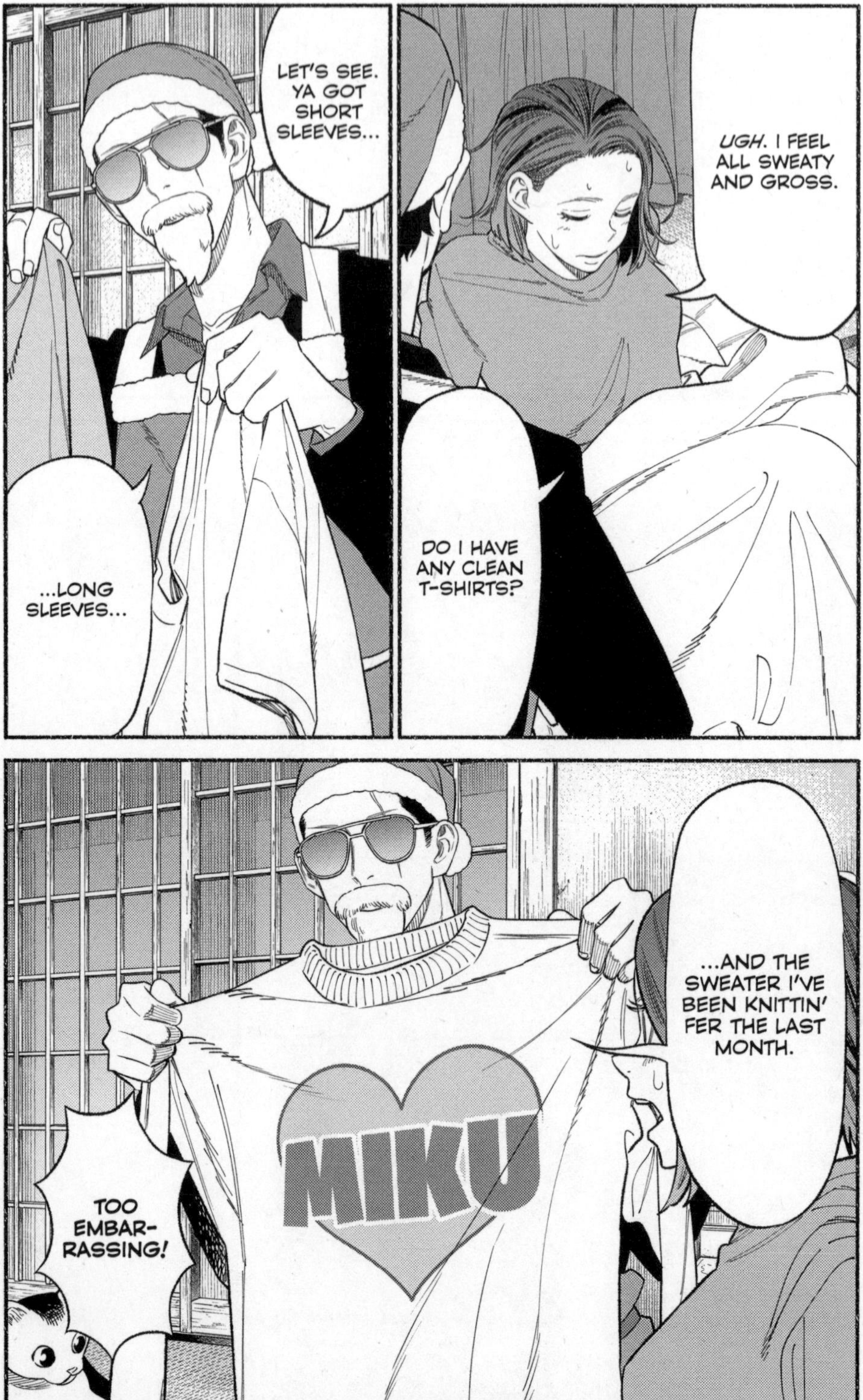
UGH. I FEEL ALL SWEATY AND GROSS.
DO I HAVE ANY CLEAN T-SHIRTS?
LET'S SEE. YA GOT SHORT SLEEVES...
...LONG SLEEVES...
...AND THE SWEATER I'VE BEEN KNITTIN' FER THE LAST MONTH.
MIKU
TOO EMBAR-RASSING!

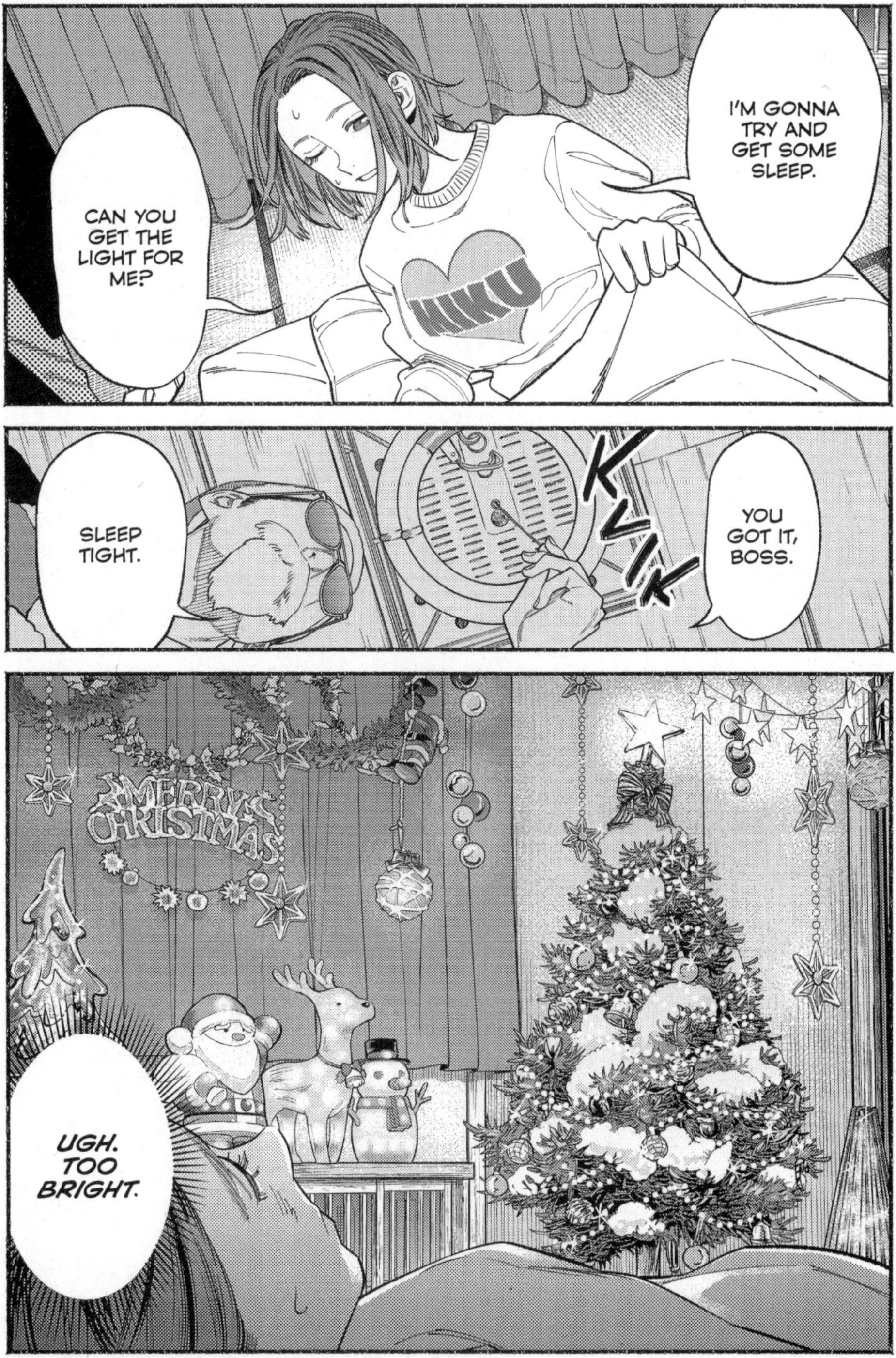
I'M GONNA TRY AND GET SOME SLEEP.
CAN YOU GET THE LIGHT FOR ME?
YOU GOT IT, BOSS.
KLIK
SLEEP TIGHT.
MERRY CHRISTMAS
UGH. TOO BRIGHT.

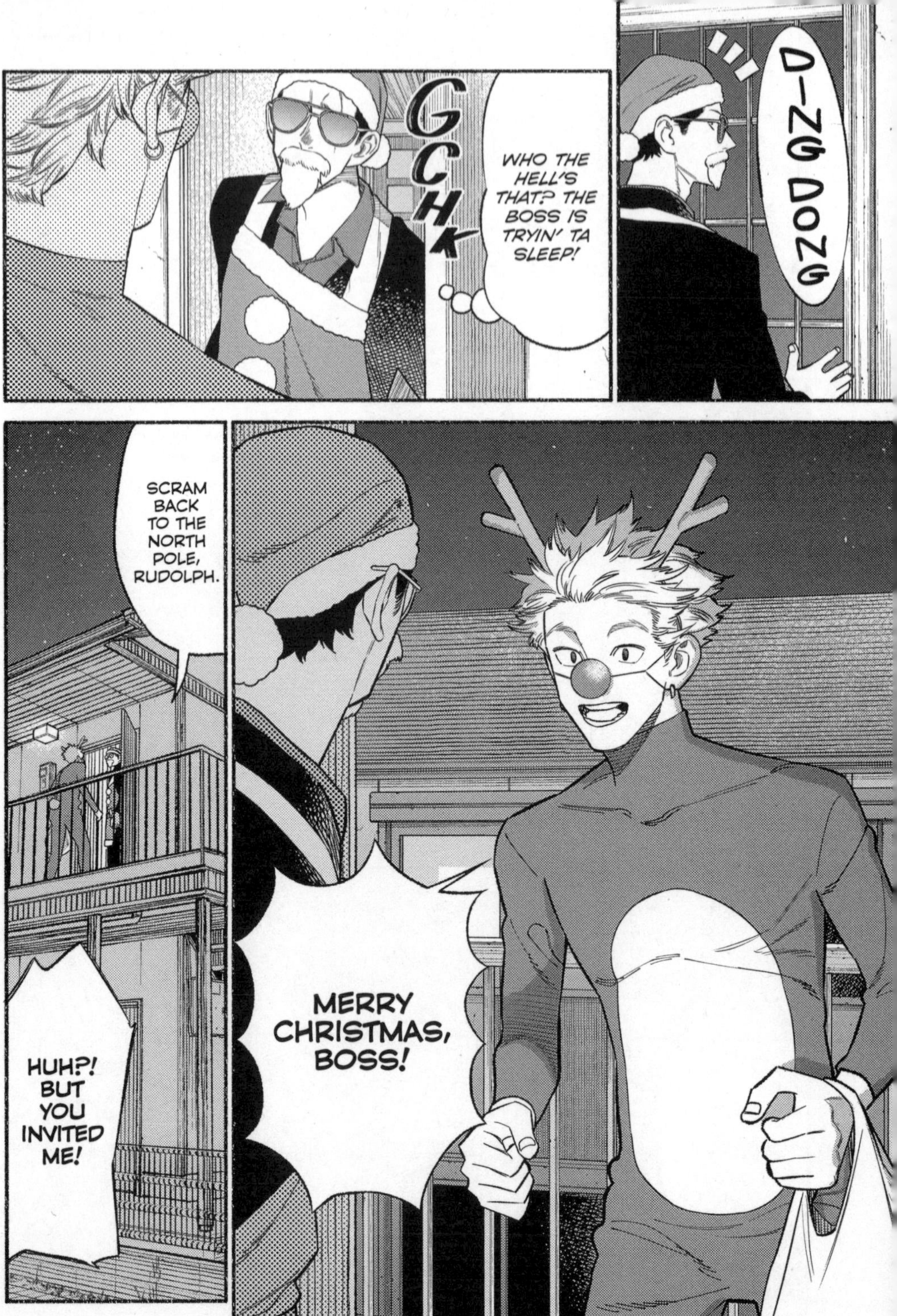
DING DONG
GCHK
WHO THE HELL'S THAT? THE BOSS IS TRYIN' TA SLEEP!
MERRY CHRISTMAS, BOSS!
SCRAM BACK TO THE NORTH POLE, RUDOLPH.
HUH?! BUT YOU INVITED ME!

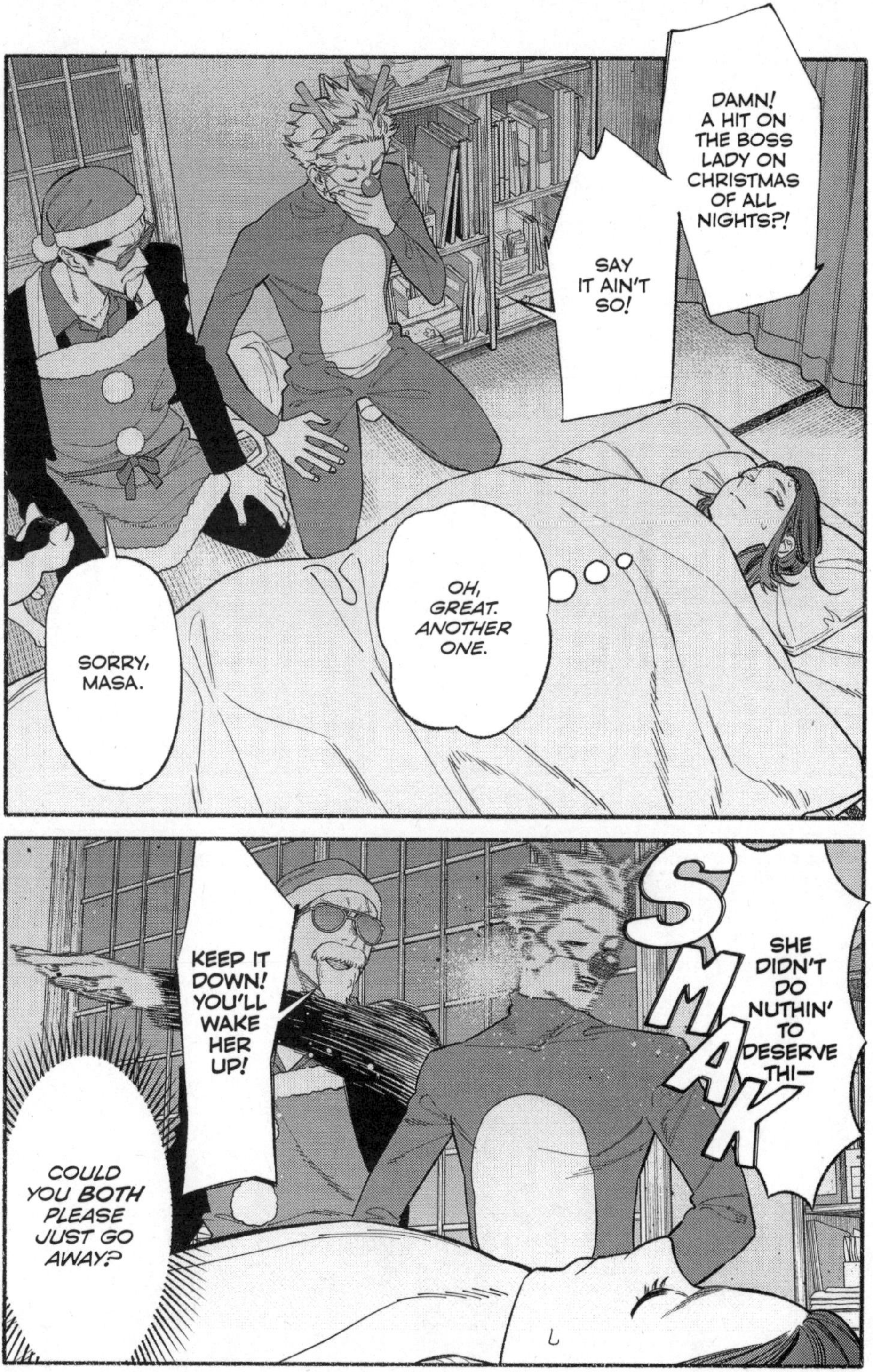
DAMN! A HIT ON THE BOSS LADY ON CHRISTMAS OF ALL NIGHTS?!
SAY IT AIN'T SO!
OH, GREAT. ANOTHER ONE.
SORRY, MASA.
SMAK
SHE DIDN'T DO NUTHIN' TO DESERVE THI—
KEEP IT DOWN! YOU'LL WAKE HER UP!
COULD YOU **BOTH** PLEASE JUST GO AWAY?

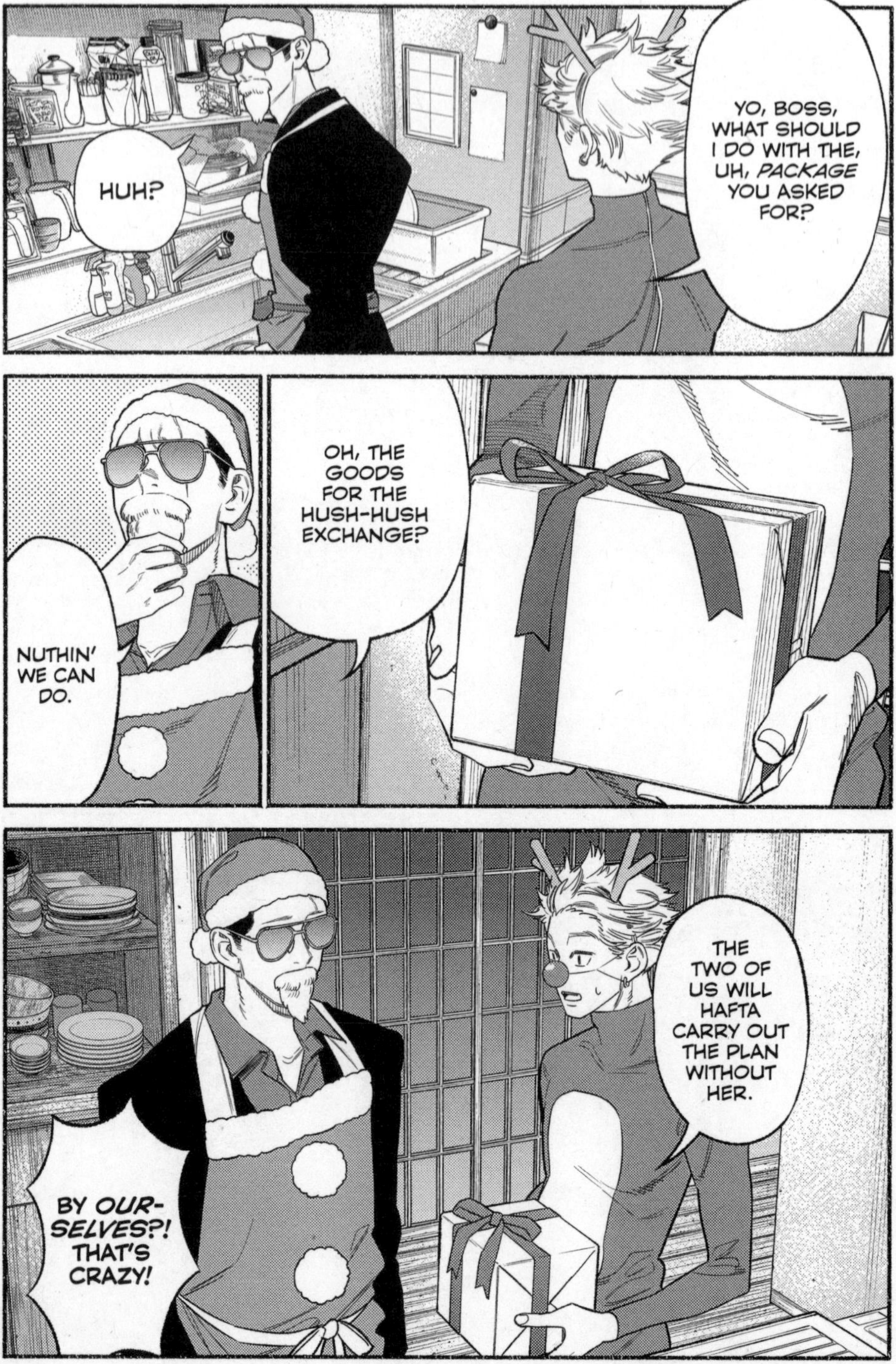
YO, BOSS, WHAT SHOULD I DO WITH THE, UH, *PACKAGE* YOU ASKED FOR?
HUH?
OH, THE GOODS FOR THE HUSH-HUSH EXCHANGE?
NUTHIN' WE CAN DO.
THE TWO OF US WILL HAFTA CARRY OUT THE PLAN WITHOUT HER.
BY *OUR-SELVES*?! THAT'S CRAZY!

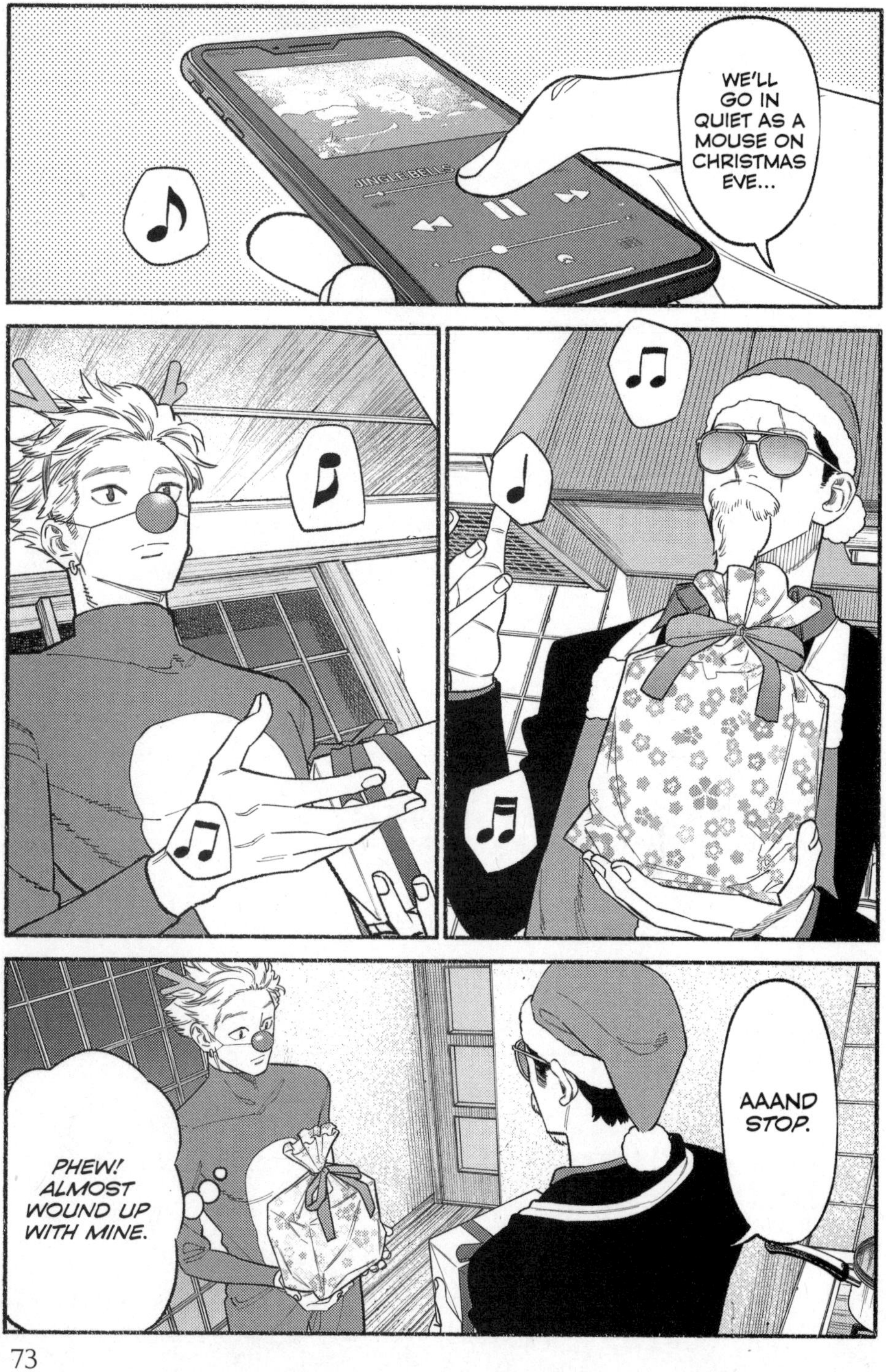
WE'LL GO IN QUIET AS A MOUSE ON CHRISTMAS EVE...
JINGLE BELLS
AAAND STOP.
PHEW! ALMOST WOUND UP WITH MINE.

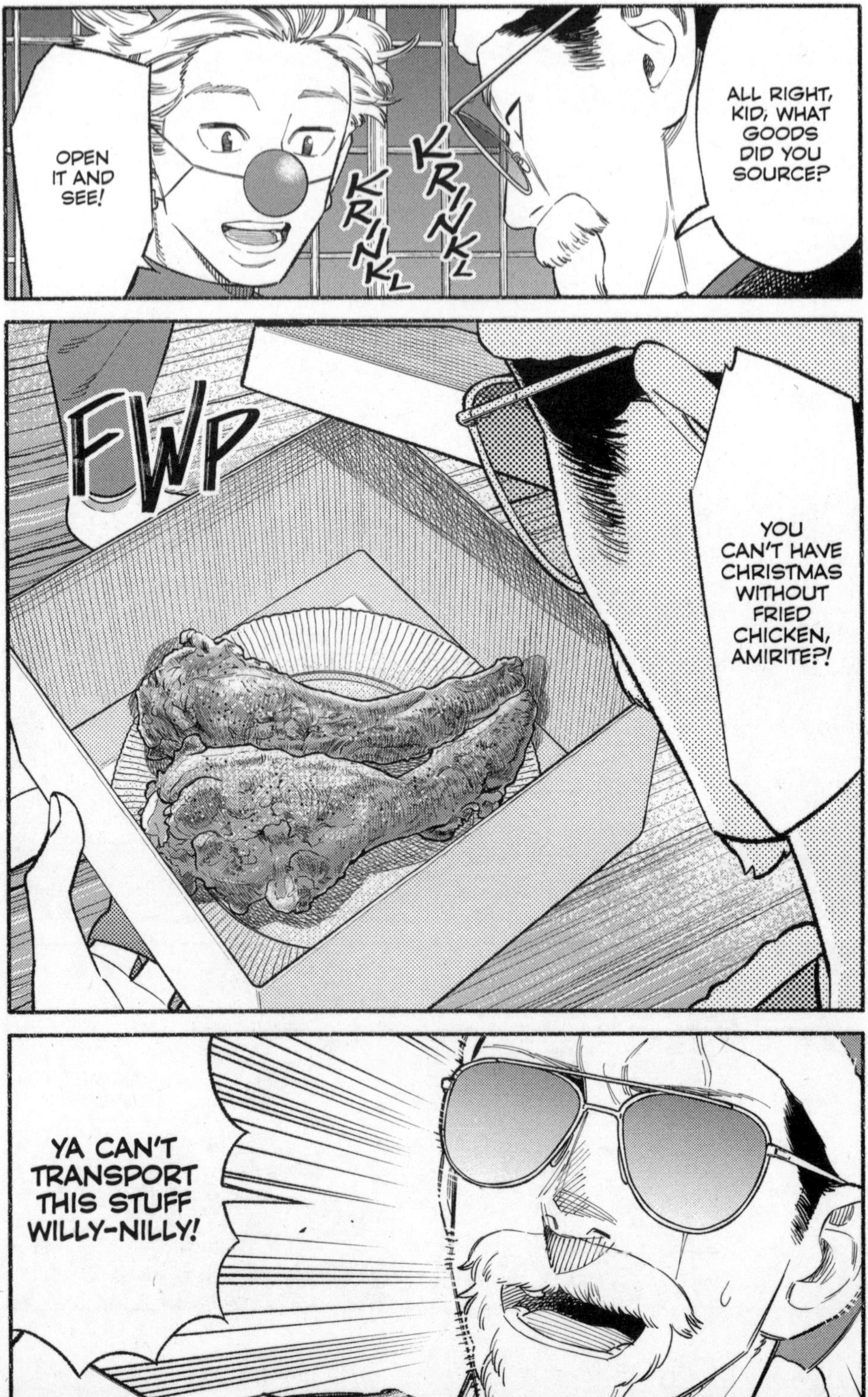
ALL RIGHT, KID; WHAT GOODS DID YOU SOURCE?
KRINKL
KRINKL
OPEN IT AND SEE!
FWP
YOU CAN'T HAVE CHRISTMAS WITHOUT FRIED CHICKEN, AMIRITE?!
YA CAN'T TRANSPORT THIS STUFF WILLY-NILLY!

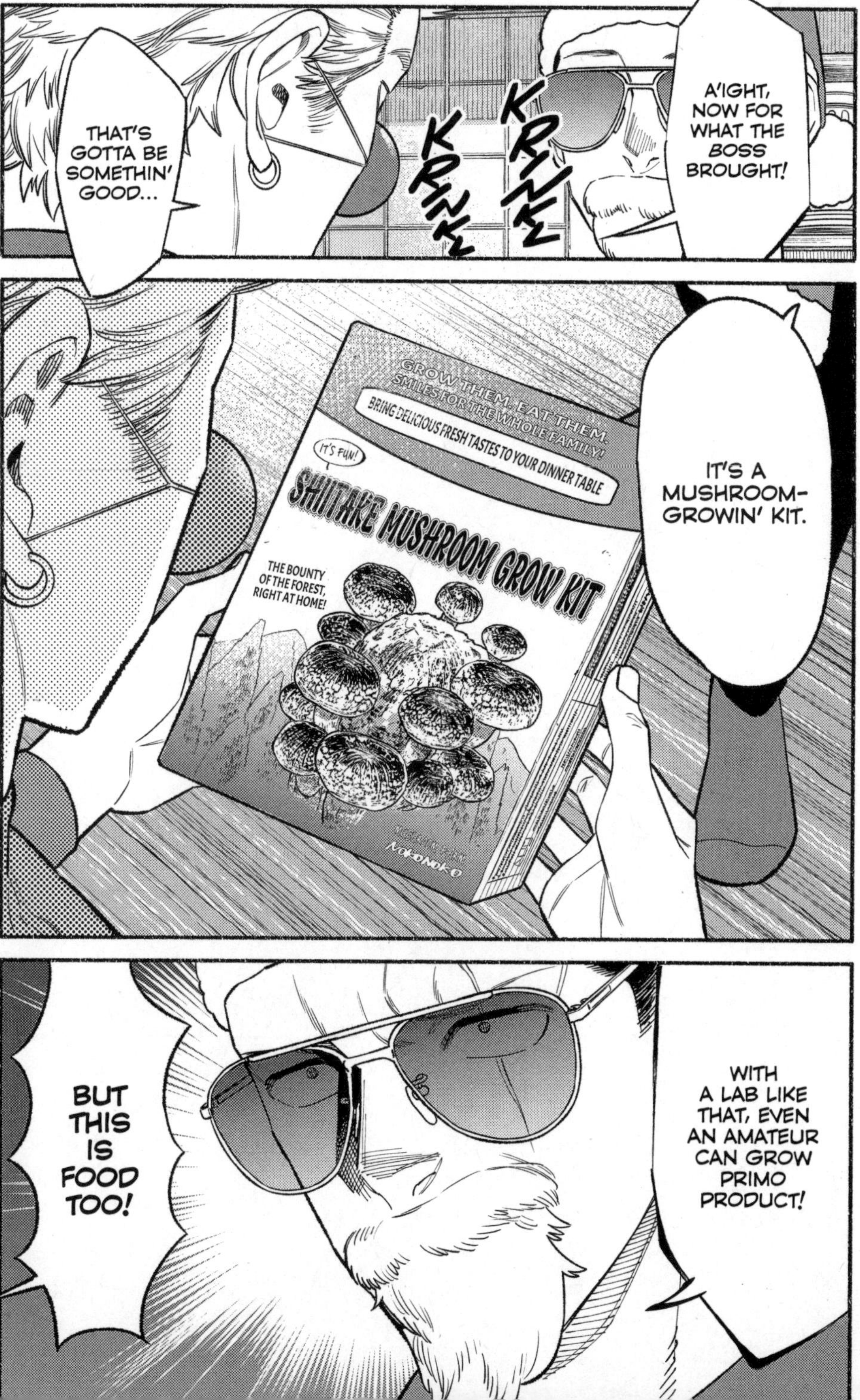
A'IGHT, NOW FOR WHAT THE *BOSS* BROUGHT!
KRINKLE
KRINKLE
THAT'S GOTTA BE SOMETHIN' GOOD...
IT'S A MUSHROOM-GROWIN' KIT.
GROW THEM. EAT THEM. SMILES FOR THE WHOLE FAMILY!
BRING DELICIOUS FRESH TASTES TO YOUR DINNER TABLE
IT'S FUN!
SHIITAKE MUSHROOM GROW KIT
THE BOUNTY OF THE FOREST, RIGHT AT HOME!
WITH A LAB LIKE THAT, EVEN AN AMATEUR CAN GROW PRIMO PRODUCT!
BUT THIS IS FOOD TOO!

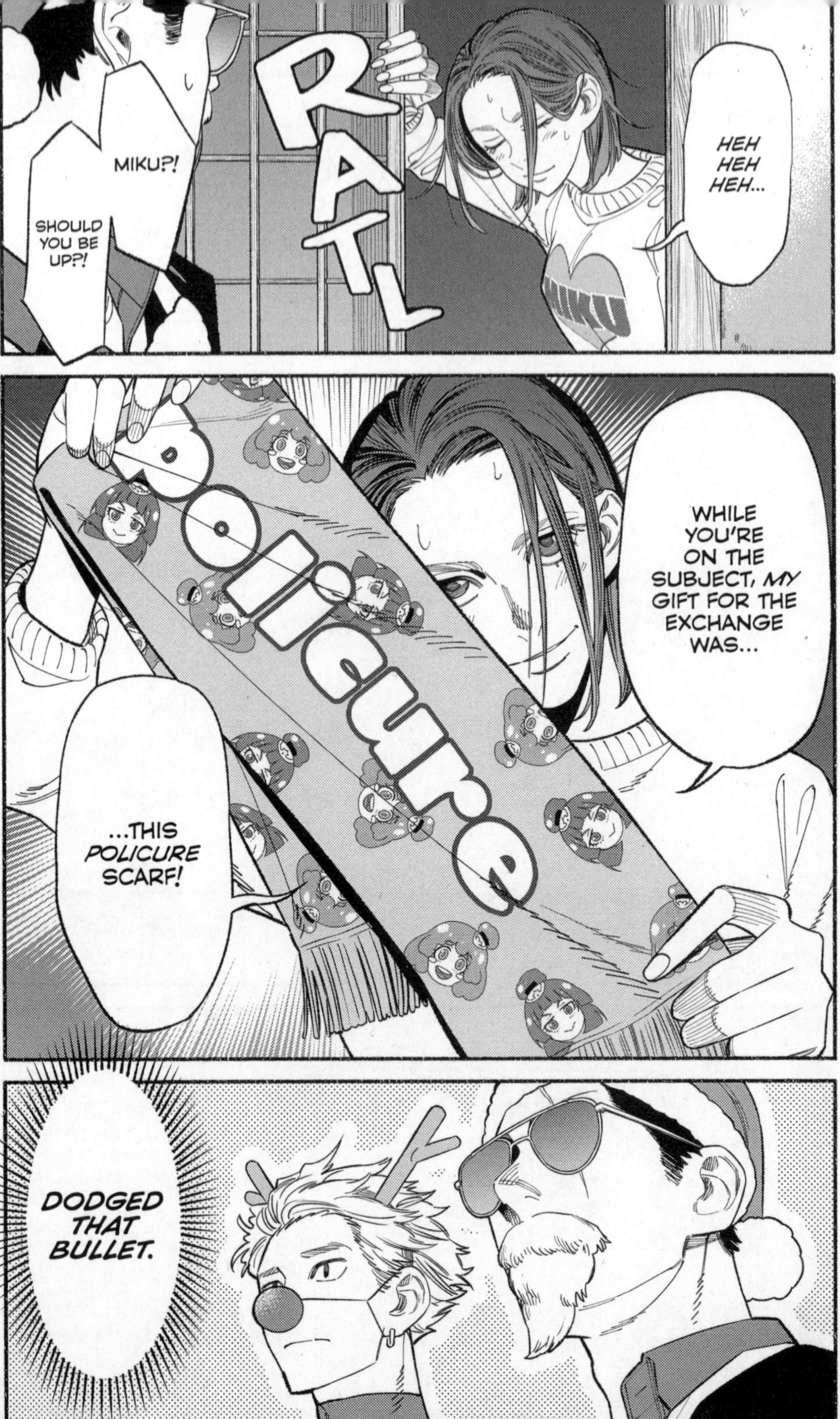
HEH HEH HEH...
RATTL
MIKU?!
SHOULD YOU BE UP?!
WHILE YOU'RE ON THE SUBJECT, *MY* GIFT FOR THE EXCHANGE WAS...
Policure
...THIS *POLICURE* SCARF!
DODGED THAT BULLET.

The Way of the Househusband

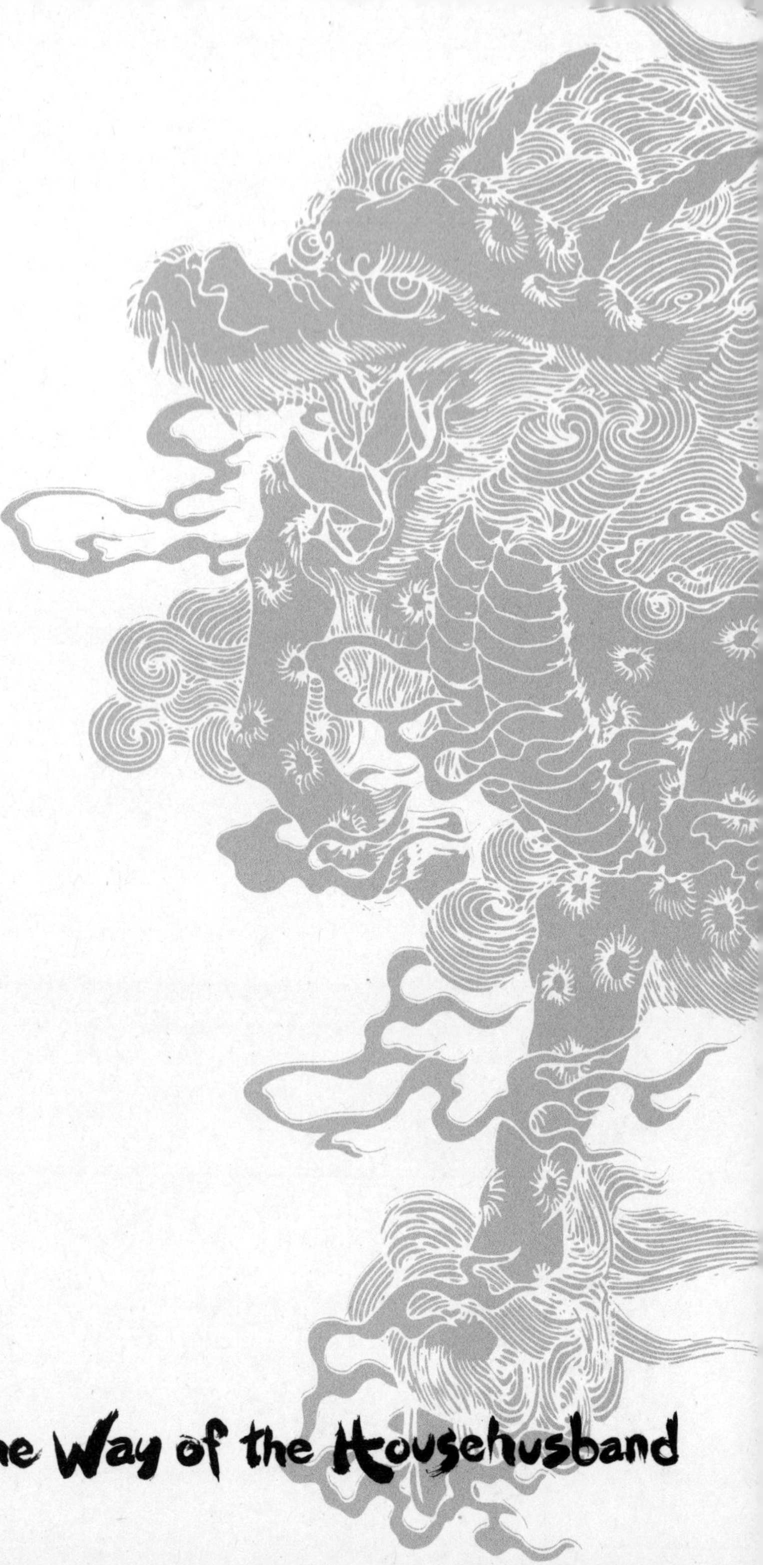

CHAPTER 87

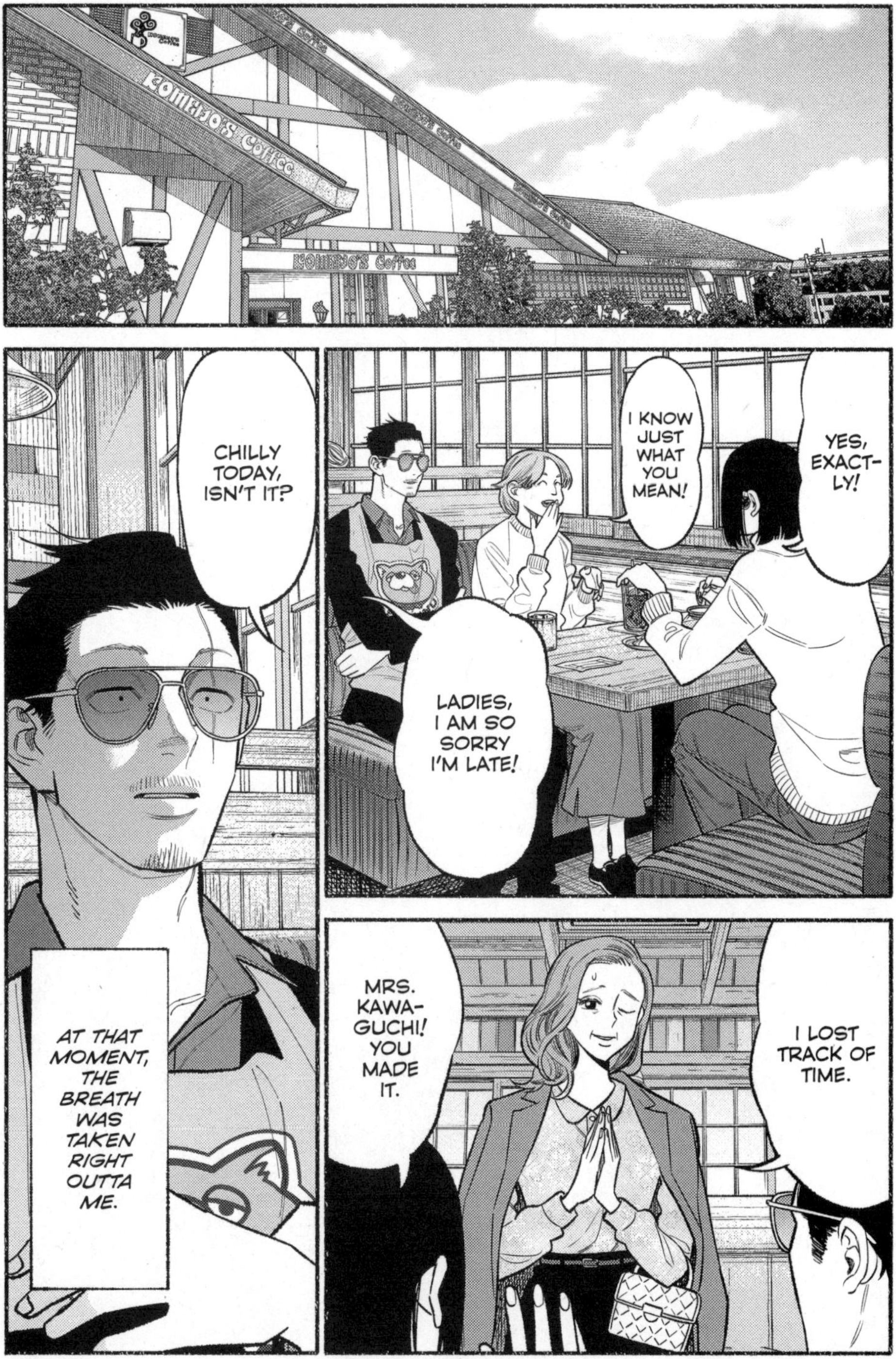
YES, EXACTLY!
I KNOW JUST WHAT YOU MEAN!
LADIES, I AM SO SORRY I'M LATE!
I LOST TRACK OF TIME.
MRS. KAWAGUCHI! YOU MADE IT.
CHILLY TODAY, ISN'T IT?
AT THAT MOMENT, THE BREATH WAS TAKEN RIGHT OUTTA ME.

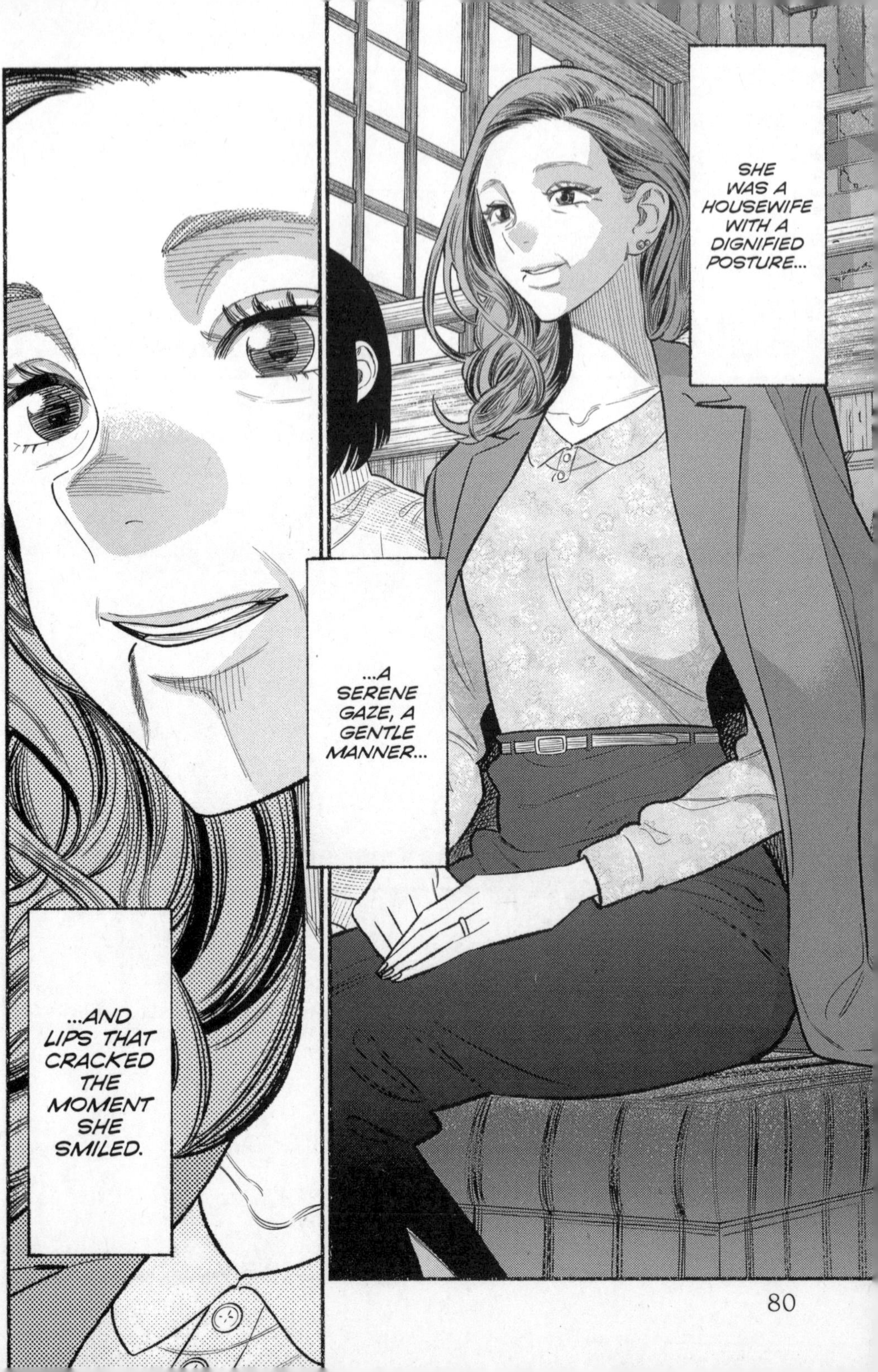
SHE WAS A HOUSEWIFE WITH A DIGNIFIED POSTURE...
...A SERENE GAZE, A GENTLE MANNER...
...AND LIPS THAT CRACKED THE MOMENT SHE SMILED.

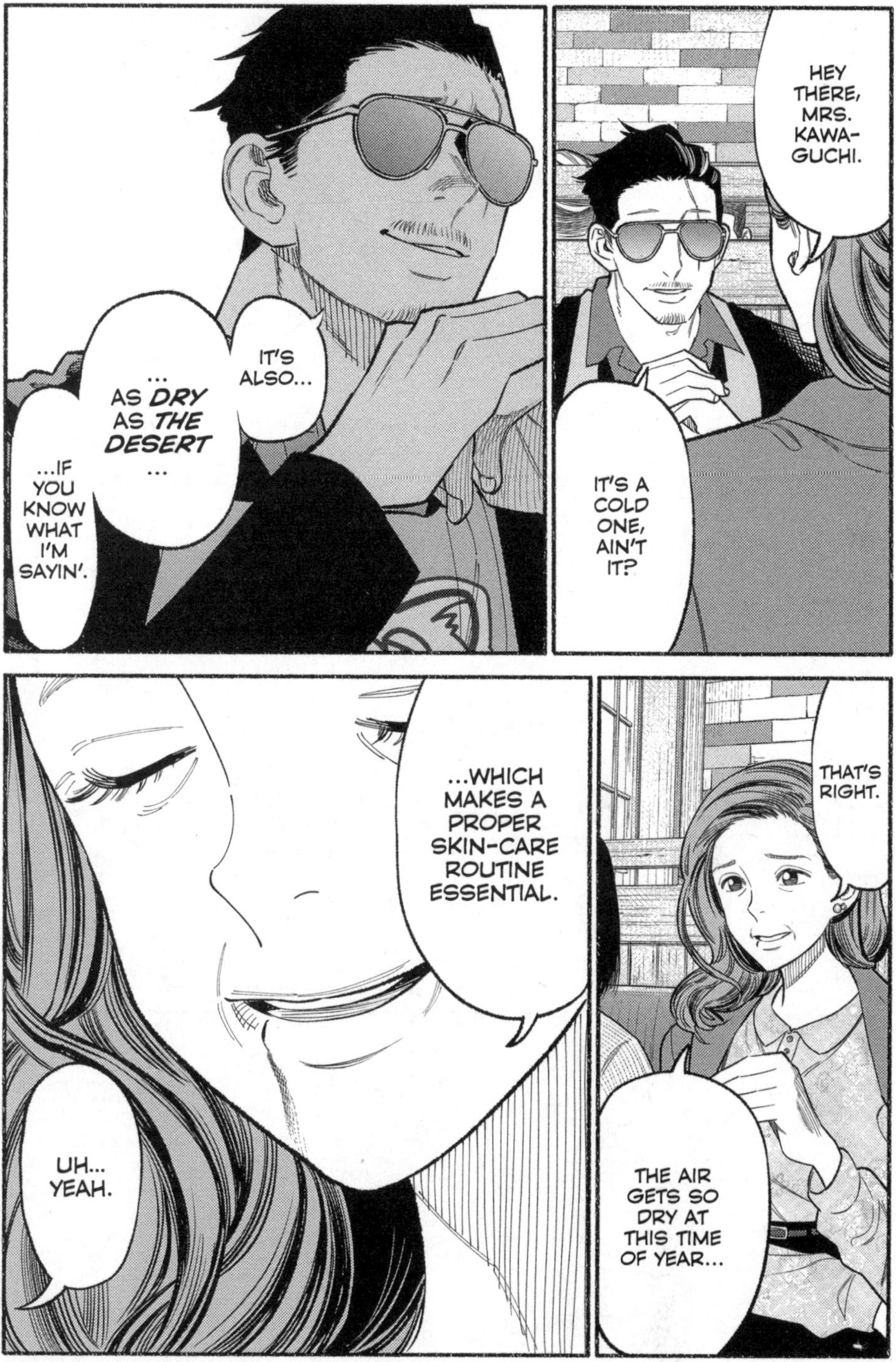
HEY THERE, MRS. KAWA-GUCHI.
IT'S A COLD ONE, AIN'T IT?
IT'S ALSO...
...AS *DRY* AS *THE DESERT*...
...IF YOU KNOW WHAT I'M SAYIN'.
THAT'S RIGHT.
THE AIR GETS SO DRY AT THIS TIME OF YEAR...
...WHICH MAKES A PROPER SKIN-CARE ROUTINE ESSENTIAL.
UH... YEAH.

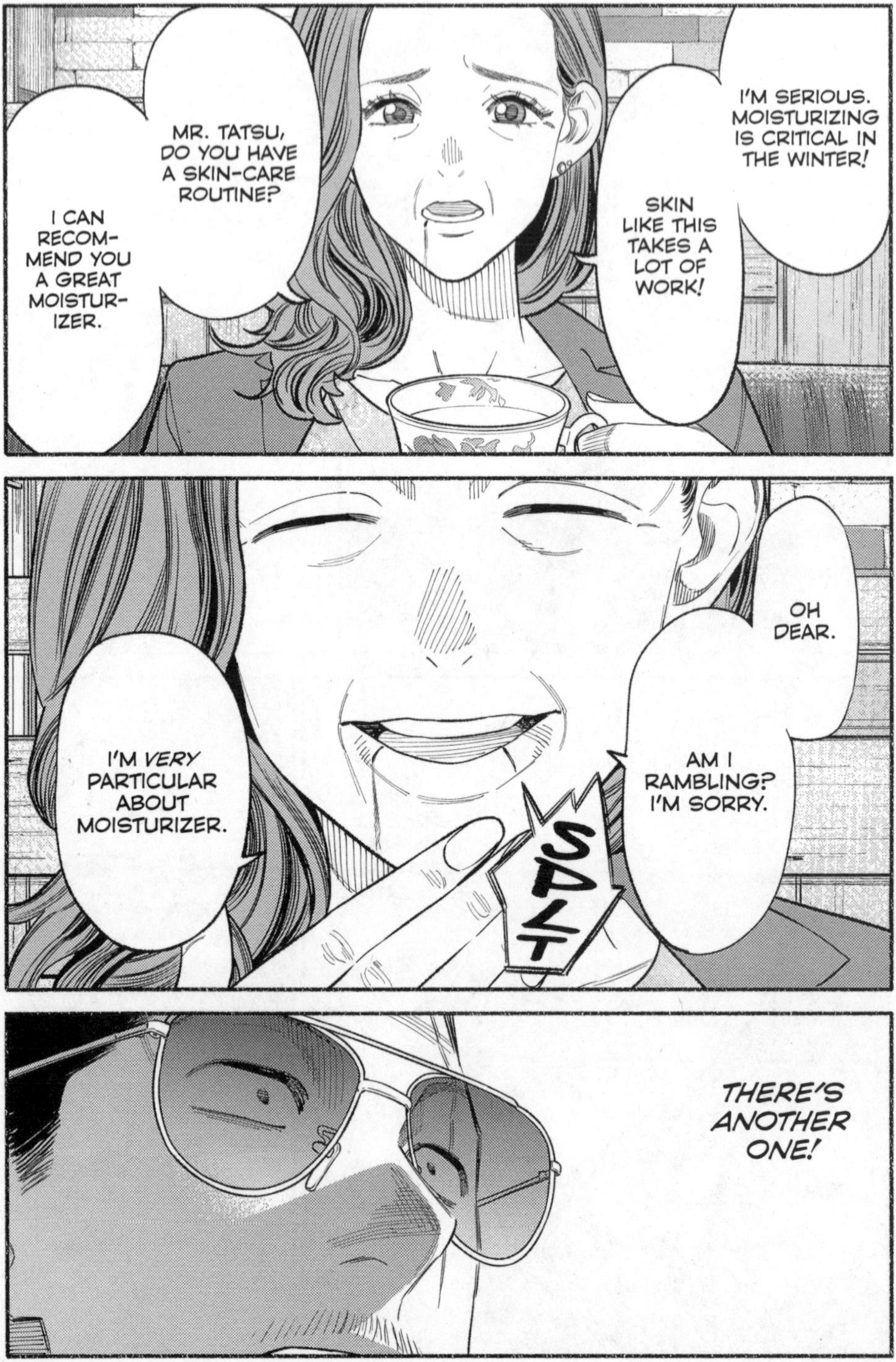
I'M SERIOUS. MOISTURIZING IS CRITICAL IN THE WINTER!
SKIN LIKE THIS TAKES A LOT OF WORK!
MR. TATSU, DO YOU HAVE A SKIN-CARE ROUTINE?
I CAN RECOMMEND YOU A GREAT MOISTURIZER.
OH DEAR.
AM I RAMBLING? I'M SORRY.
SPLT
I'M *VERY* PARTICULAR ABOUT MOISTURIZER.
THERE'S ANOTHER ONE!

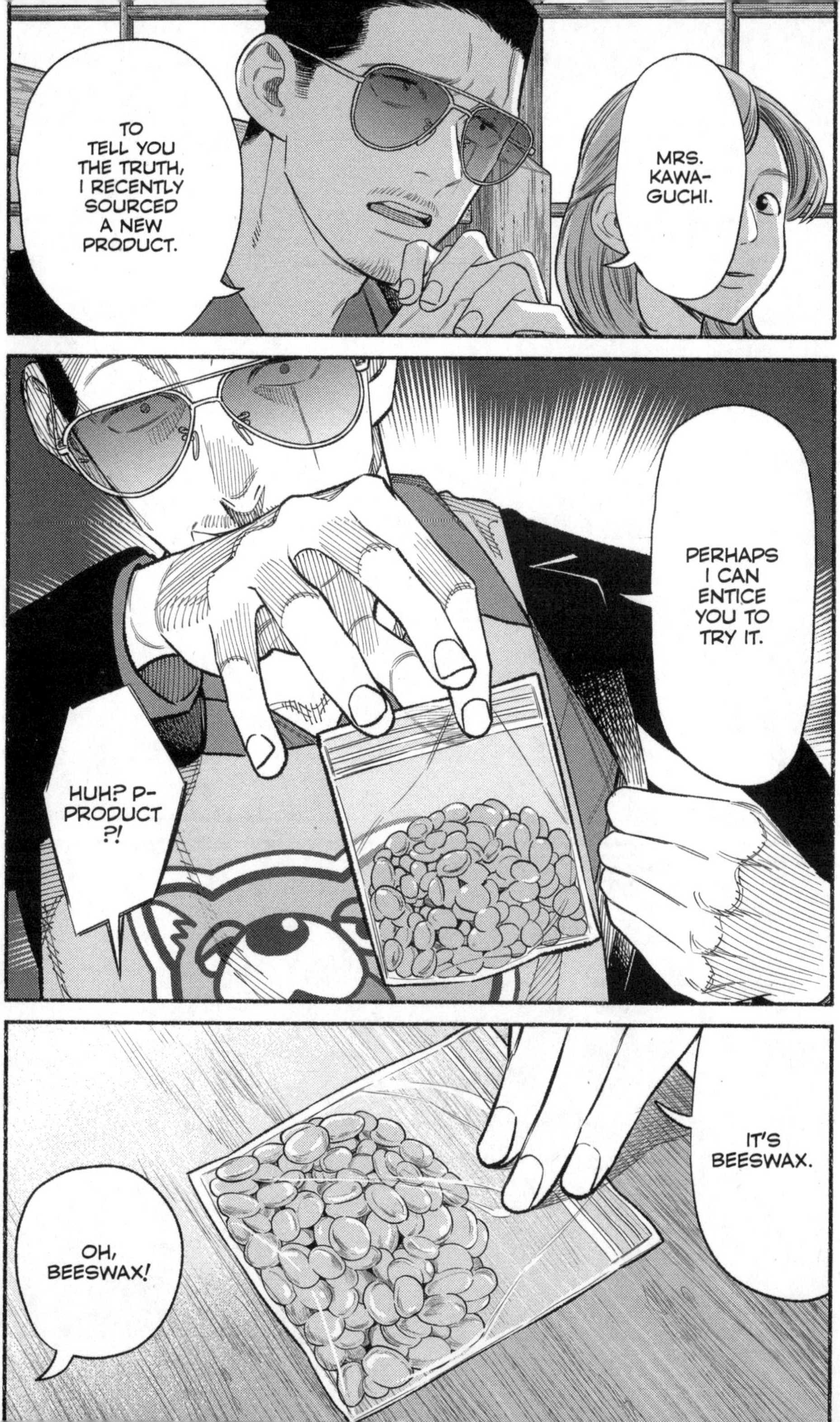
MRS. KAWA-GUCHI.
TO TELL YOU THE TRUTH, I RECENTLY SOURCED A NEW PRODUCT.
PERHAPS I CAN ENTICE YOU TO TRY IT.
HUH? P-PRODUCT?!
IT'S BEESWAX.
OH, BEESWAX!

PREPARING THE PRODUCT IS SIMPLE.

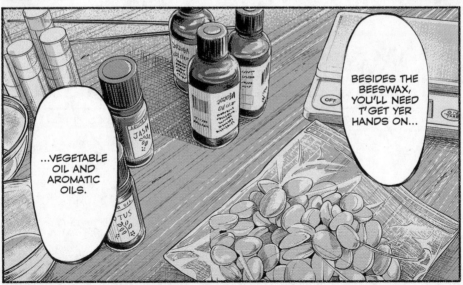

BESIDES THE BEESWAX, YOU'LL NEED T'GET YER HANDS ON...

...VEGETABLE OIL AND AROMATIC OILS.

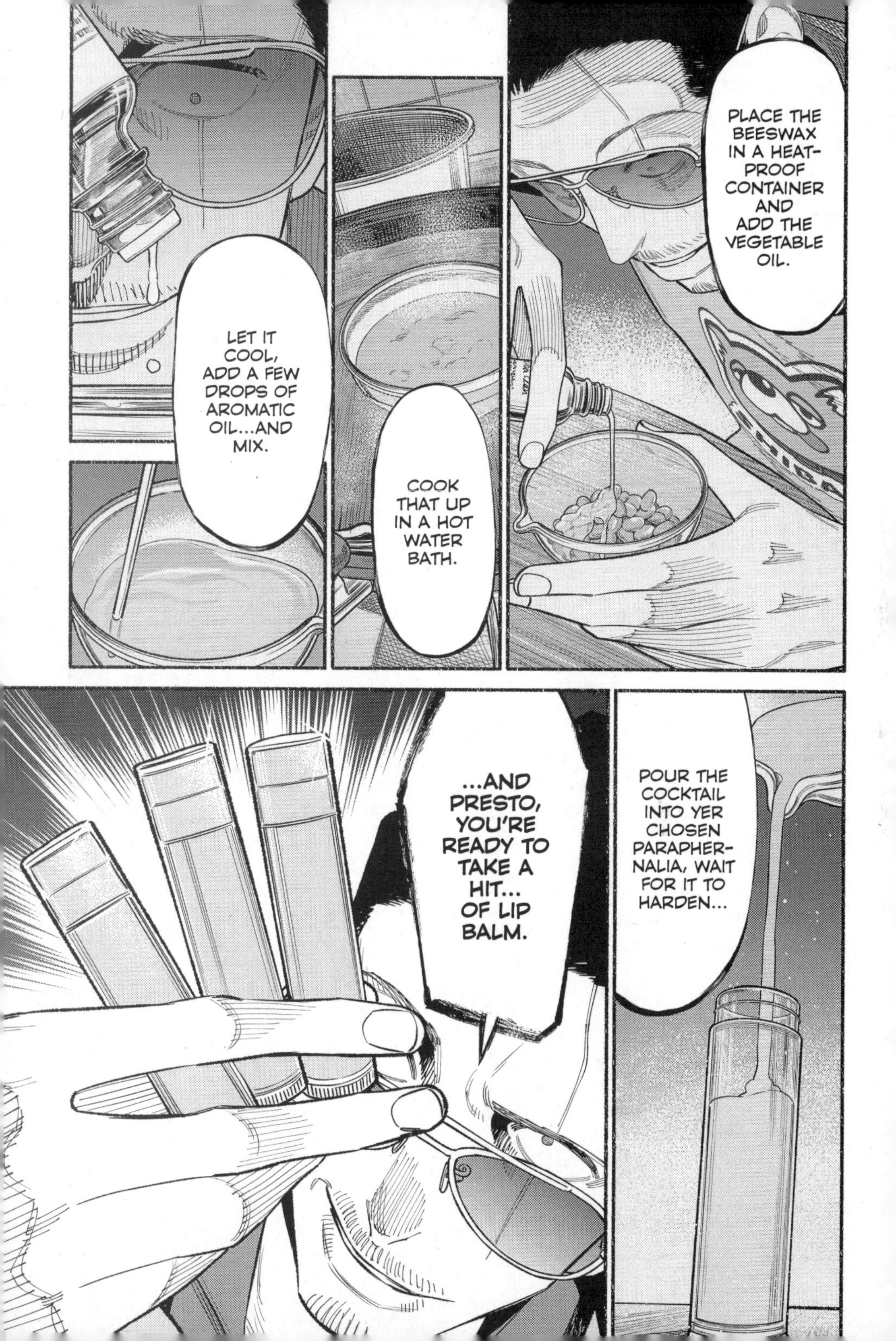
PLACE THE BEESWAX IN A HEAT-PROOF CONTAINER AND ADD THE VEGETABLE OIL.
COOK THAT UP IN A HOT WATER BATH.
LET IT COOL, ADD A FEW DROPS OF AROMATIC OIL...AND MIX.
POUR THE COCKTAIL INTO YER CHOSEN PARAPHER-NALIA, WAIT FOR IT TO HARDEN...
...AND PRESTO, YOU'RE READY TO TAKE A HIT... OF LIP BALM.

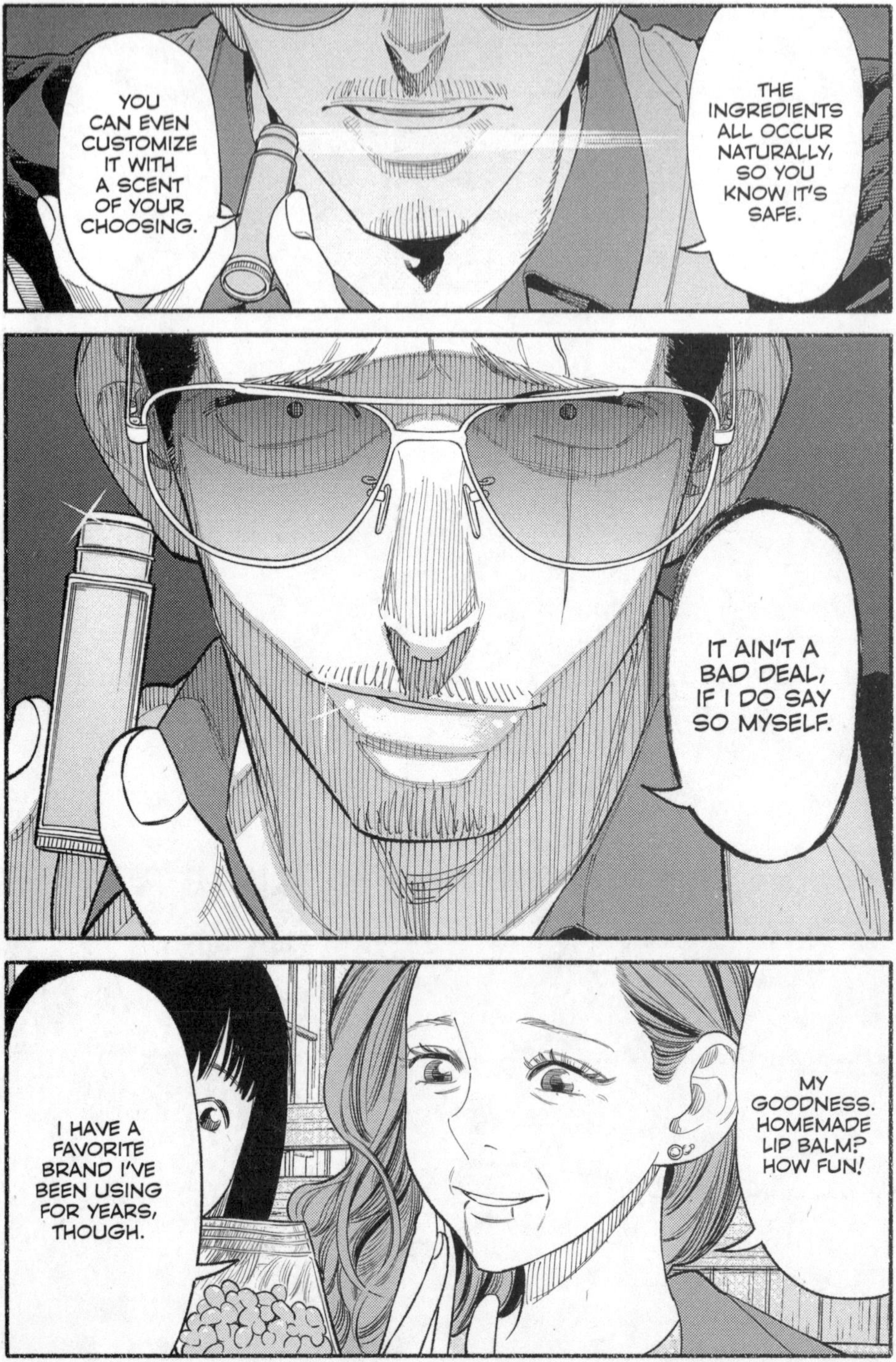
THE INGREDIENTS ALL OCCUR NATURALLY, SO YOU KNOW IT'S SAFE.
YOU CAN EVEN CUSTOMIZE IT WITH A SCENT OF YOUR CHOOSING.
IT AIN'T A BAD DEAL, IF I DO SAY SO MYSELF.
MY GOODNESS. HOMEMADE LIP BALM? HOW FUN!
I HAVE A FAVORITE BRAND I'VE BEEN USING FOR YEARS, THOUGH.

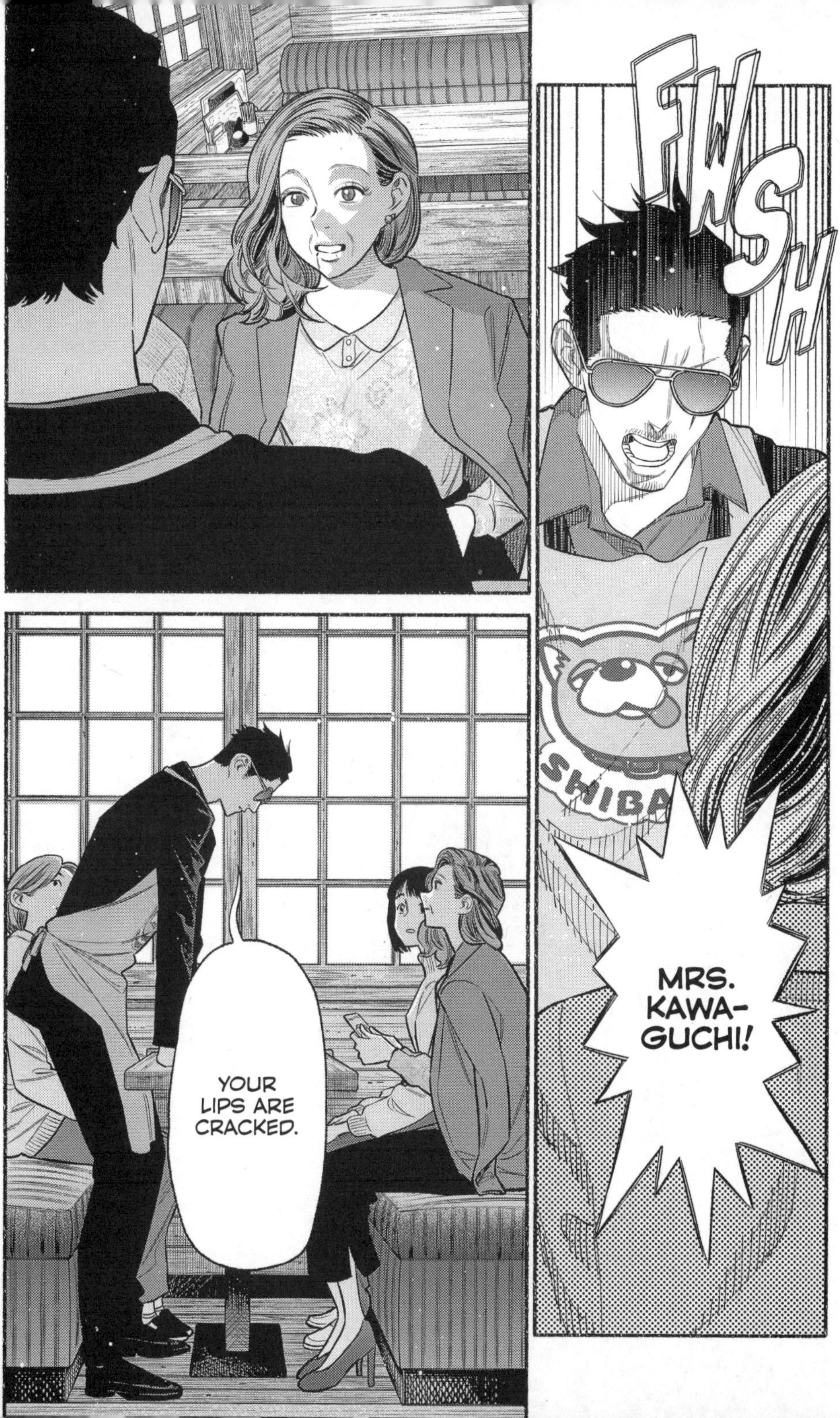
FWSH
SHIBA
MRS. KAWA-GUCHI!
YOUR LIPS ARE CRACKED.

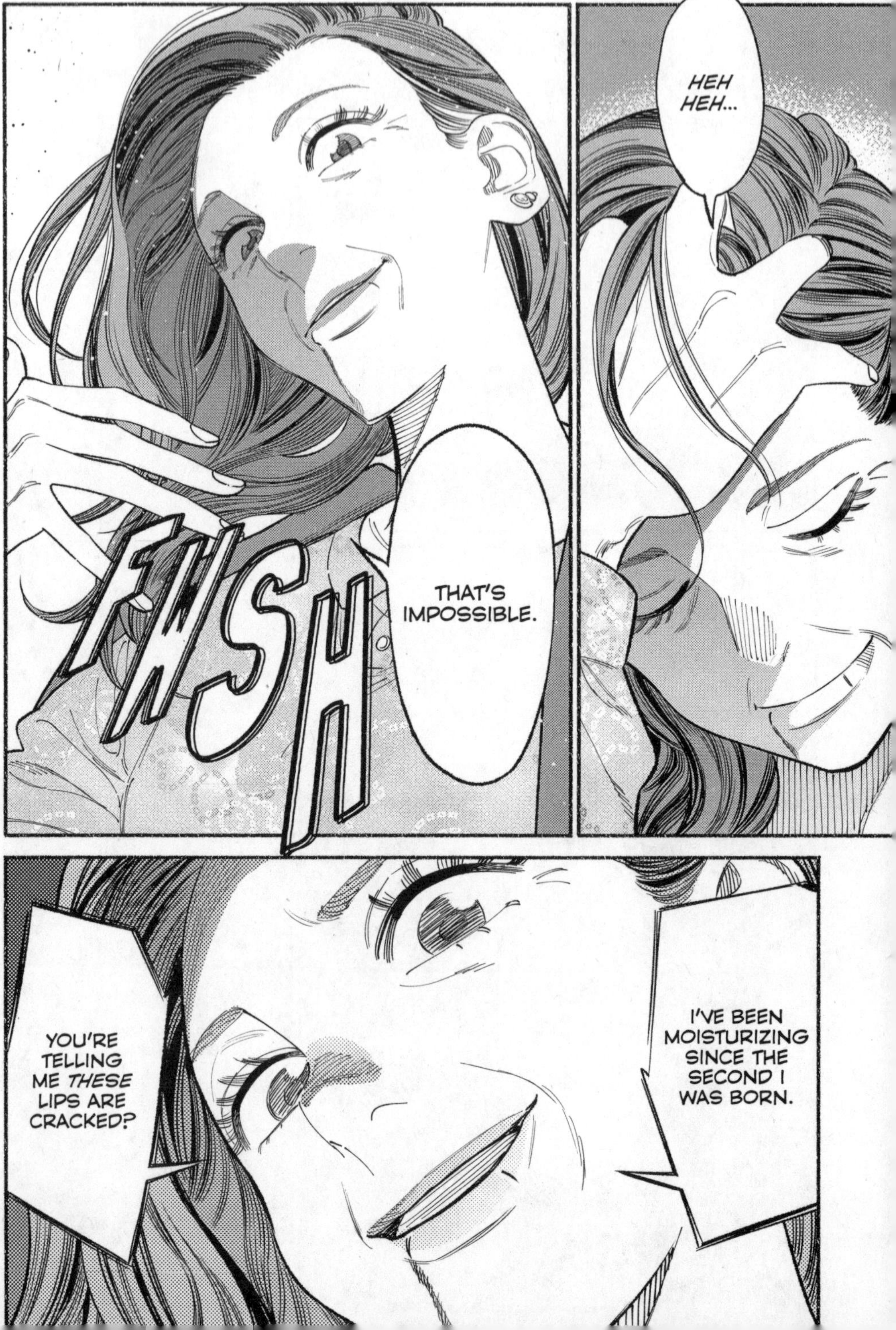
HEH HEH...
FWSH
THAT'S IMPOSSIBLE.
I'VE BEEN MOISTURIZING SINCE THE SECOND I WAS BORN.
YOU'RE TELLING ME *THESE* LIPS ARE CRACKED?

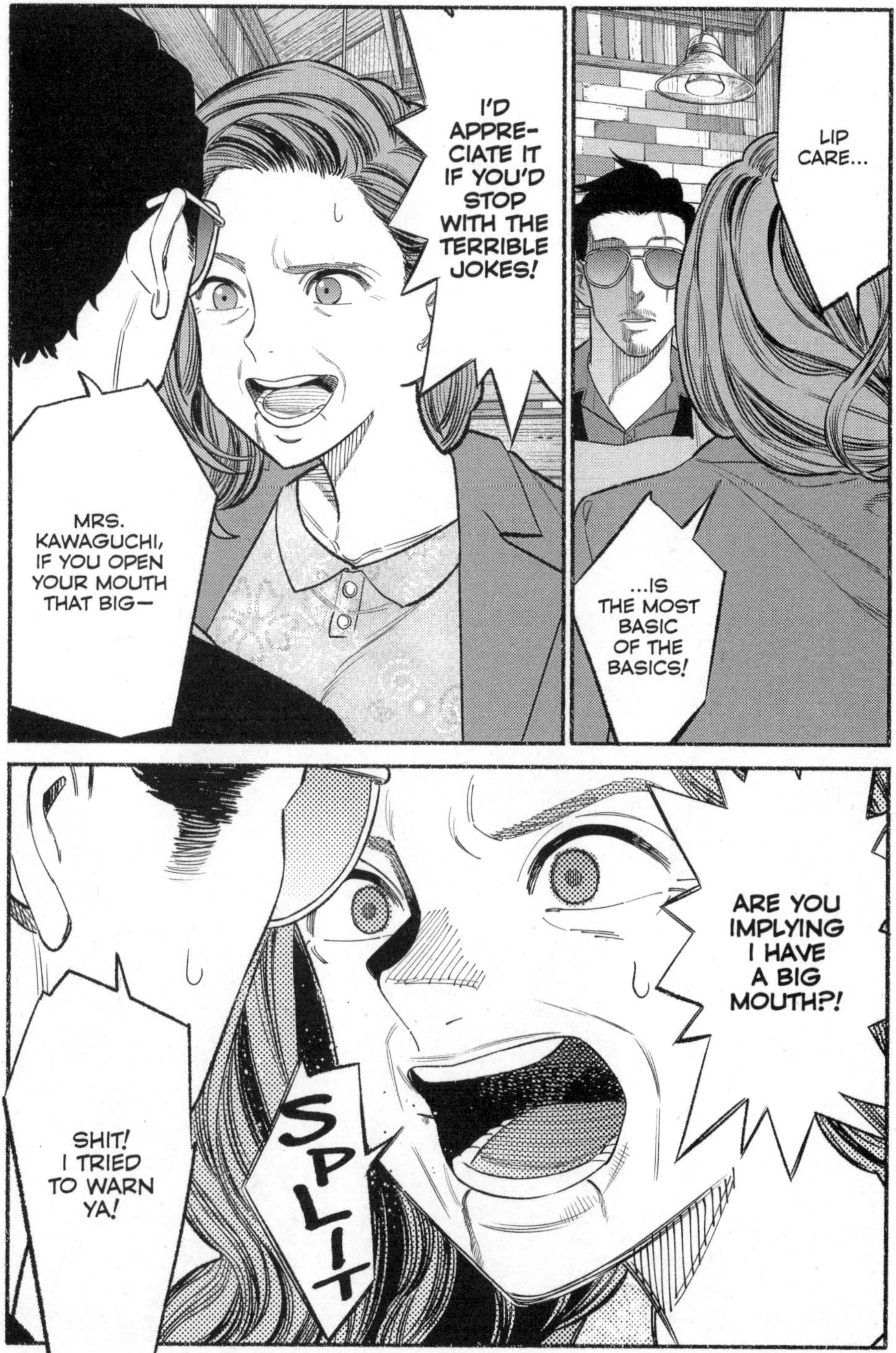
LIP CARE...
...IS THE MOST BASIC OF THE BASICS!
I'D APPRE-CIATE IT IF YOU'D STOP WITH THE TERRIBLE JOKES!
MRS. KAWAGUCHI, IF YOU OPEN YOUR MOUTH THAT BIG—
ARE YOU IMPLYING I HAVE A BIG MOUTH?!
SPLIT
SHIT! I TRIED TO WARN YA!

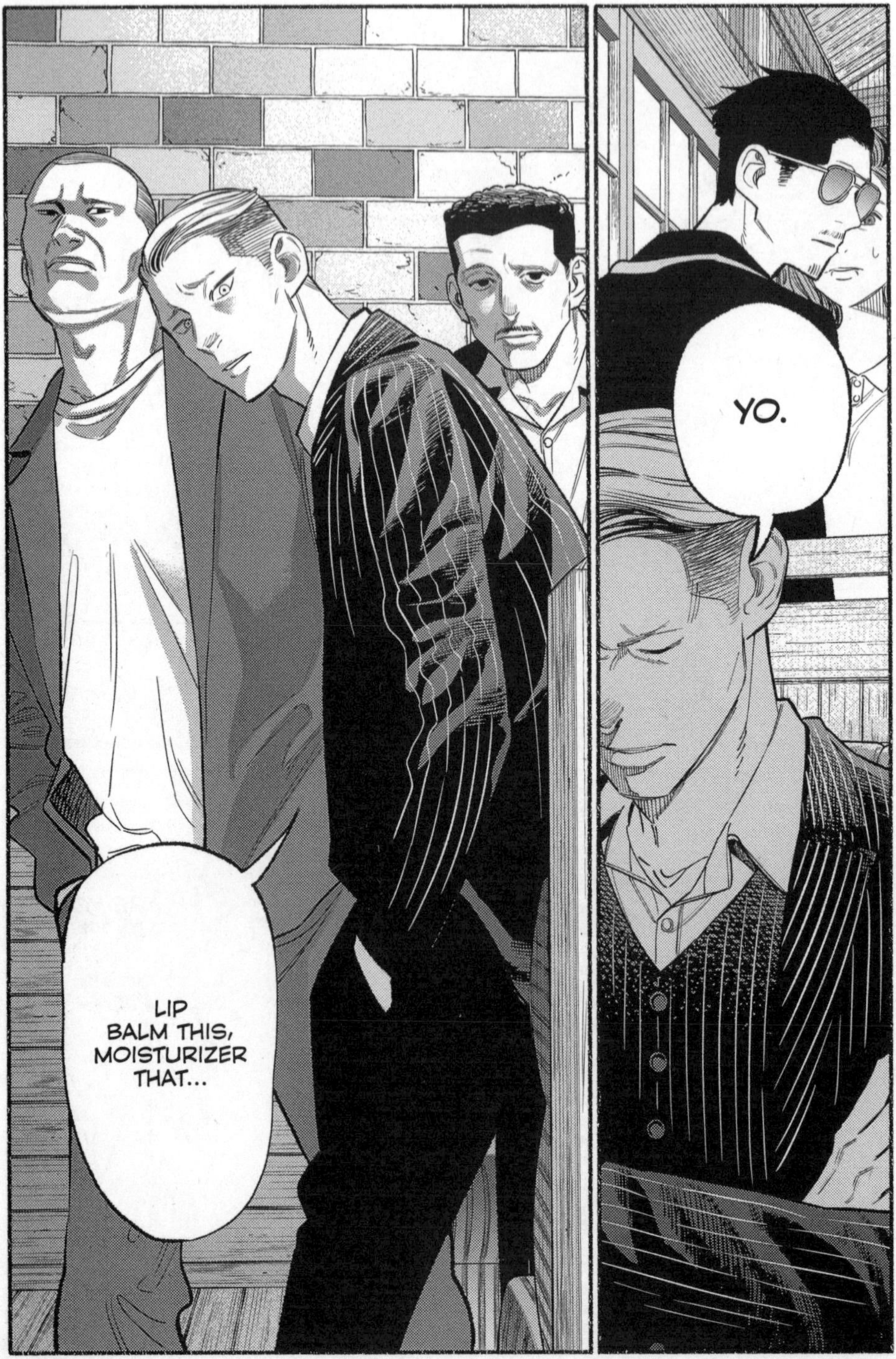
YO.
LIP BALM THIS, MOISTURIZER THAT...

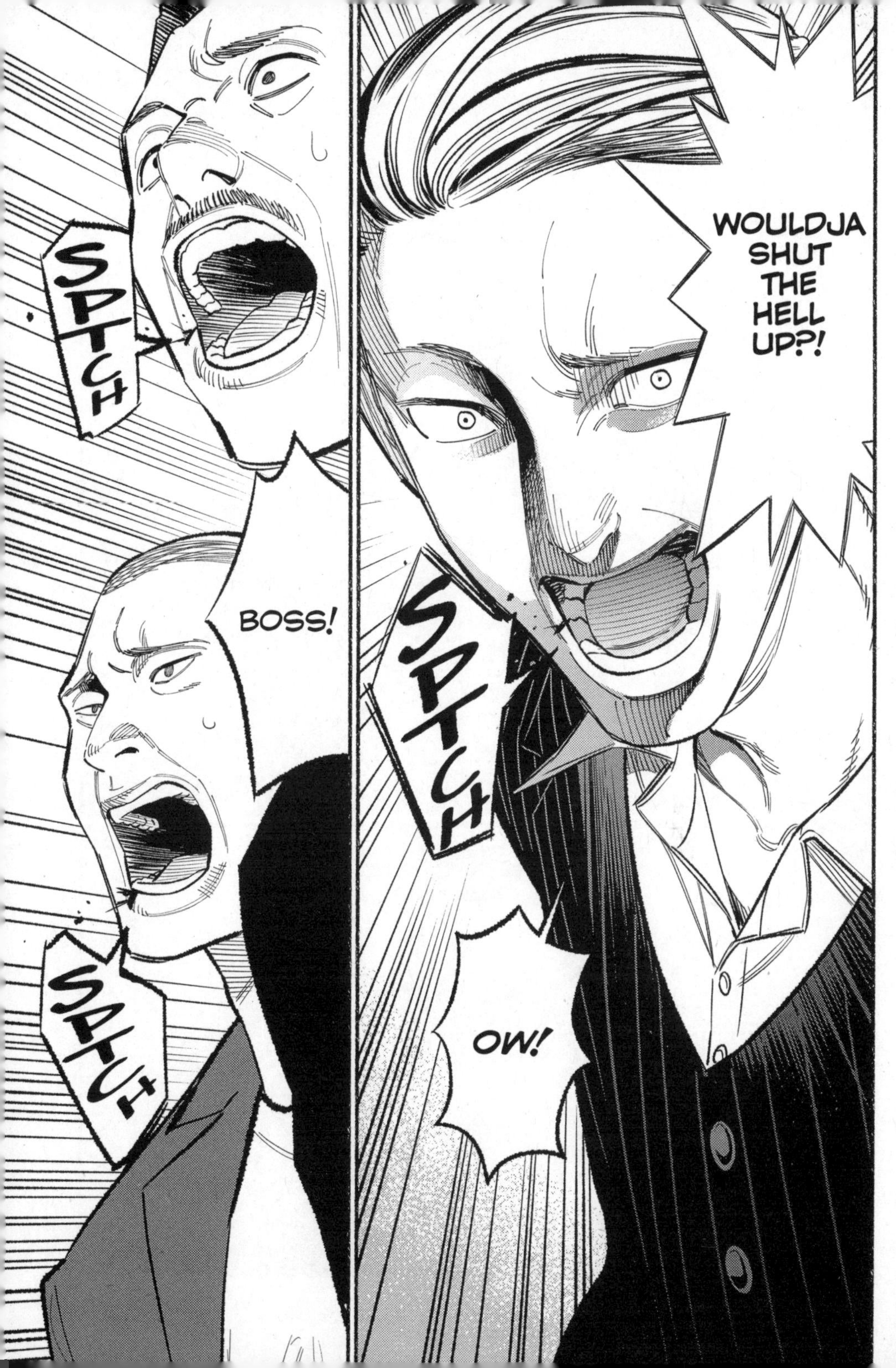
WOULDJA SHUT THE HELL UP?!
SPTCH
OW!
SPTCH
BOSS!
SPTCH

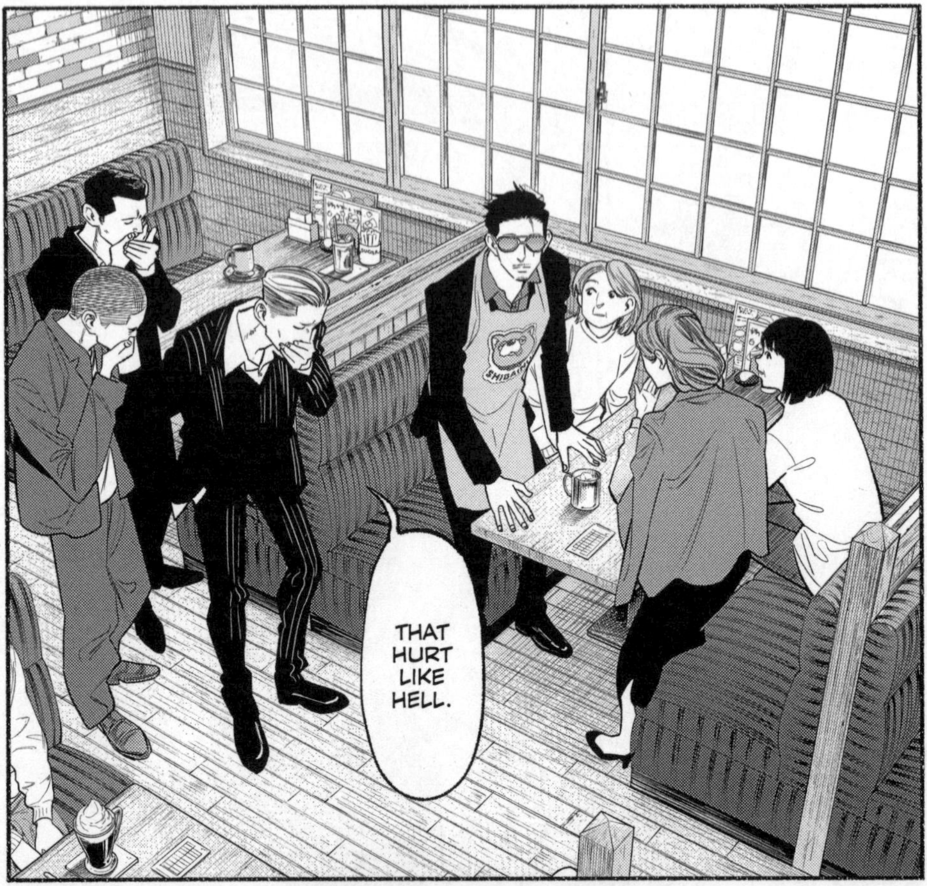
THAT HURT LIKE HELL.

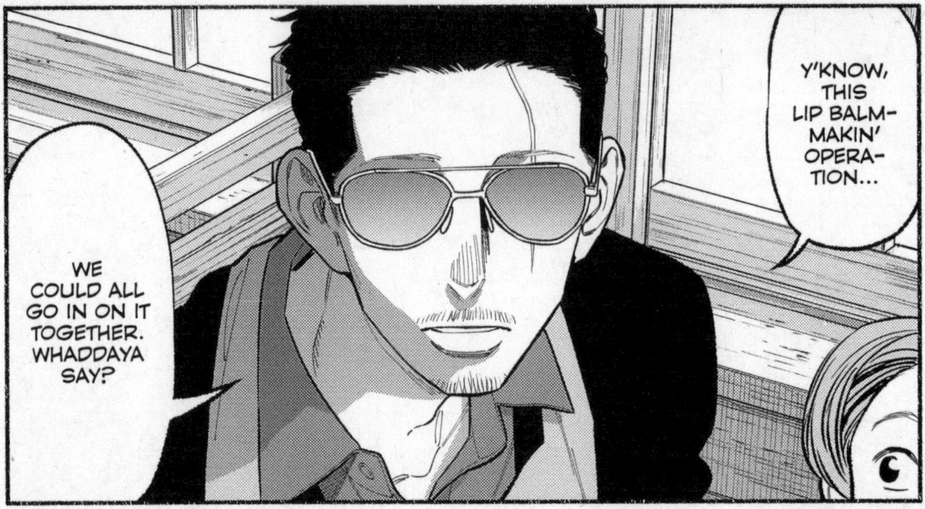
Y'KNOW, THIS LIP BALM-MAKIN' OPERATION...
WE COULD ALL GO IN ON IT TOGETHER. WHADDAYA SAY?

MRS.
KAWAGUCHI

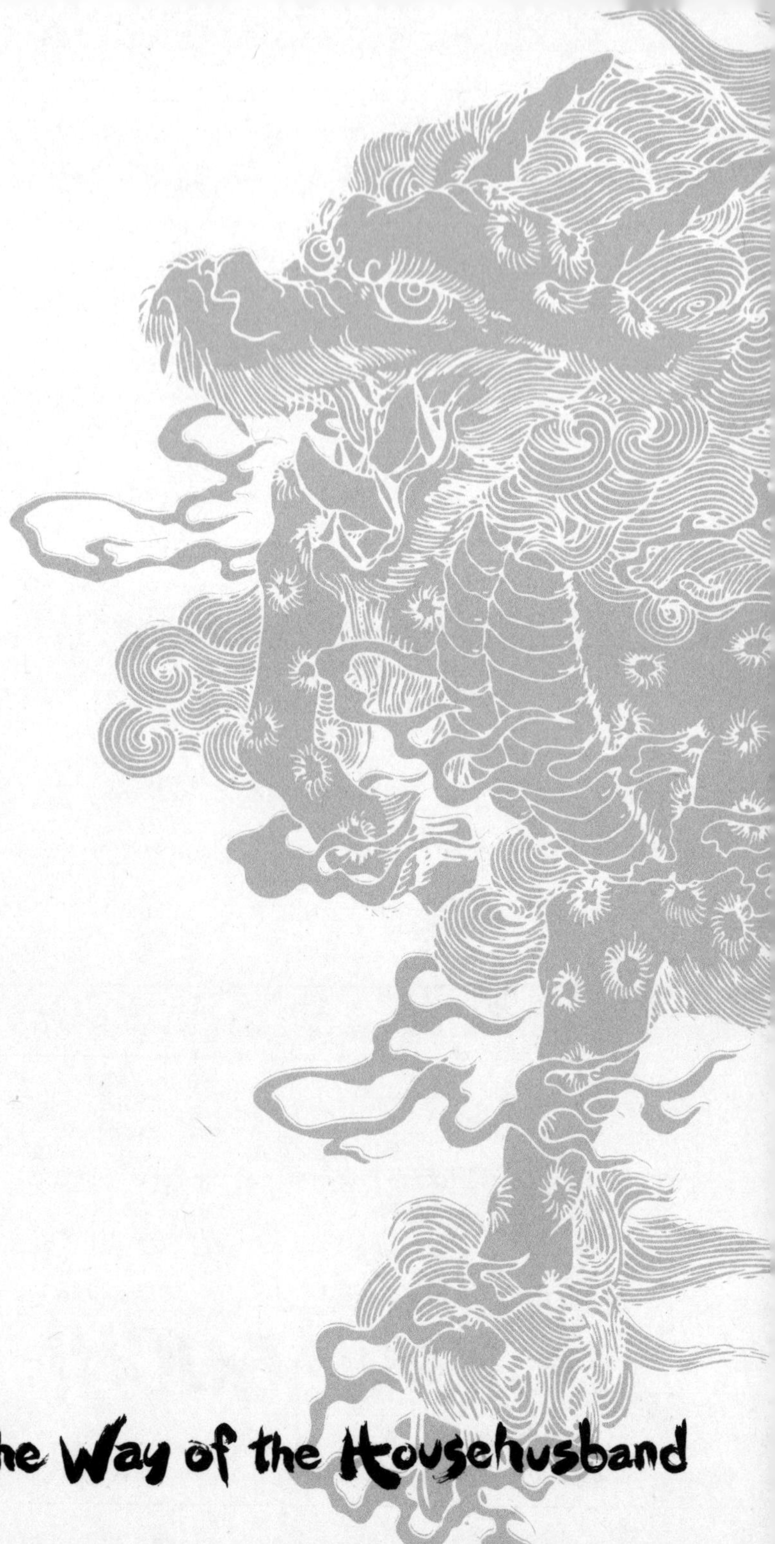

The Way of the Househusband

CHAPTER 88

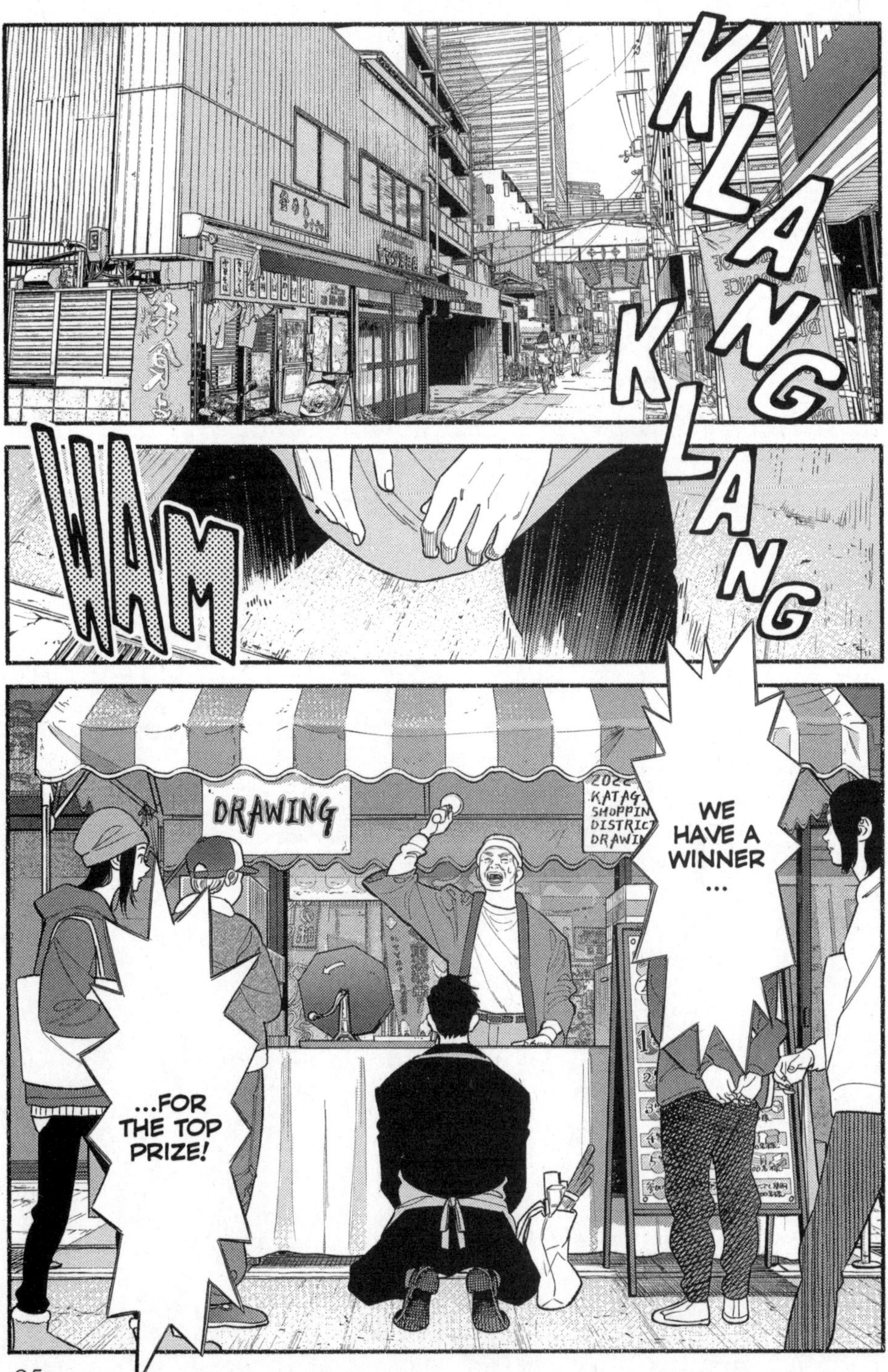
KLANG
KLANG
WAM
DRAWING
WE HAVE A WINNER ...
...FOR THE TOP PRIZE!

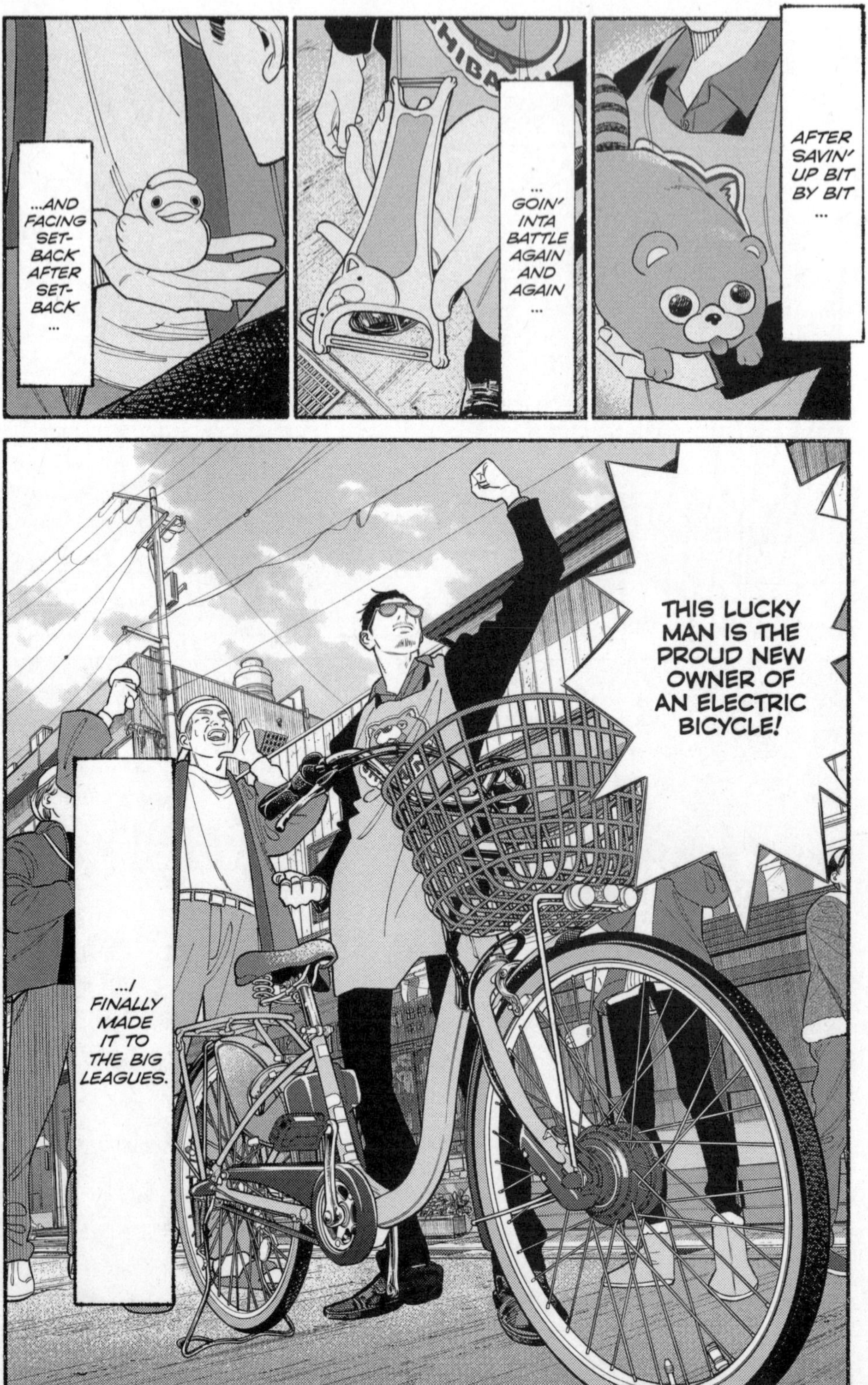
AFTER SAVIN' UP BIT BY BIT ...
... GOIN' INTA BATTLE AGAIN AND AGAIN ...
...AND FACING SET-BACK AFTER SET-BACK ...
THIS LUCKY MAN IS THE PROUD NEW OWNER OF AN ELECTRIC BICYCLE!
...I FINALLY MADE IT TO THE BIG LEAGUES.

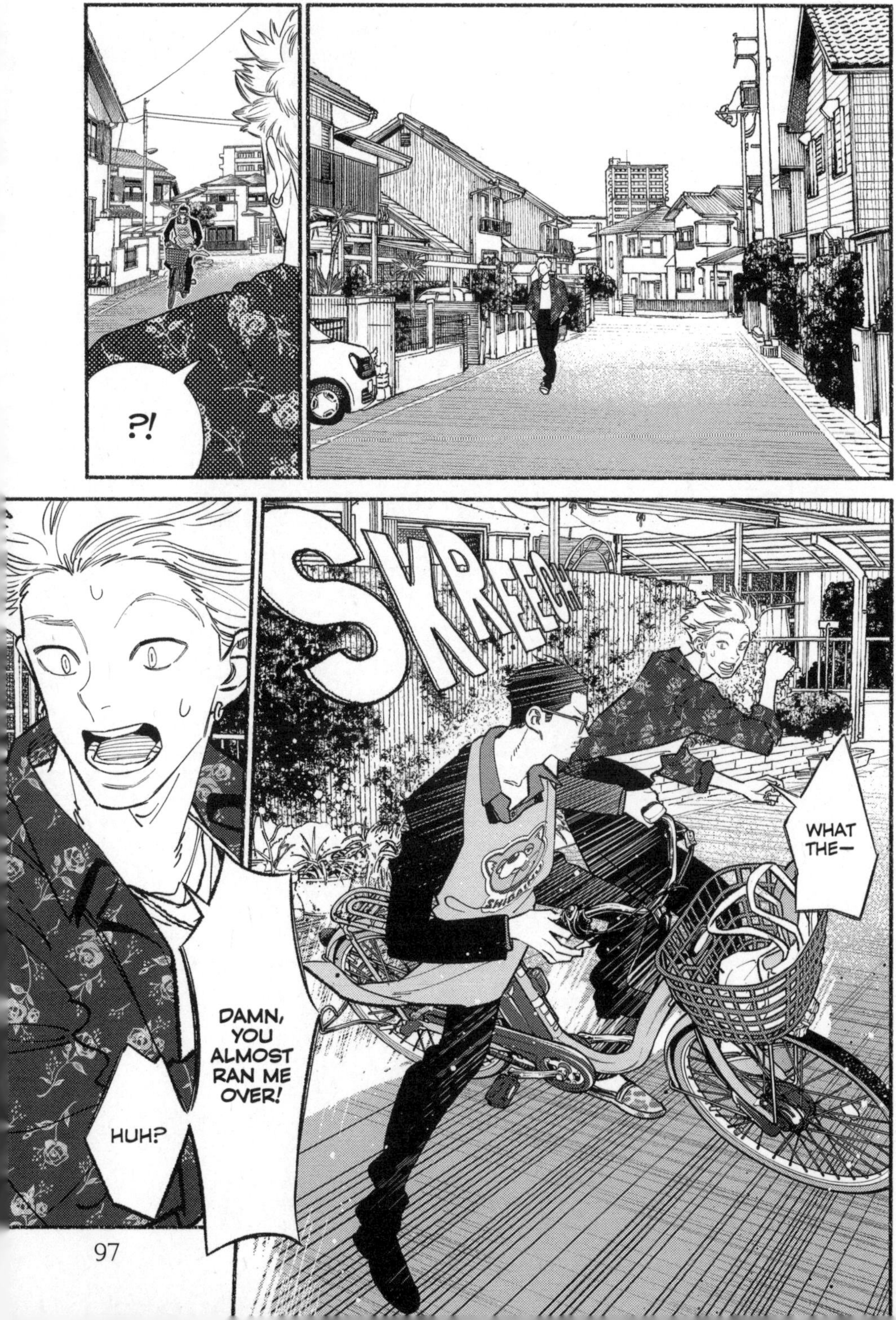
?!
SKREECH
WHAT THE—
DAMN, YOU ALMOST RAN ME OVER!
HUH?

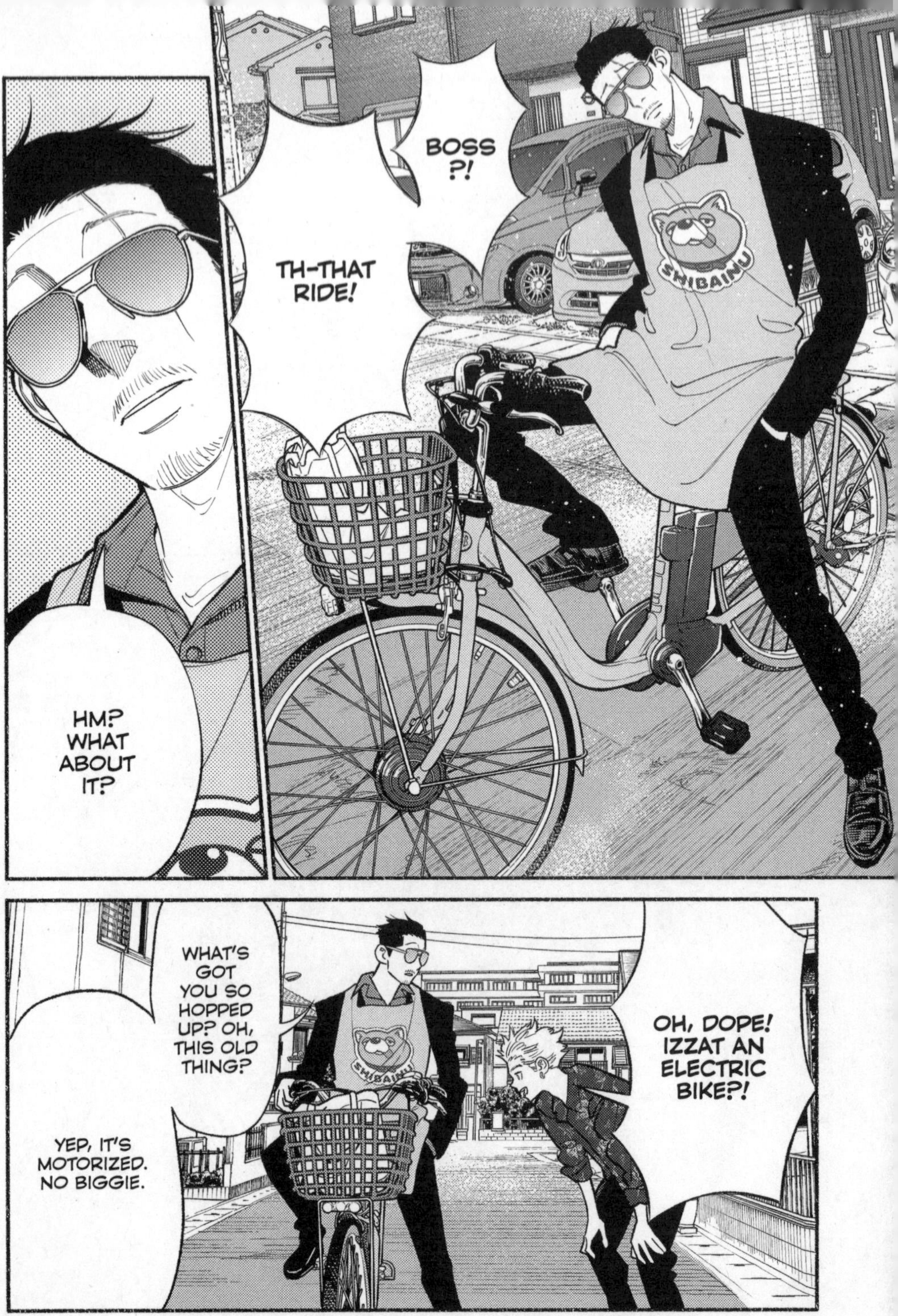
BOSS?!
TH-THAT RIDE!
HM? WHAT ABOUT IT?
OH, DOPE! IZZAT AN ELECTRIC BIKE?!
WHAT'S GOT YOU SO HOPPED UP? OH, THIS OLD THING?
YEP, IT'S MOTORIZED. NO BIGGIE.

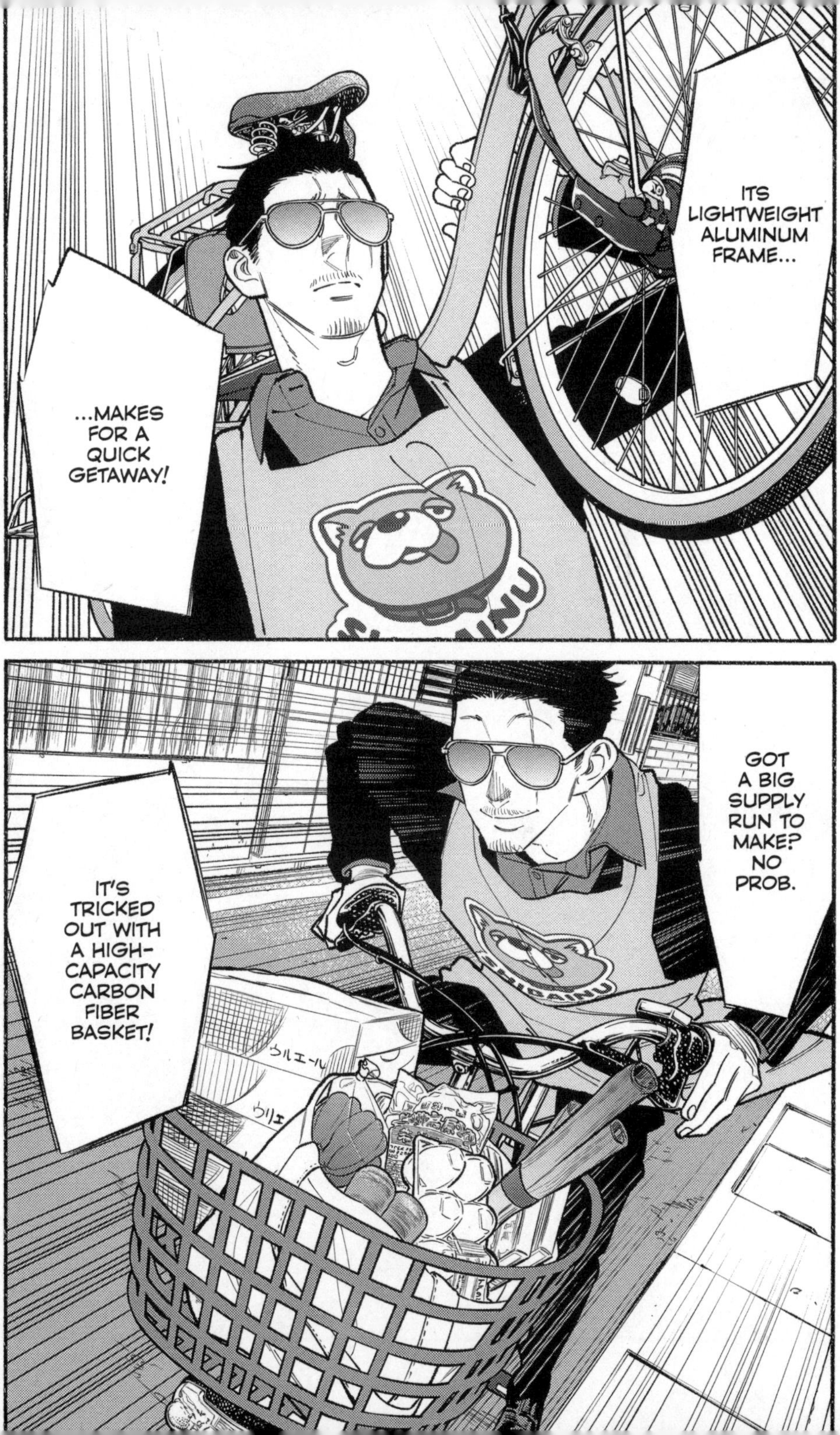
ITS LIGHTWEIGHT ALUMINUM FRAME...
...MAKES FOR A QUICK GETAWAY!
GOT A BIG SUPPLY RUN TO MAKE? NO PROB.
IT'S TRICKED OUT WITH A HIGH-CAPACITY CARBON FIBER BASKET!

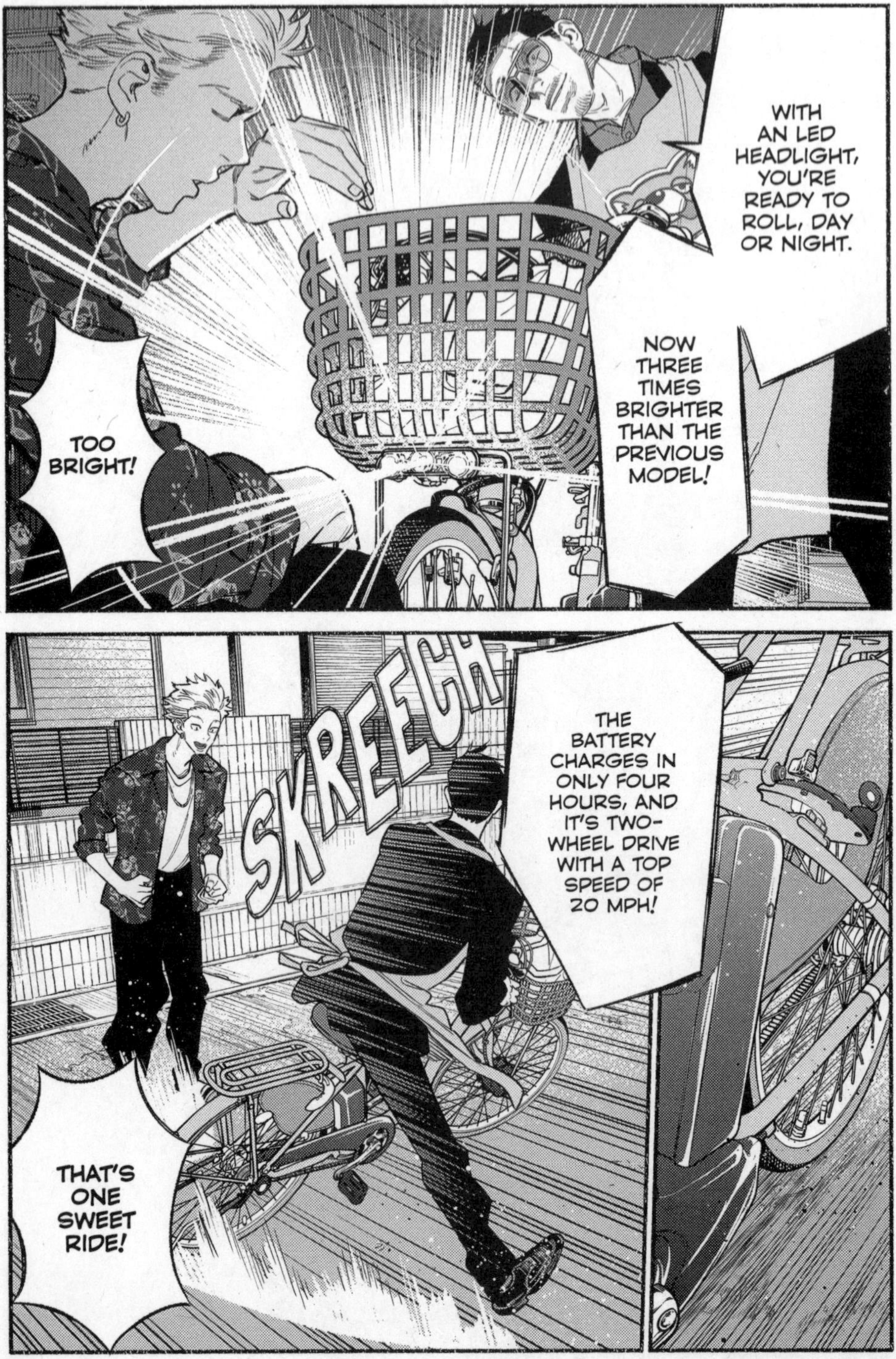
WITH AN LED HEADLIGHT, YOU'RE READY TO ROLL, DAY OR NIGHT.
NOW THREE TIMES BRIGHTER THAN THE PREVIOUS MODEL!
TOO BRIGHT!
THE BATTERY CHARGES IN ONLY FOUR HOURS, AND IT'S TWO-WHEEL DRIVE WITH A TOP SPEED OF 20 MPH!
SKREECH
THAT'S ONE SWEET RIDE!

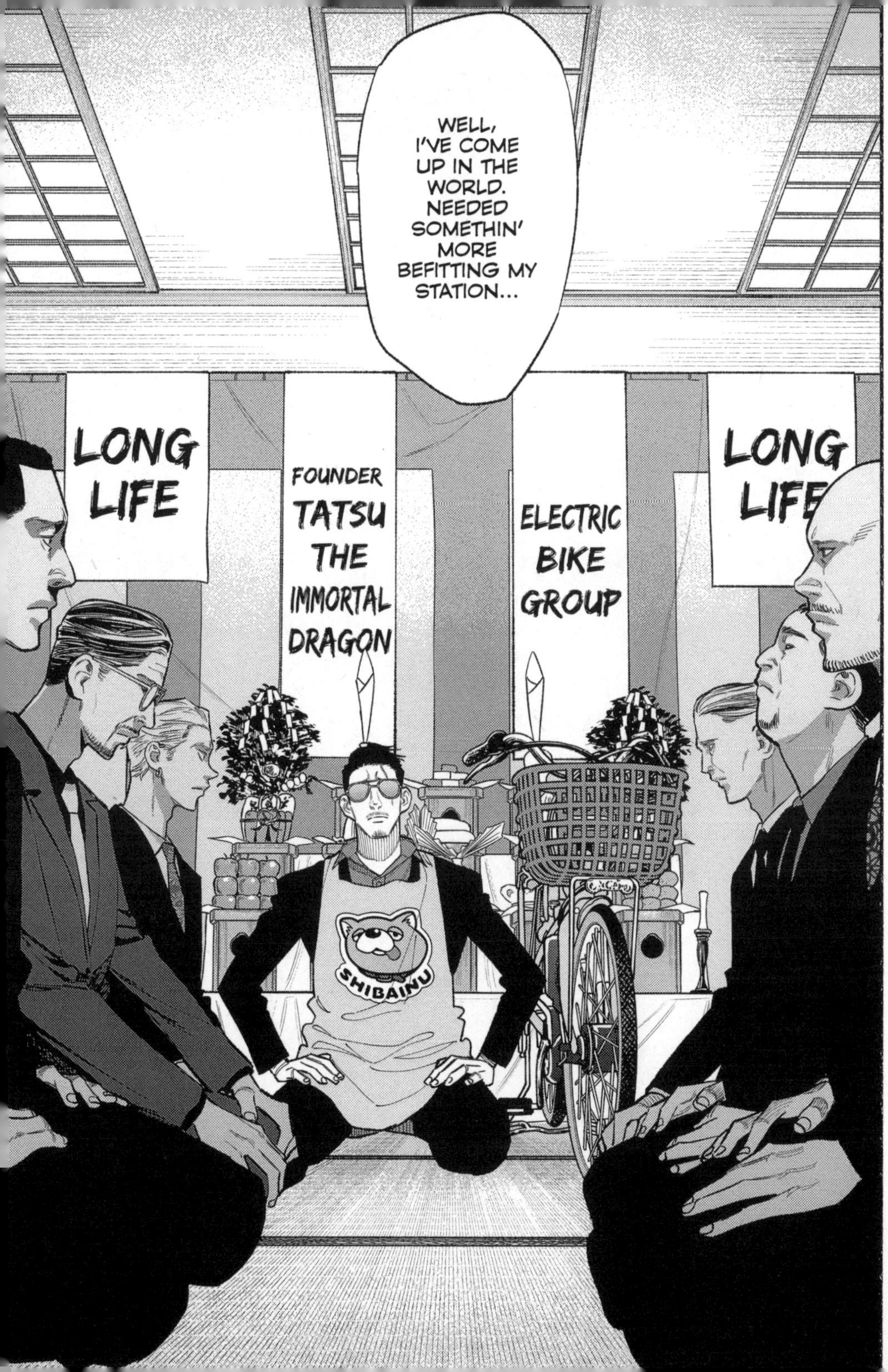
WELL, I'VE COME UP IN THE WORLD. NEEDED SOMETHIN' MORE BEFITTING MY STATION...
LONG LIFE
FOUNDER TATSU THE IMMORTAL DRAGON
ELECTRIC BIKE GROUP
LONG LIFE
SHIBAINU

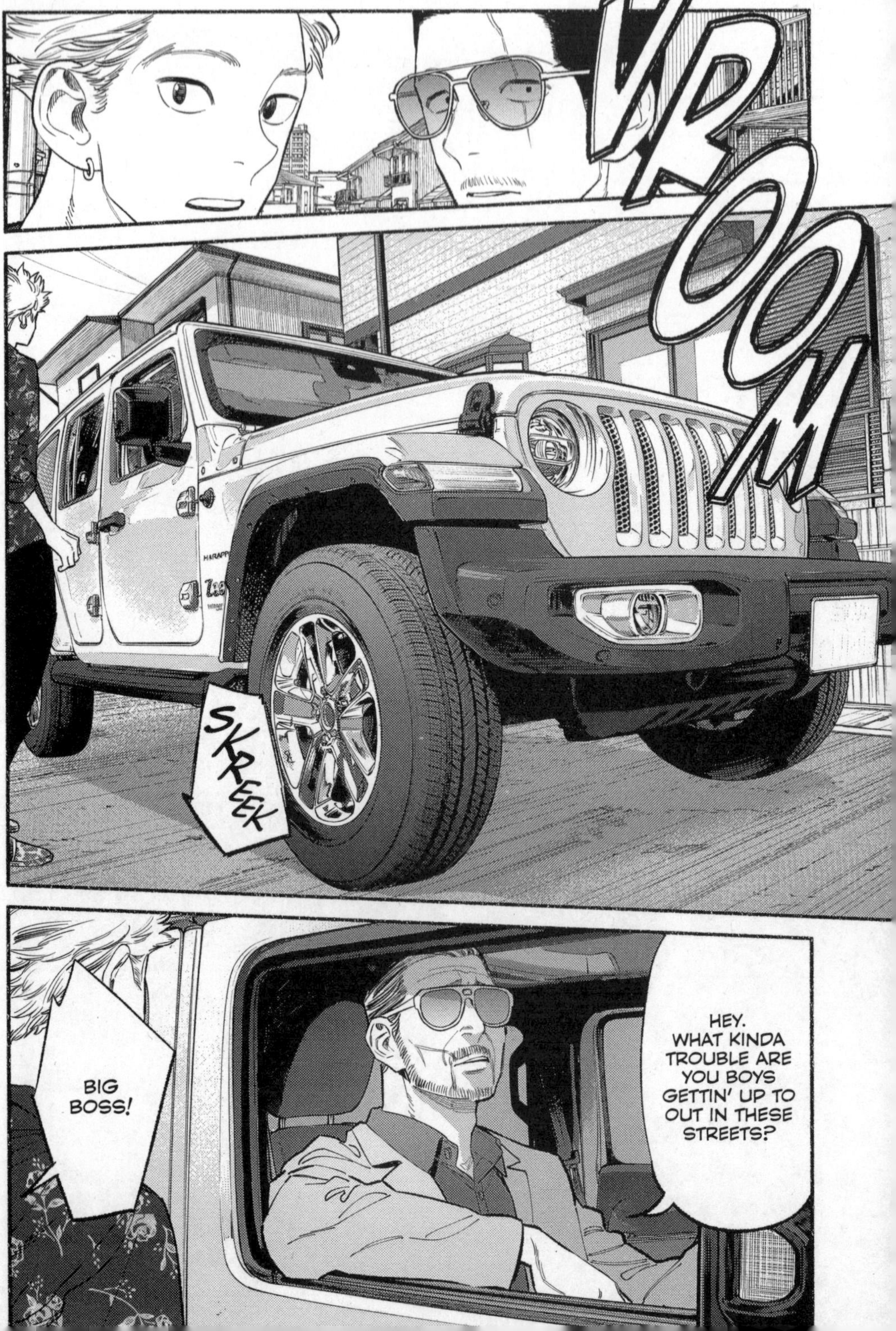
VROOOM
SKREEK
HEY. WHAT KINDA TROUBLE ARE YOU BOYS GETTIN' UP TO OUT IN THESE STREETS?
BIG BOSS!

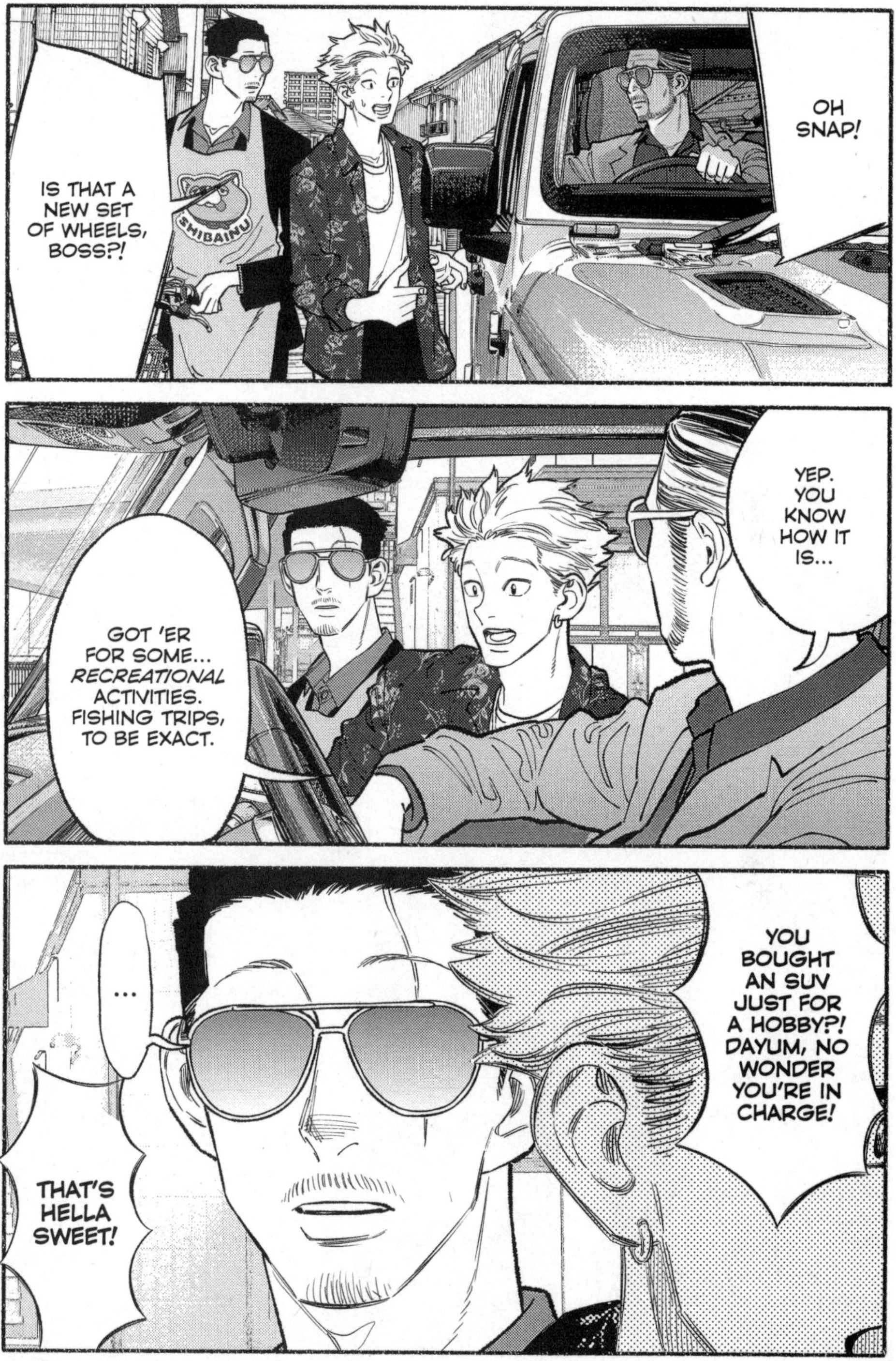
OH SNAP!
IS THAT A NEW SET OF WHEELS, BOSS?!
YEP. YOU KNOW HOW IT IS...
GOT 'ER FOR SOME... *RECREATIONAL* ACTIVITIES. FISHING TRIPS, TO BE EXACT.
YOU BOUGHT AN SUV JUST FOR A HOBBY?! DAYUM, NO WONDER YOU'RE IN CHARGE!
...
THAT'S HELLA SWEET!

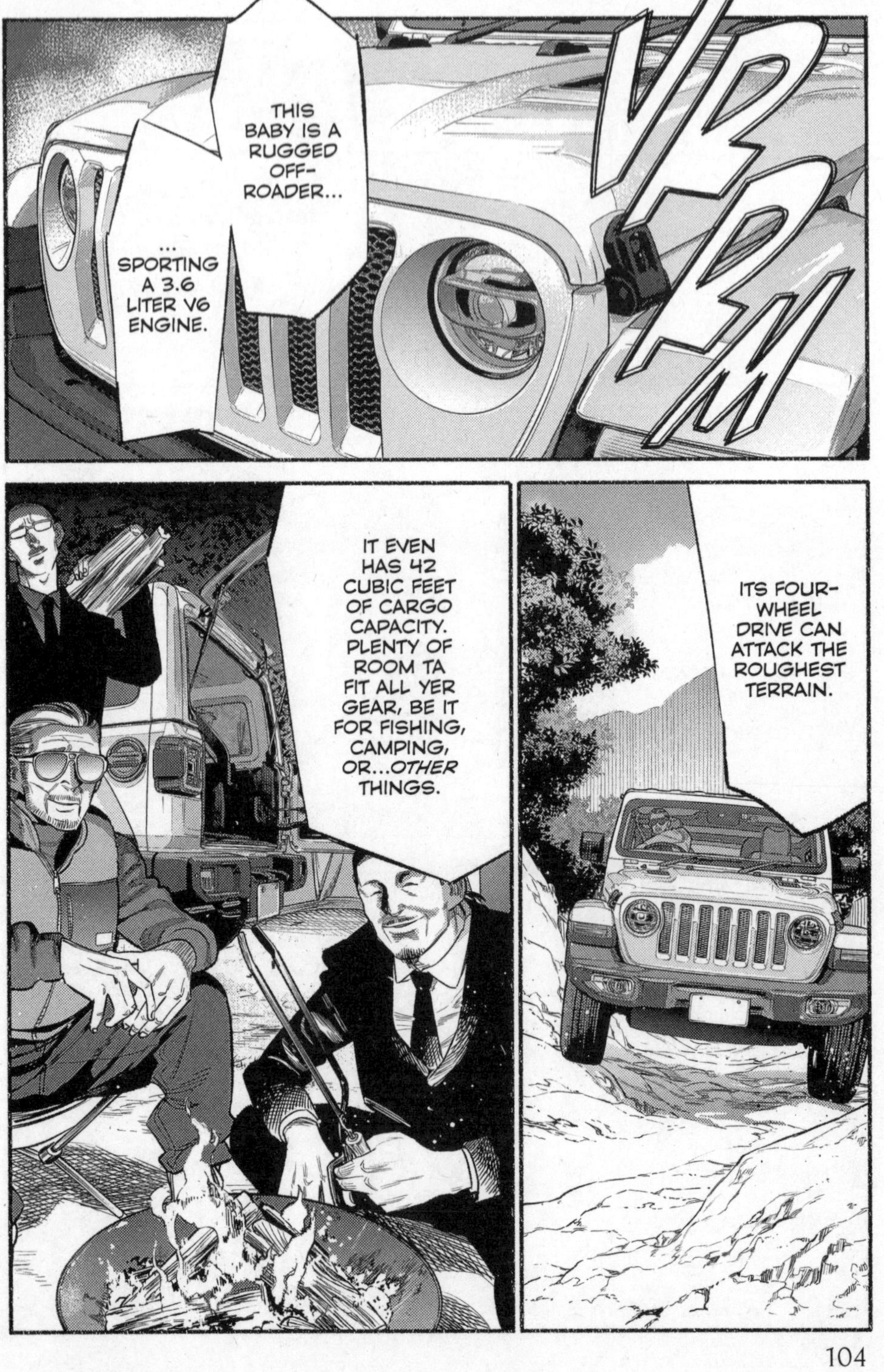
THIS BABY IS A RUGGED OFF-ROADER...
...SPORTING A 3.6 LITER V6 ENGINE.
ITS FOUR-WHEEL DRIVE CAN ATTACK THE ROUGHEST TERRAIN.
IT EVEN HAS 42 CUBIC FEET OF CARGO CAPACITY. PLENTY OF ROOM TA FIT ALL YER GEAR, BE IT FOR FISHING, CAMPING, OR...*OTHER* THINGS.

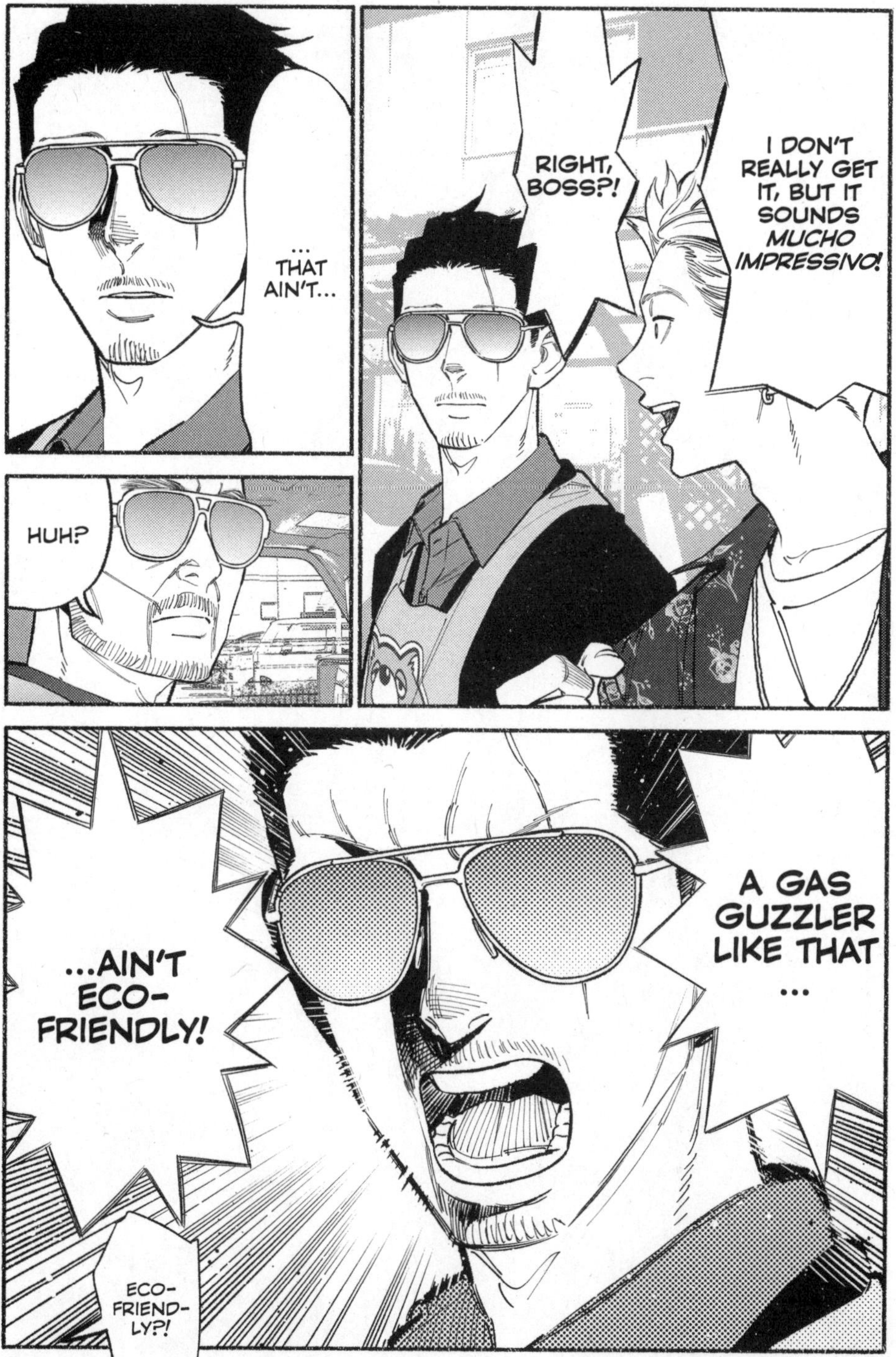
I DON'T REALLY GET IT, BUT IT SOUNDS *MUCHO IMPRESSIVO!*
RIGHT, BOSS?!
... THAT AIN'T...
HUH?
A GAS GUZZLER LIKE THAT ...
...AIN'T ECO-FRIENDLY!
ECO-FRIENDLY?!

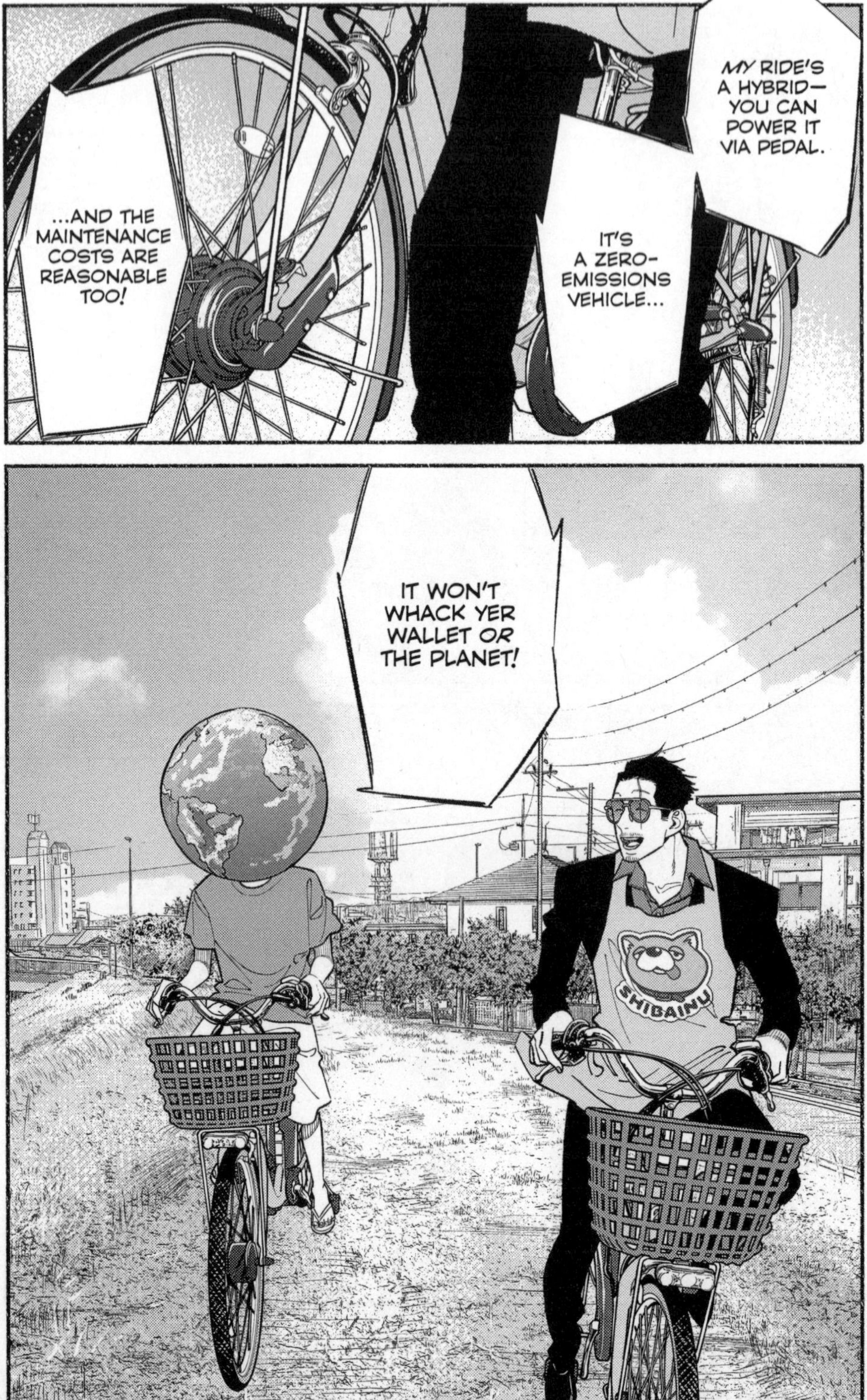
MY RIDE'S A HYBRID—YOU CAN POWER IT VIA PEDAL.
IT'S A ZERO-EMISSIONS VEHICLE...
...AND THE MAINTENANCE COSTS ARE REASONABLE TOO!
IT WON'T WHACK YER WALLET *OR* THE PLANET!
SHIBAINU

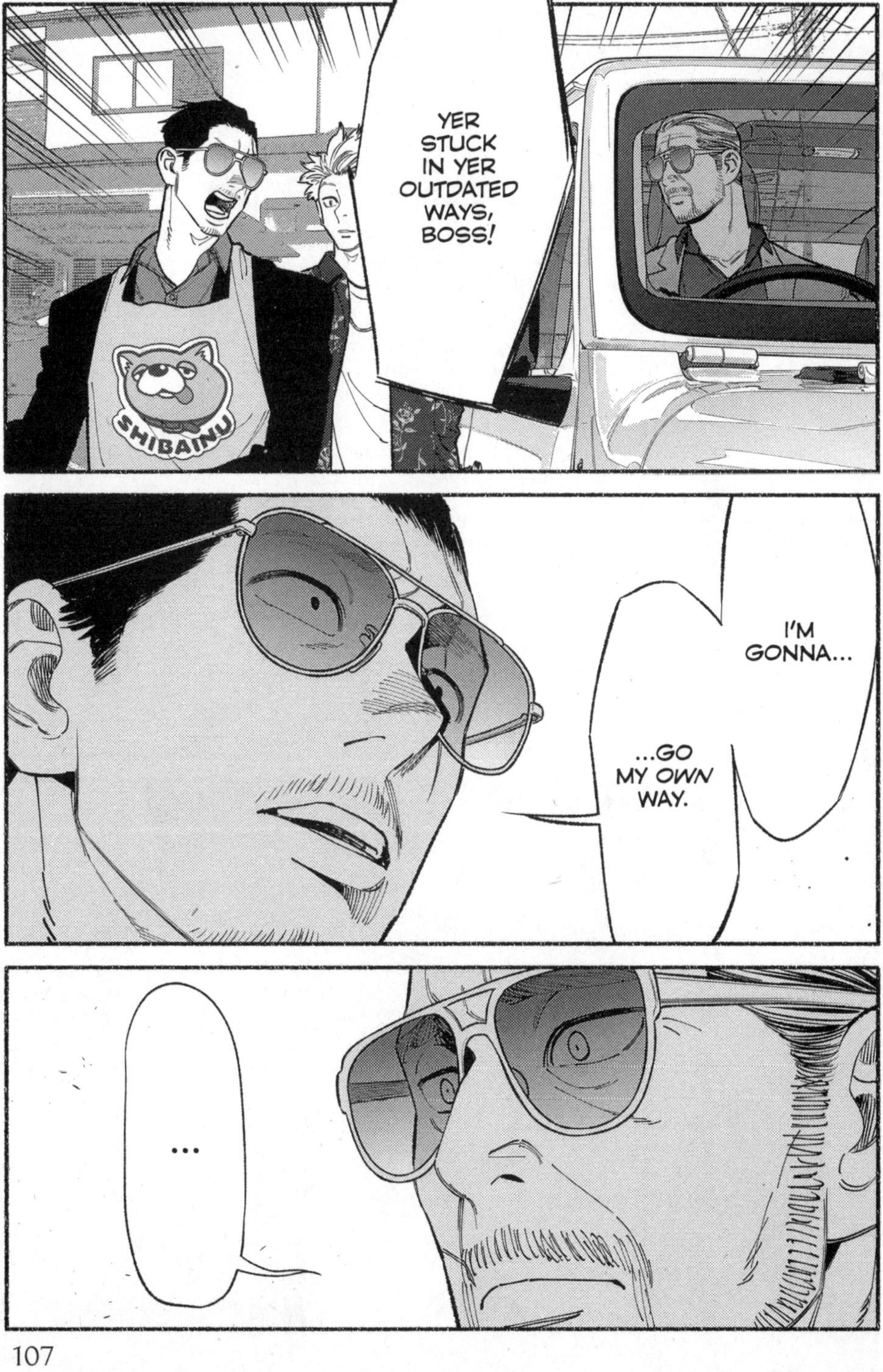
YER STUCK IN YER OUTDATED WAYS, BOSS!
SHIBAINU
I'M GONNA...
...GO MY OWN WAY.
...

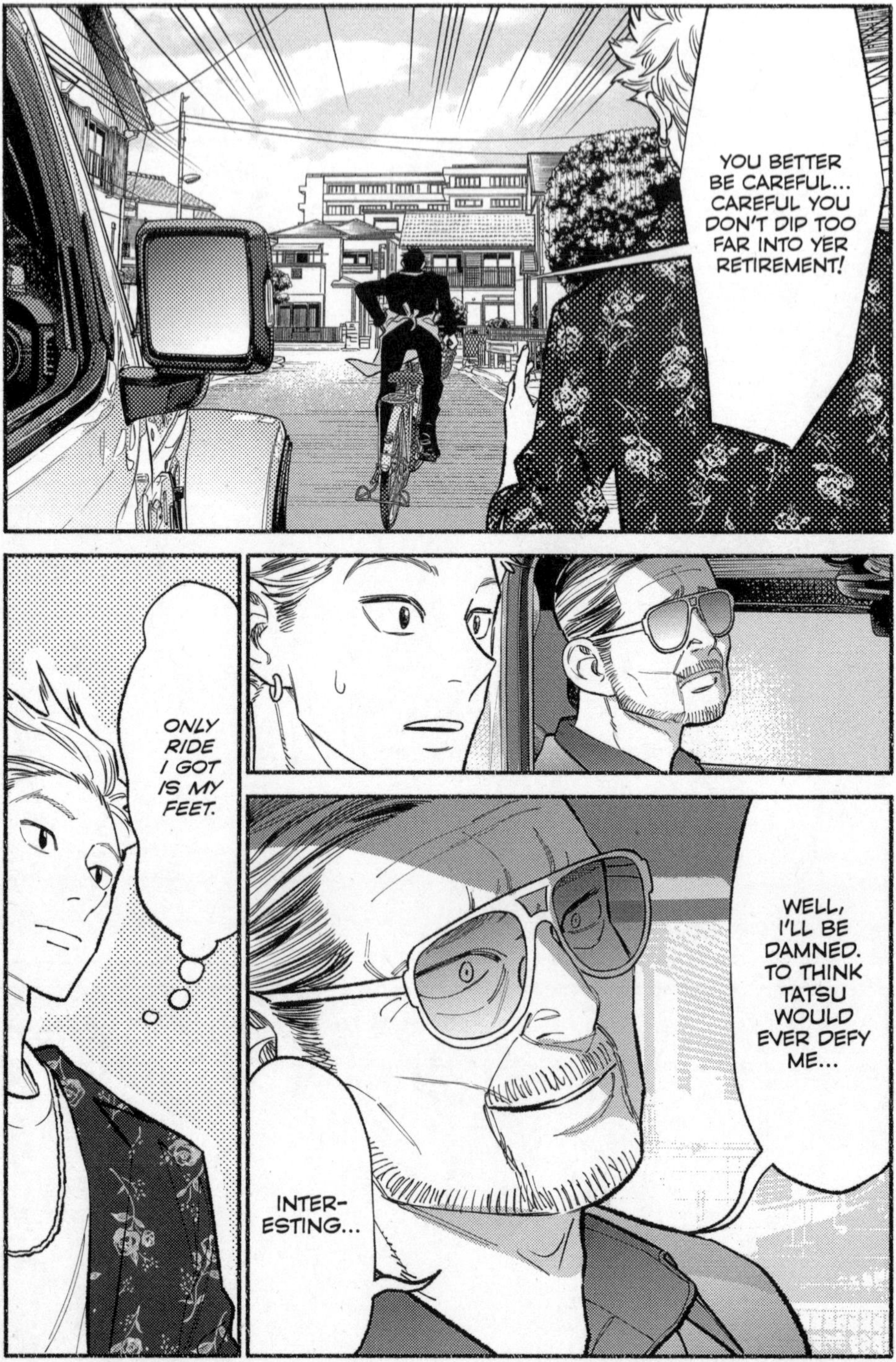
YOU BETTER BE CAREFUL... CAREFUL YOU DON'T DIP TOO FAR INTO YER RETIREMENT!
WELL, I'LL BE DAMNED. TO THINK TATSU WOULD EVER DEFY ME...
INTER-ESTING...
ONLY RIDE I GOT IS MY FEET.

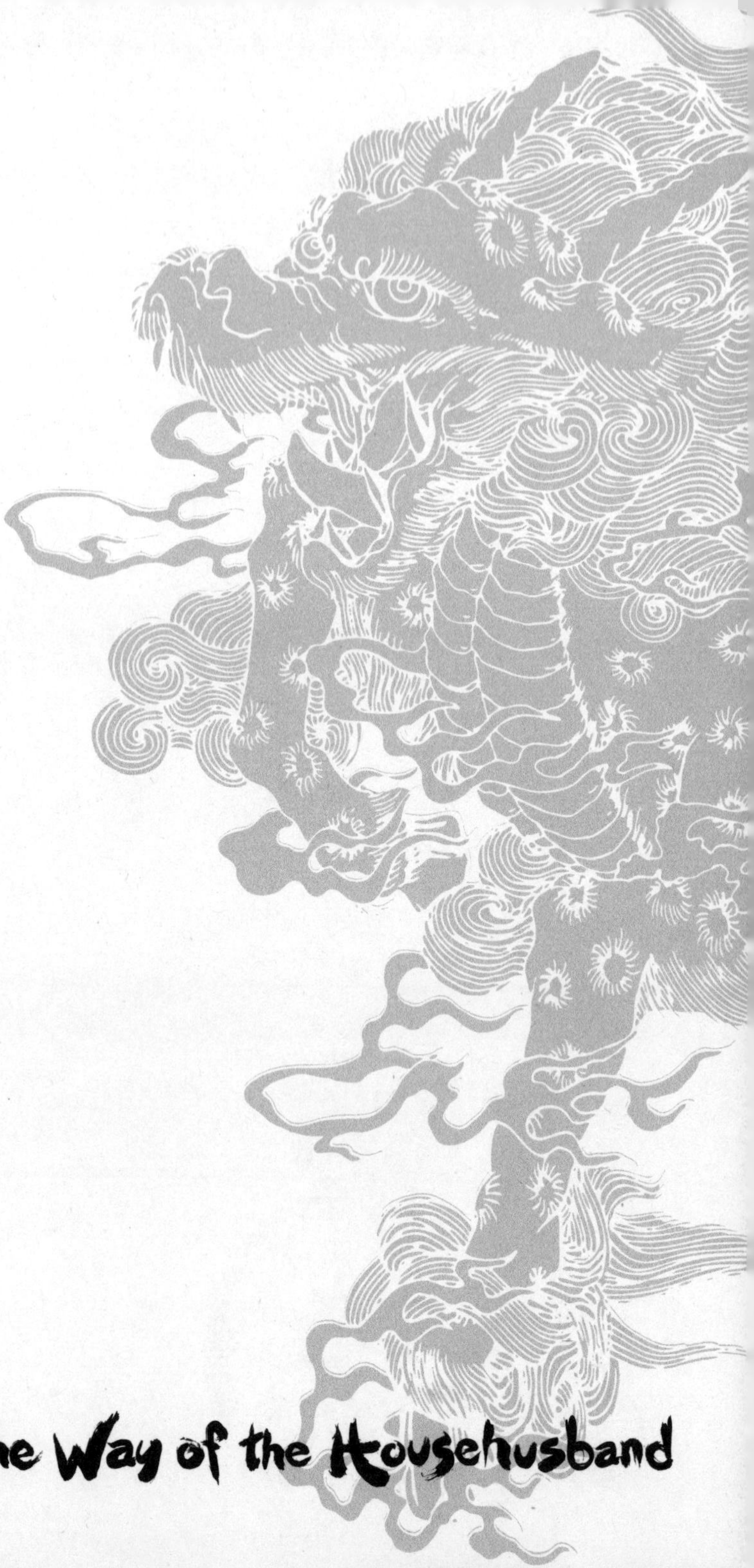

The Way of the Househusband

CHAPTER 89

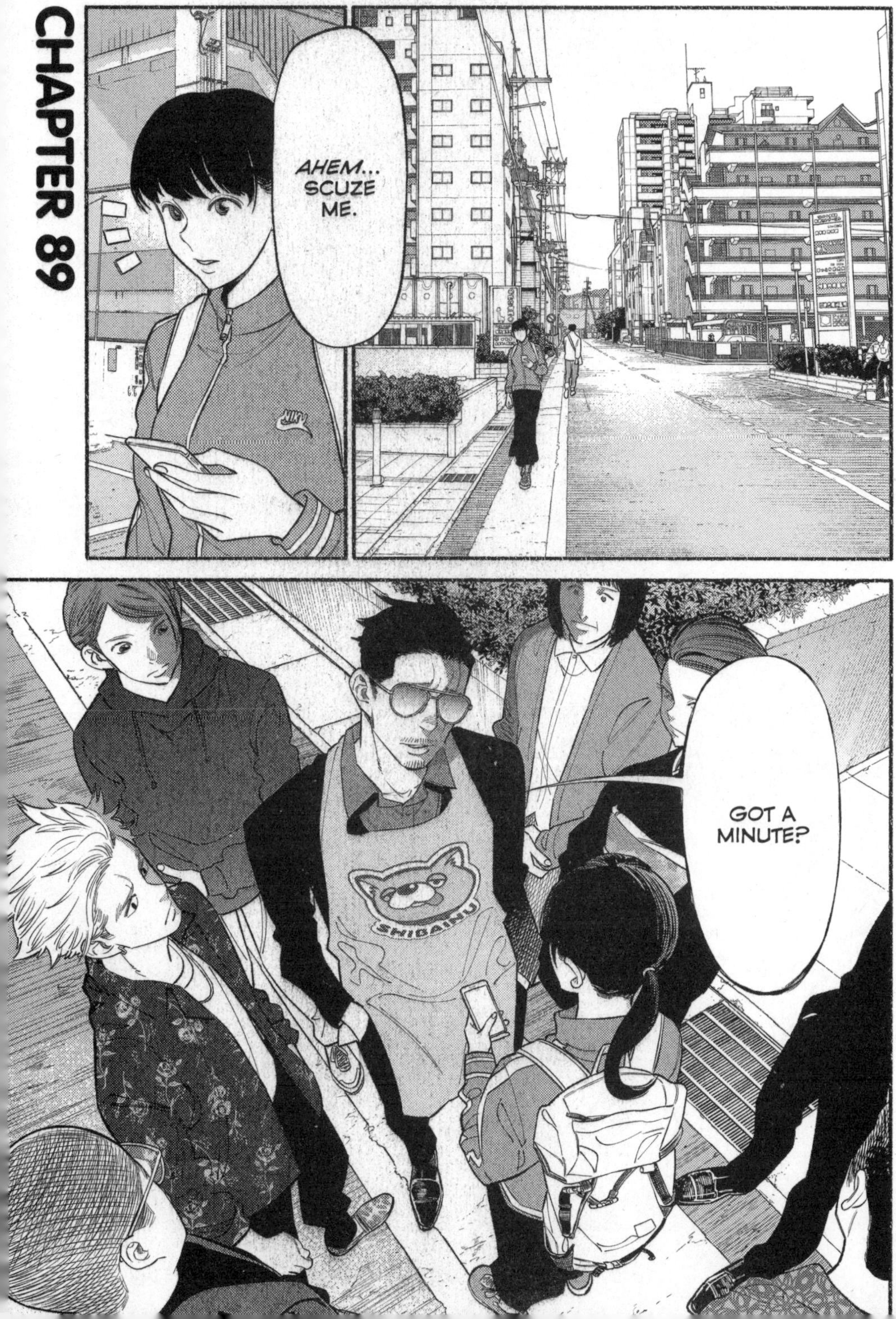
AHEM... SCUZE ME.
GOT A MINUTE?

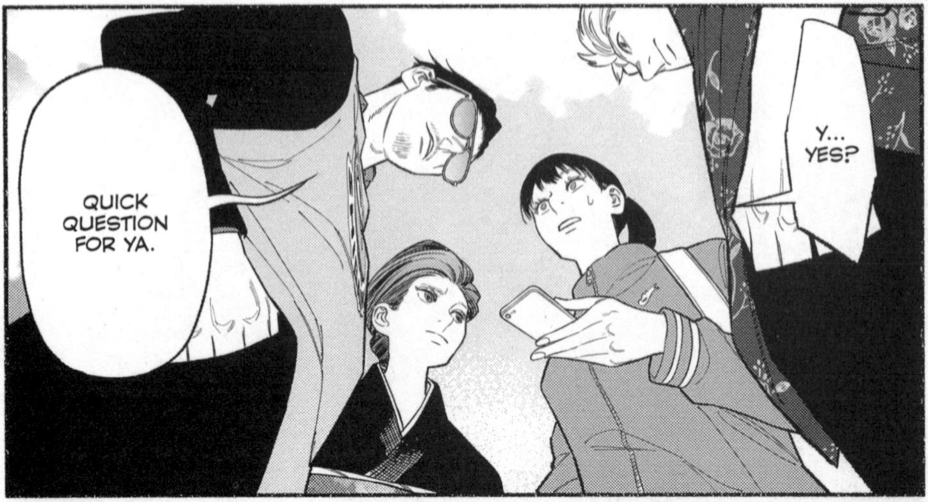
Y... YES?
QUICK QUESTION FOR YA.

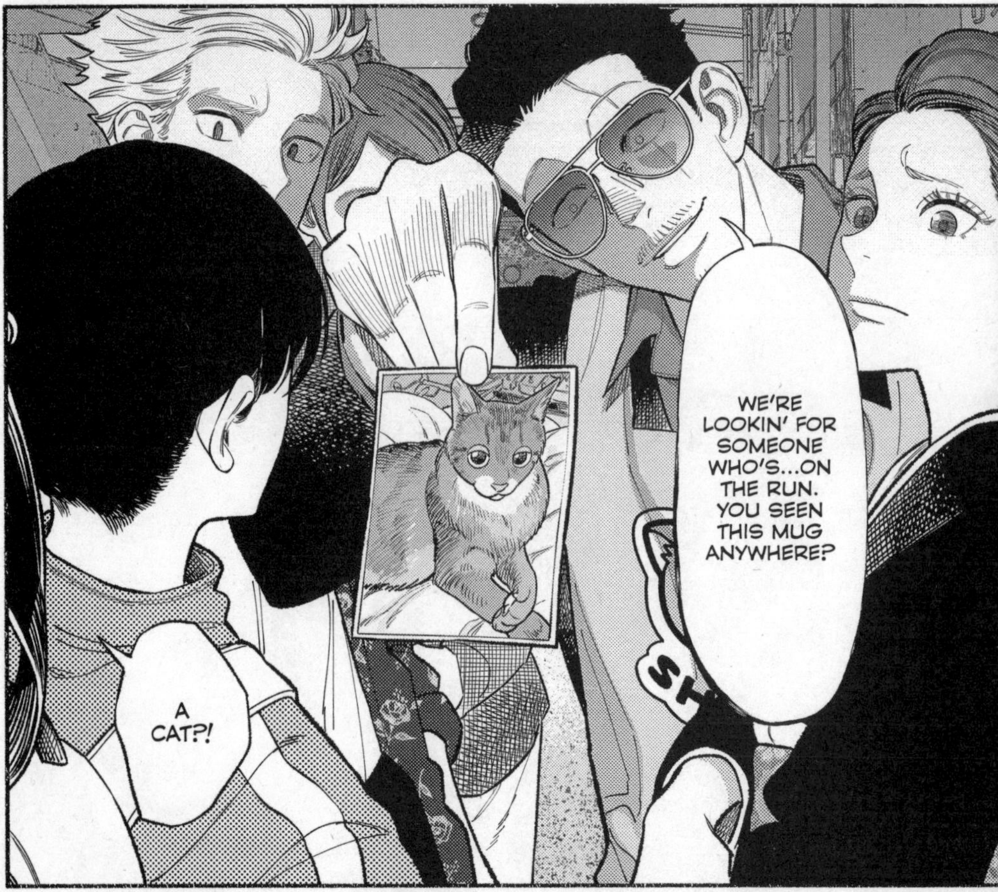
WE'RE LOOKIN' FOR SOMEONE WHO'S...ON THE RUN. YOU SEEN THIS MUG ANYWHERE?
A CAT?!

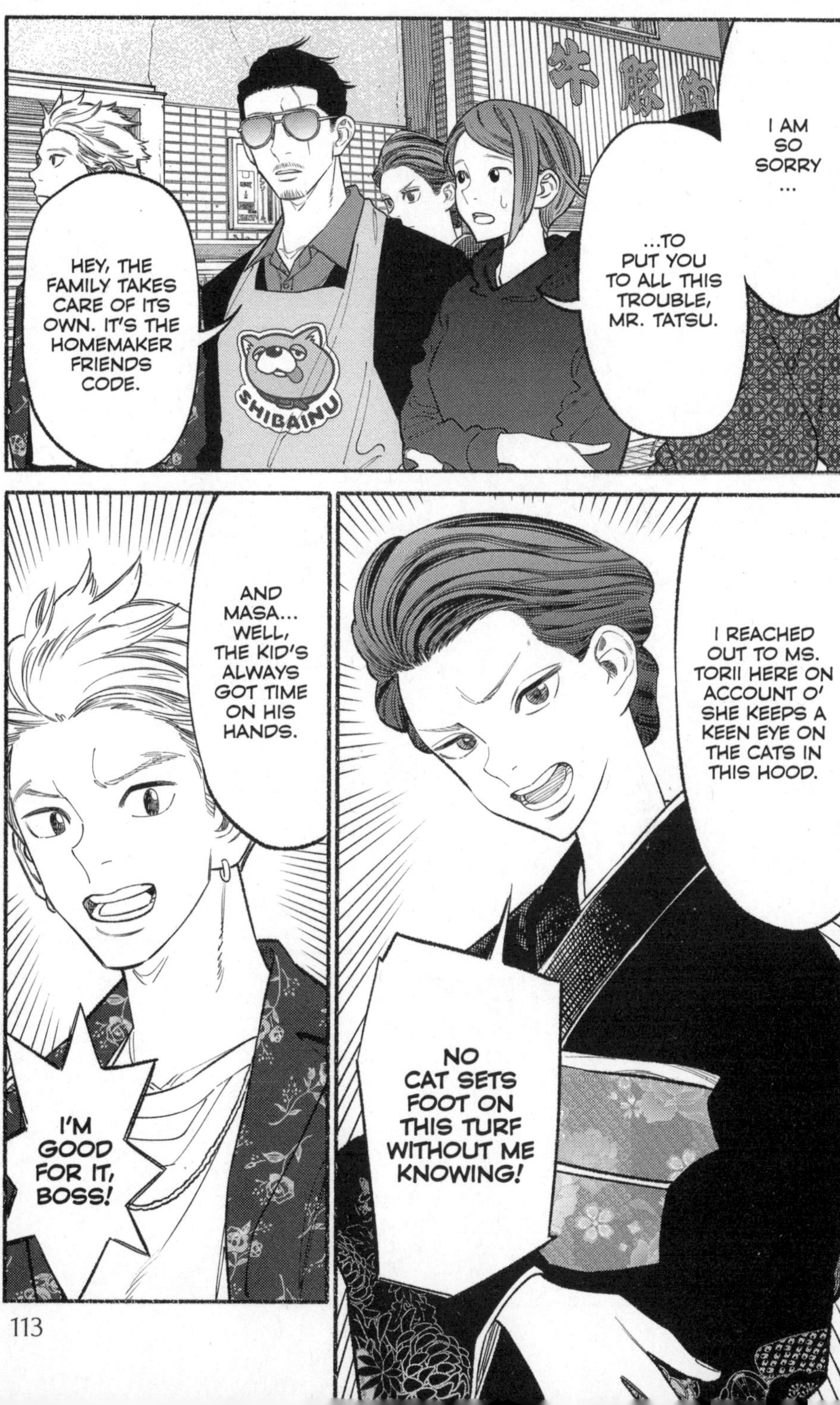
I AM SO SORRY ...
...TO PUT YOU TO ALL THIS TROUBLE, MR. TATSU.
HEY, THE FAMILY TAKES CARE OF ITS OWN. IT'S THE HOMEMAKER FRIENDS CODE.
SHIBAINU
I REACHED OUT TO MS. TORII HERE ON ACCOUNT O' SHE KEEPS A KEEN EYE ON THE CATS IN THIS HOOD.
NO CAT SETS FOOT ON THIS TURF WITHOUT ME KNOWING!
AND MASA... WELL, THE KID'S ALWAYS GOT TIME ON HIS HANDS.
I'M GOOD FOR IT, BOSS!

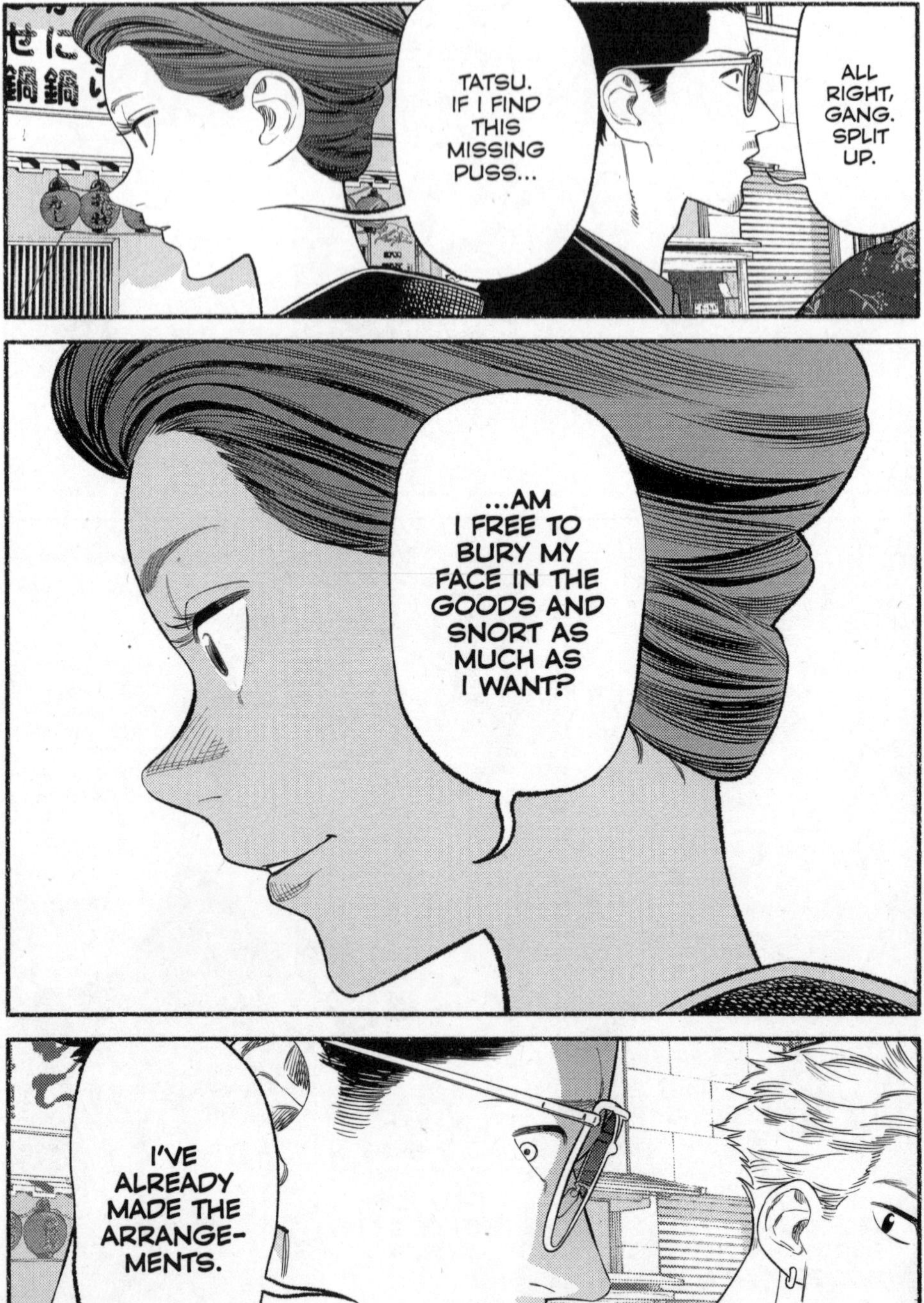
ALL RIGHT, GANG. SPLIT UP.
TATSU. IF I FIND THIS MISSING PUSS...
...AM I FREE TO BURY MY FACE IN THE GOODS AND SNORT AS MUCH AS I WANT?
I'VE ALREADY MADE THE ARRANGE-MENTS.

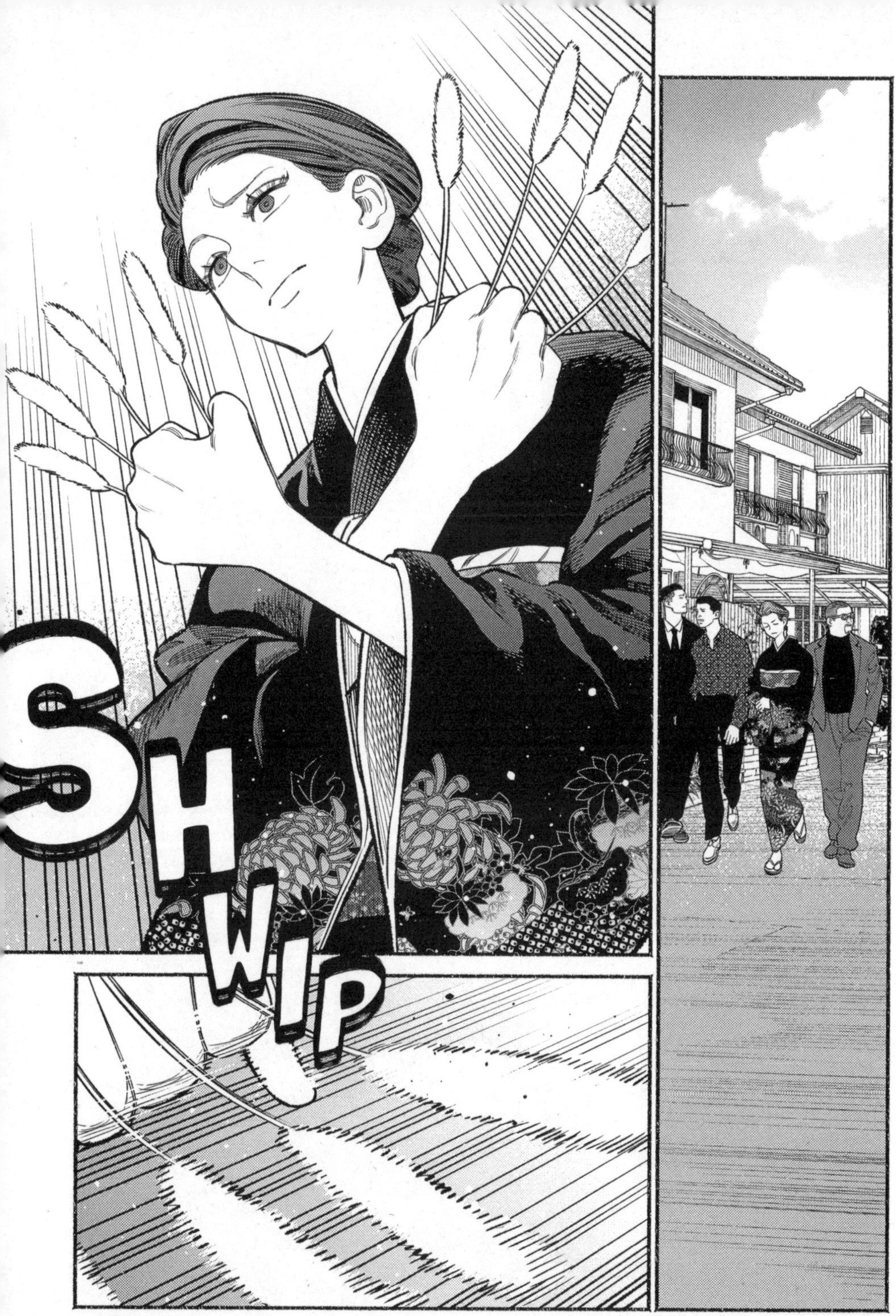
SHWIP

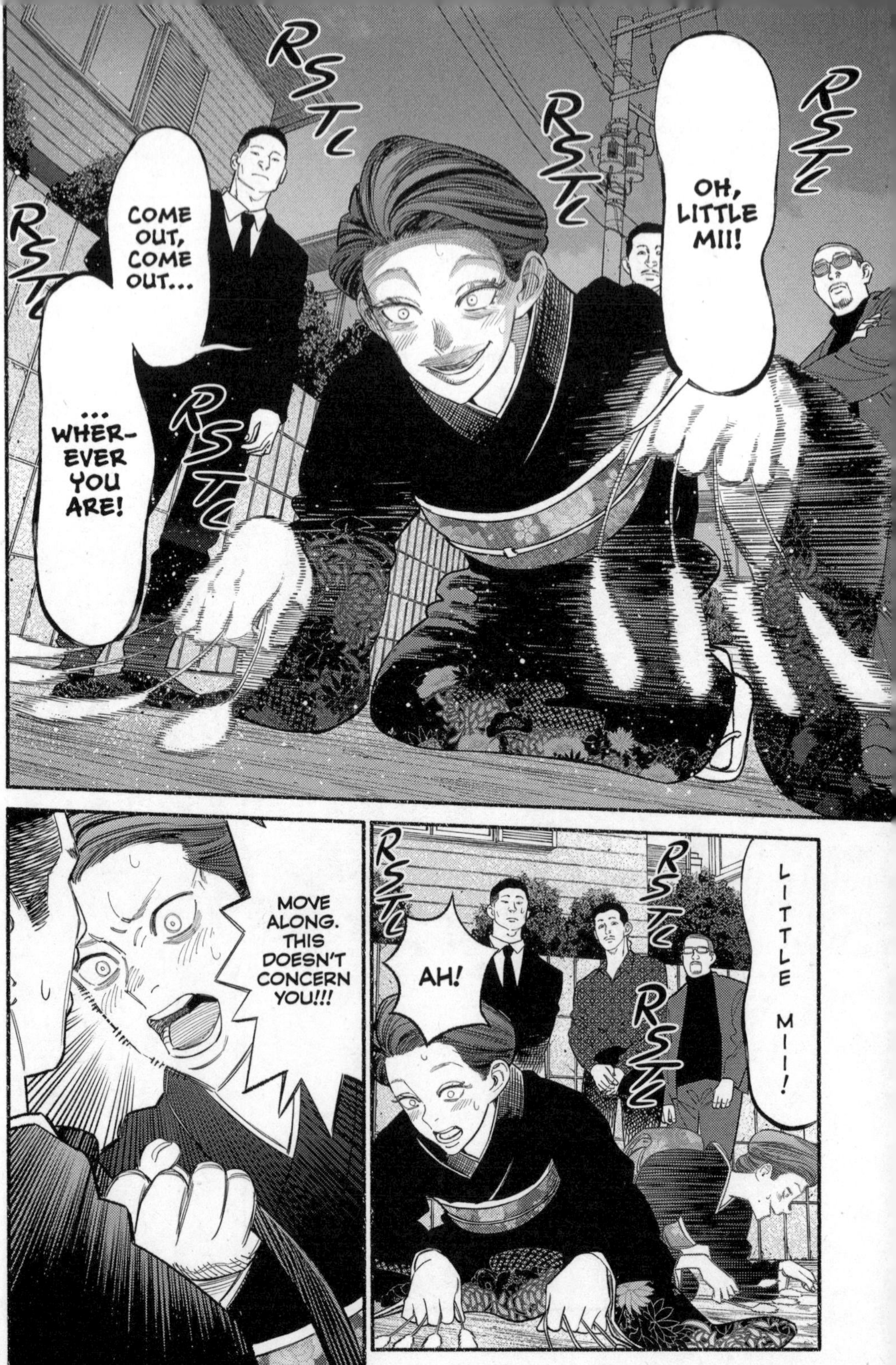
RSTL
RSTL
RSTL
OH, LITTLE MII!
COME OUT, COME OUT...
...WHEREVER YOU ARE!
RSTL
RSTL
RSTL
RSTL
LITTLE MII!
RSTL
AH!
MOVE ALONG. THIS DOESN'T CONCERN YOU!!!

MII?
ペットボトル
お茶飲料
MII?
MIIIIIIIII!

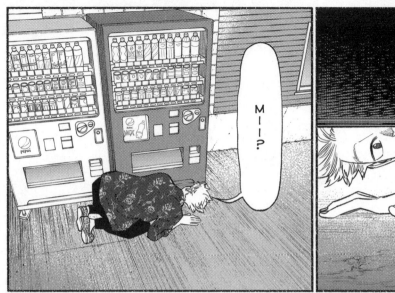

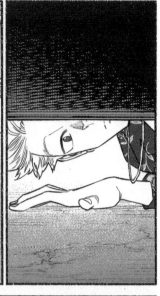

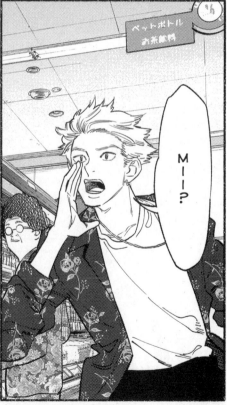

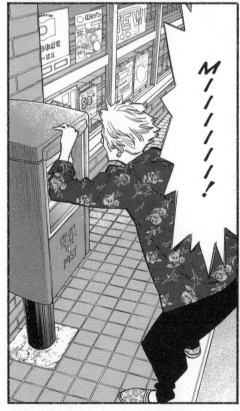

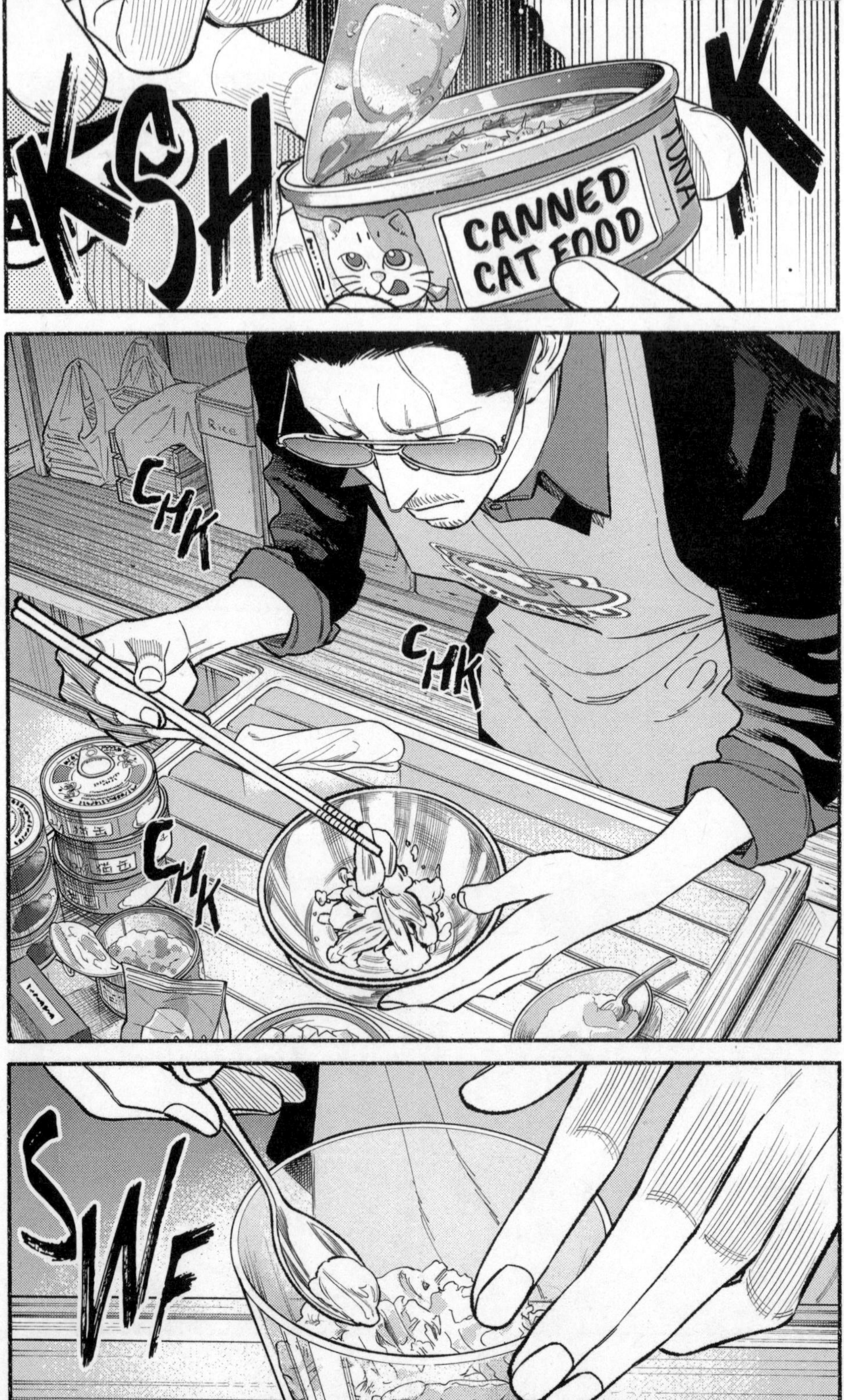
KSH
K
TUNA
CANNED CAT FOOD
CHK
CHK
CHK
SWF

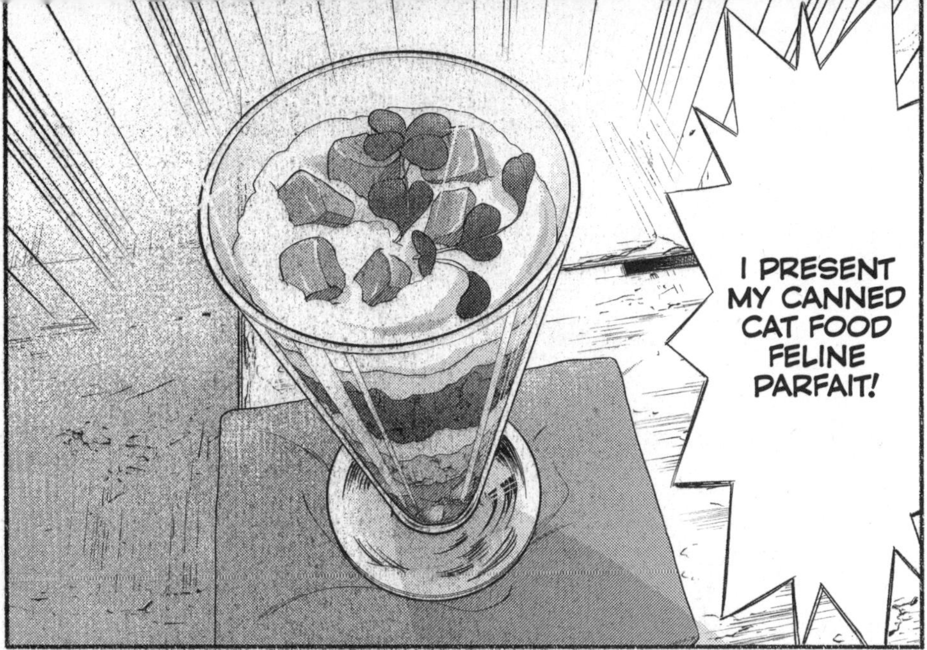
I PRESENT MY CANNED CAT FOOD FELINE PARFAIT!
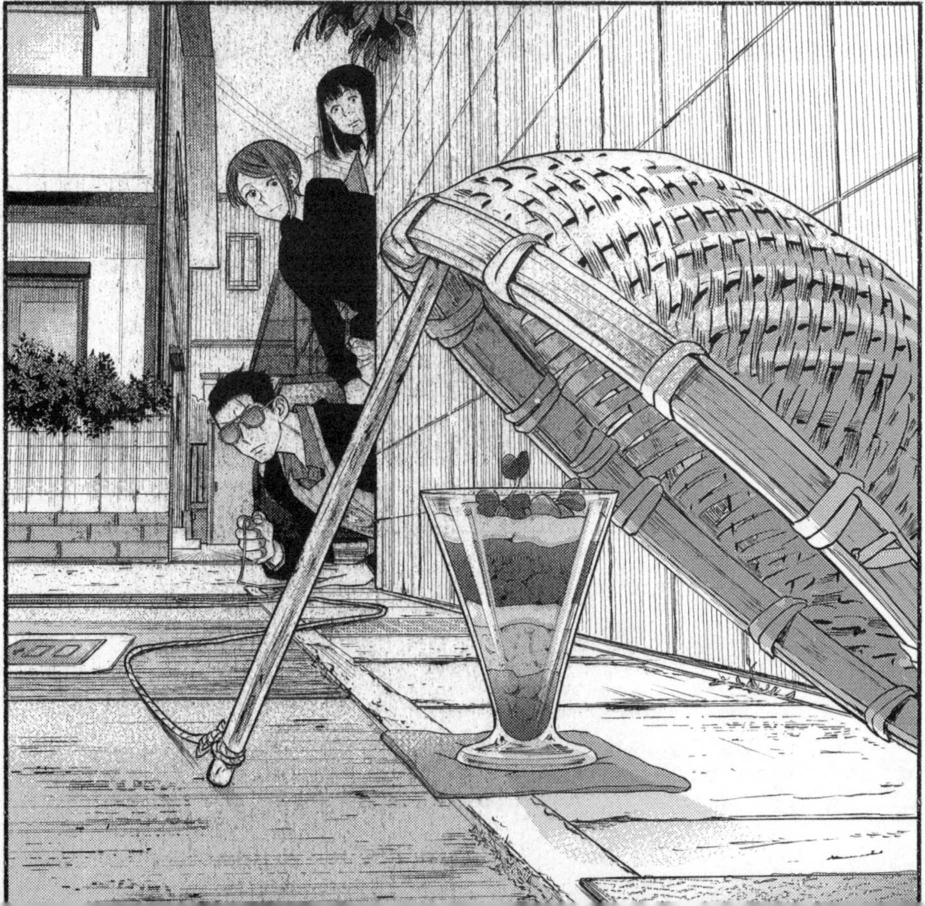

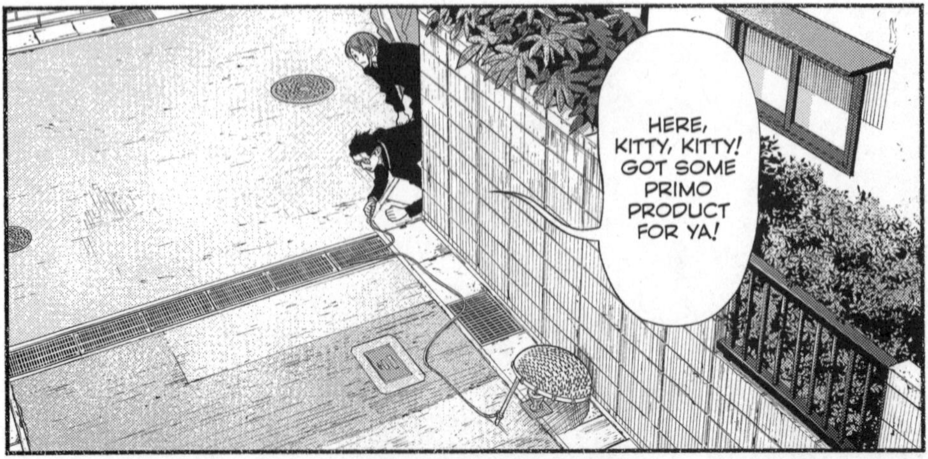
HERE, KITTY, KITTY! GOT SOME PRIMO PRODUCT FOR YA!
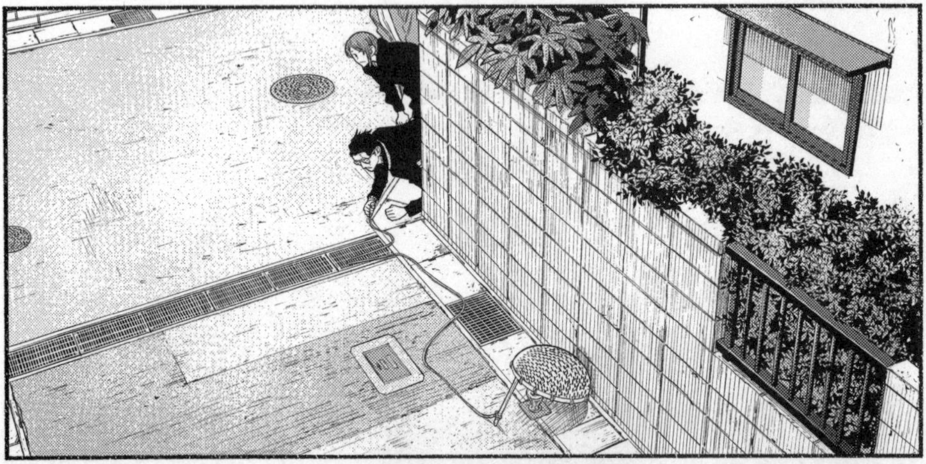
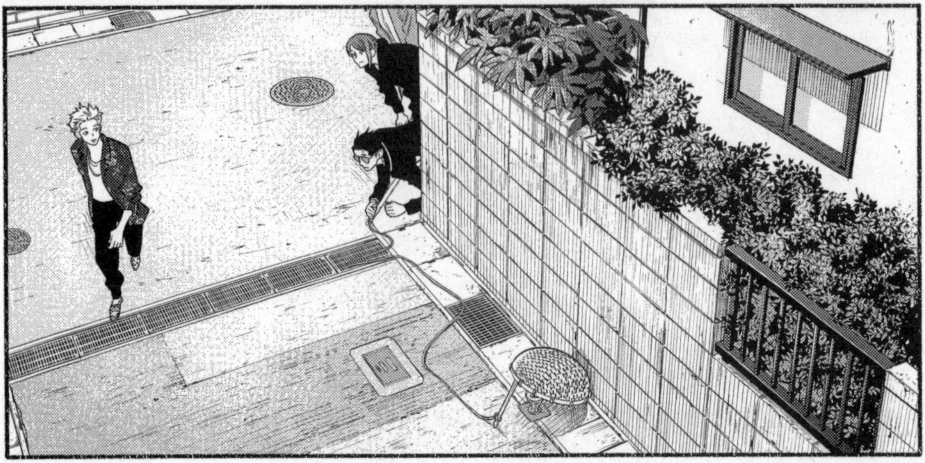

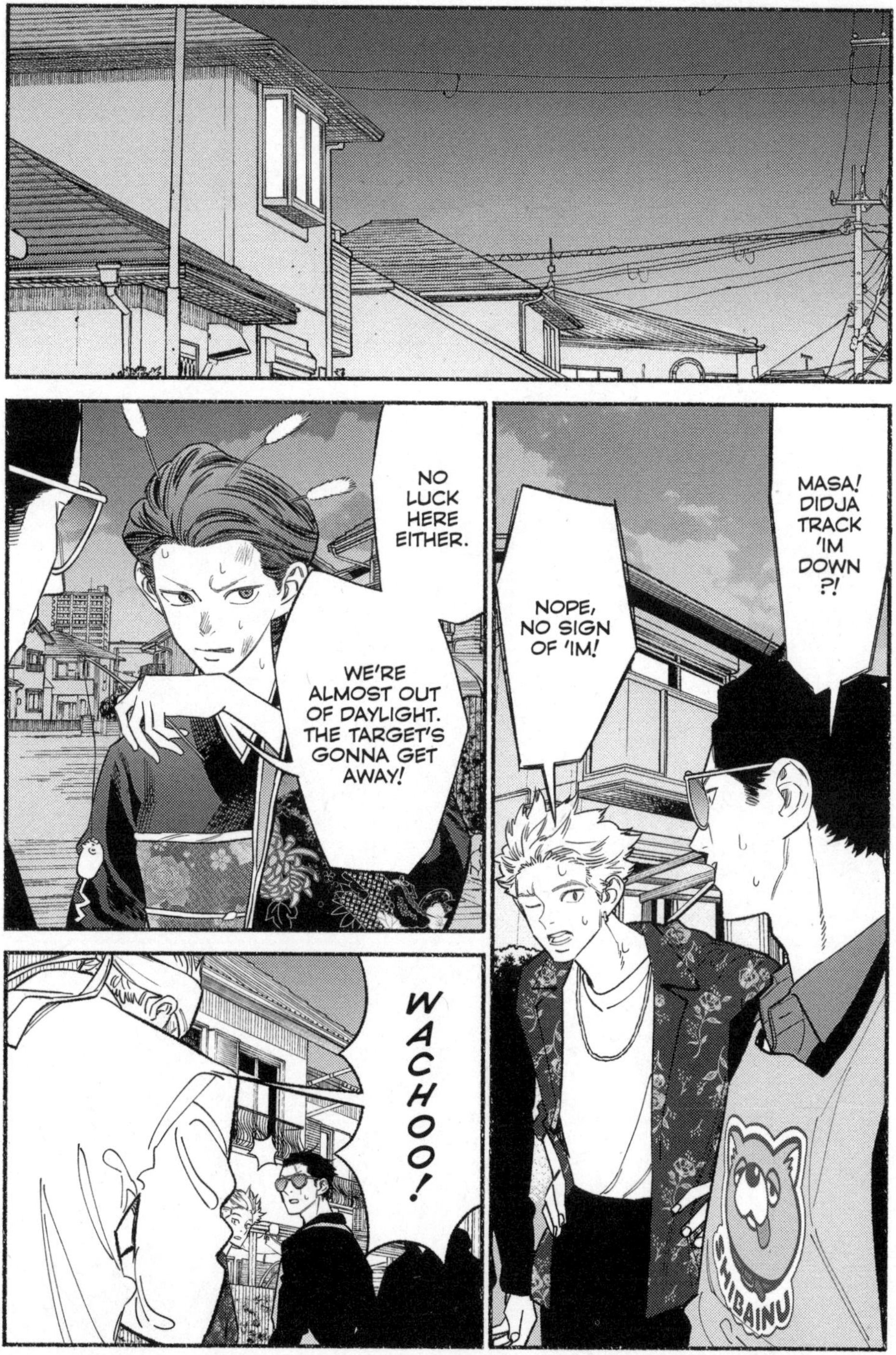
MASA! DIDJA TRACK 'IM DOWN?!
NOPE, NO SIGN OF 'IM!
NO LUCK HERE EITHER.
WE'RE ALMOST OUT OF DAYLIGHT. THE TARGET'S GONNA GET AWAY!
WACHOO!
SHIBAINU

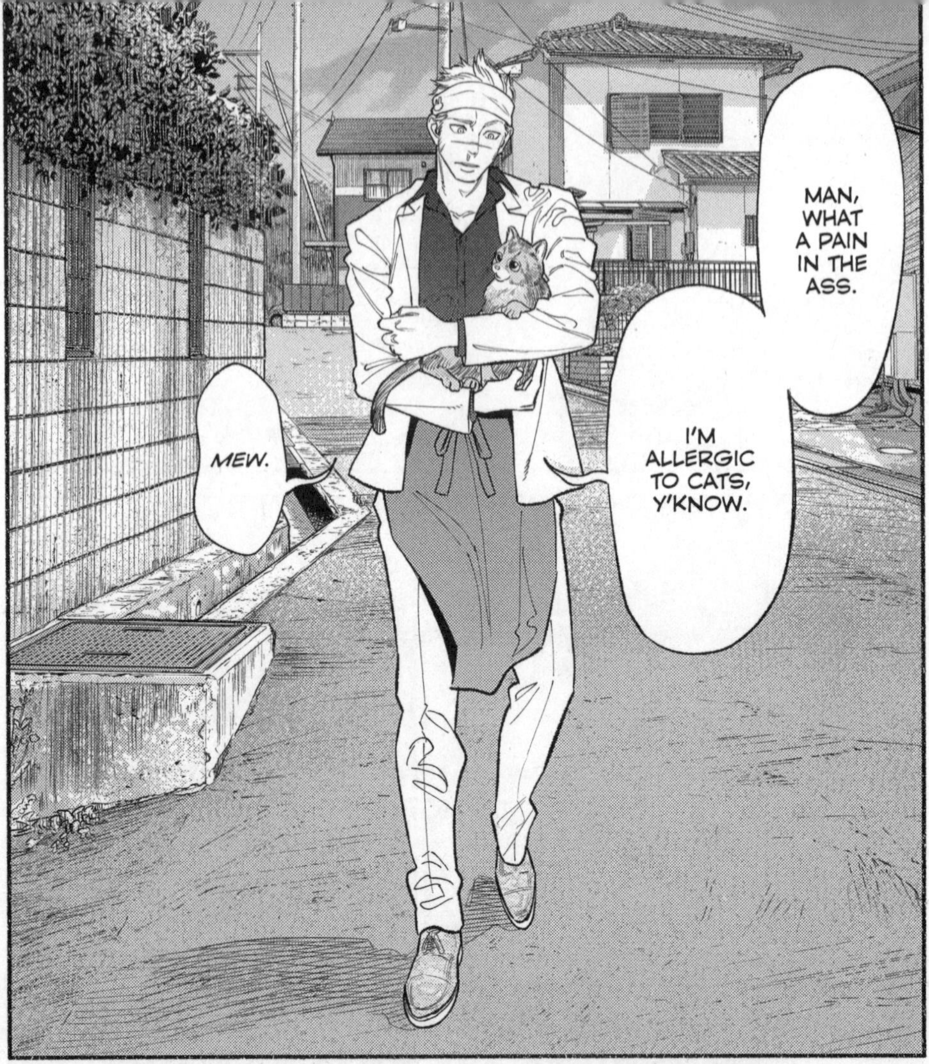
MAN, WHAT A PAIN IN THE ASS.
I'M ALLERGIC TO CATS, Y'KNOW.
MEW.
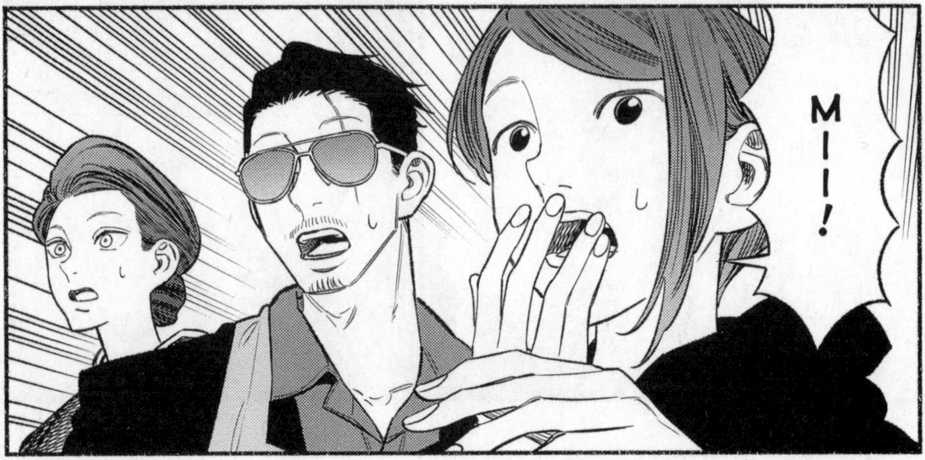
MIII!

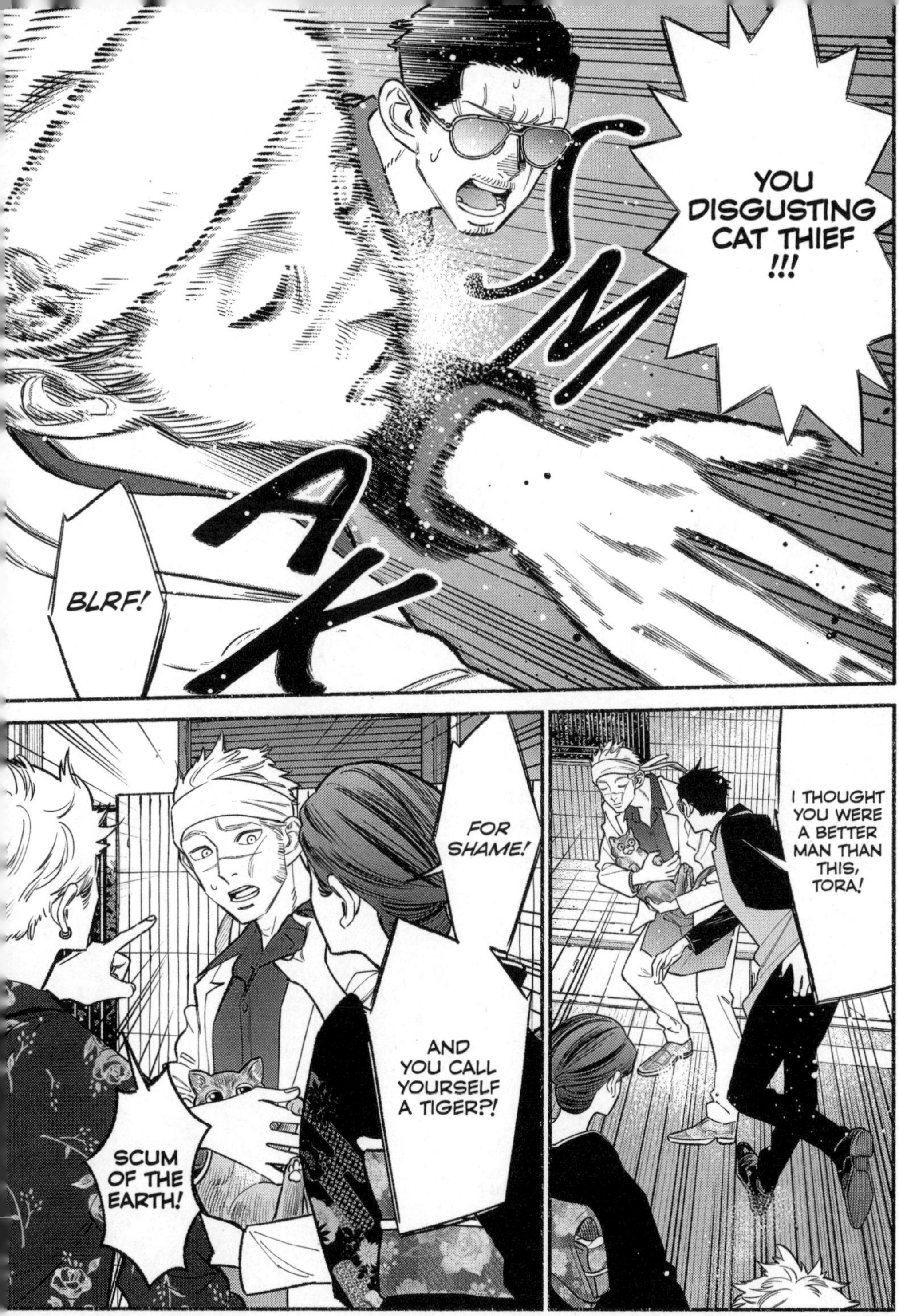
YOU DISGUSTING CAT THIEF!!!
SMACK
BLRF!
I THOUGHT YOU WERE A BETTER MAN THAN THIS, TORA!
FOR SHAME!
AND YOU CALL YOURSELF A TIGER?!
SCUM OF THE EARTH!

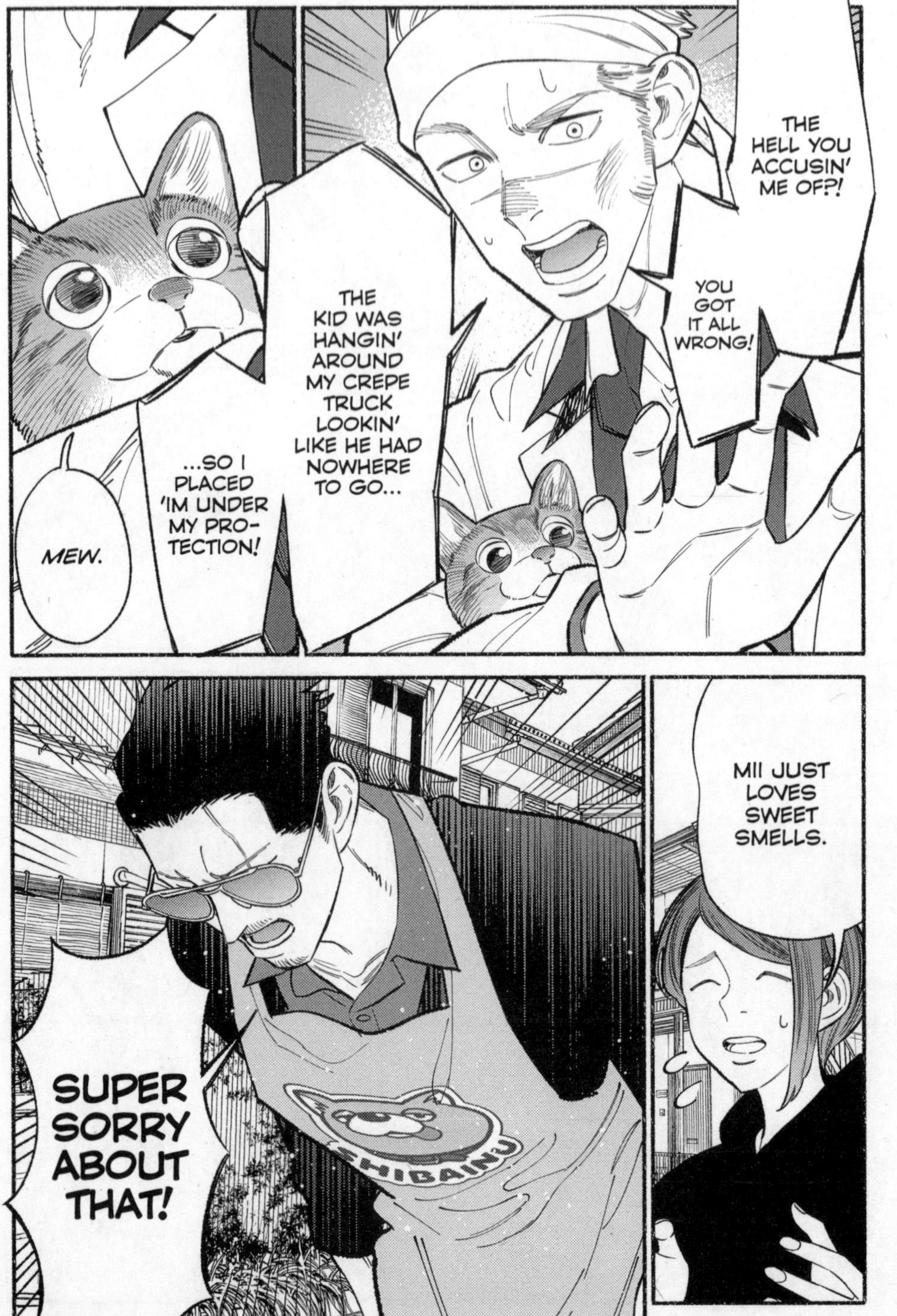
THE HELL YOU ACCUSIN' ME OF?!
YOU GOT IT ALL WRONG!
THE KID WAS HANGIN' AROUND MY CREPE TRUCK LOOKIN' LIKE HE HAD NOWHERE TO GO...
...SO I PLACED 'IM UNDER MY PRO-TECTION!
MEW.
MII JUST LOVES SWEET SMELLS.
SUPER SORRY ABOUT THAT!
SHIBAINU

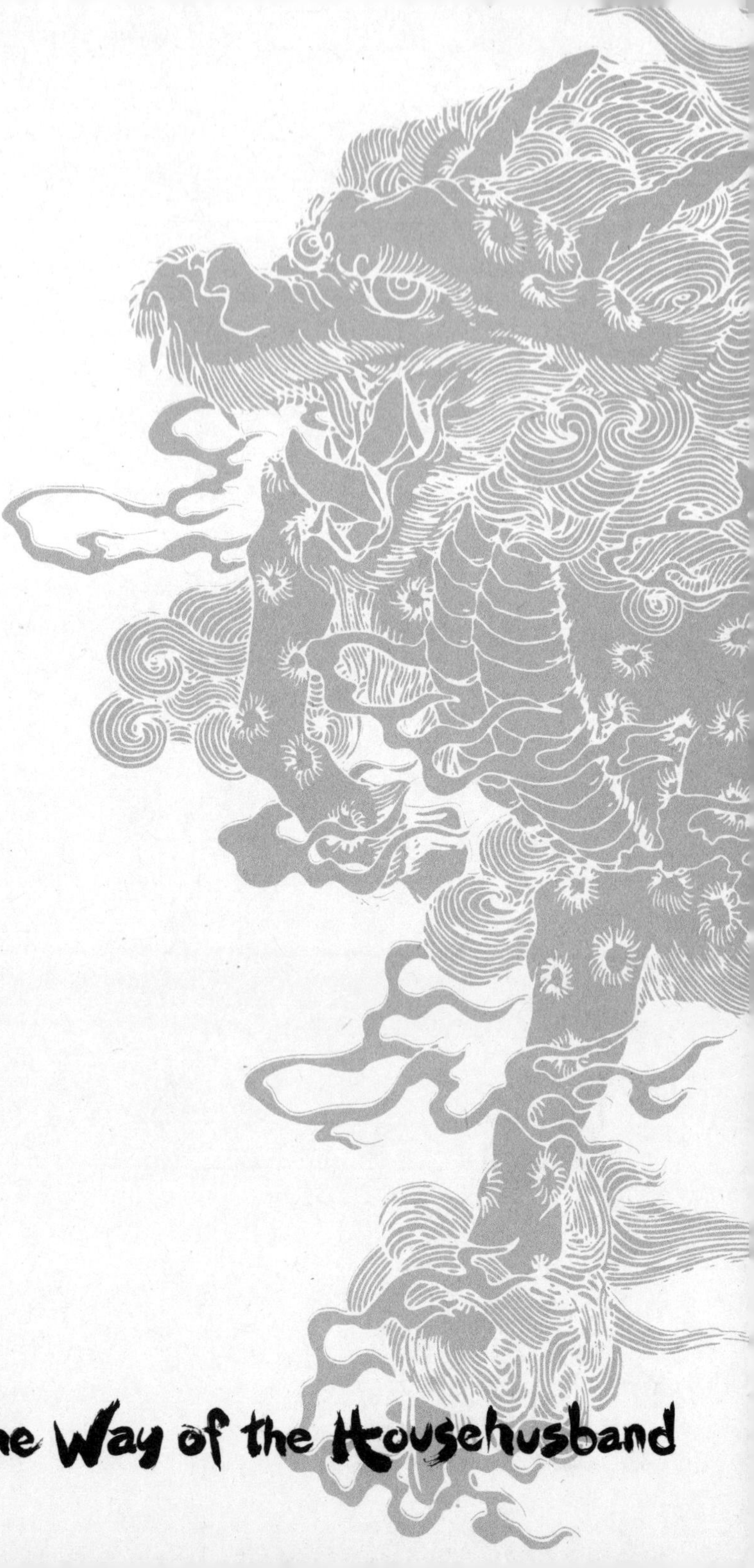

The Way of the Househusband

CHAPTER 90

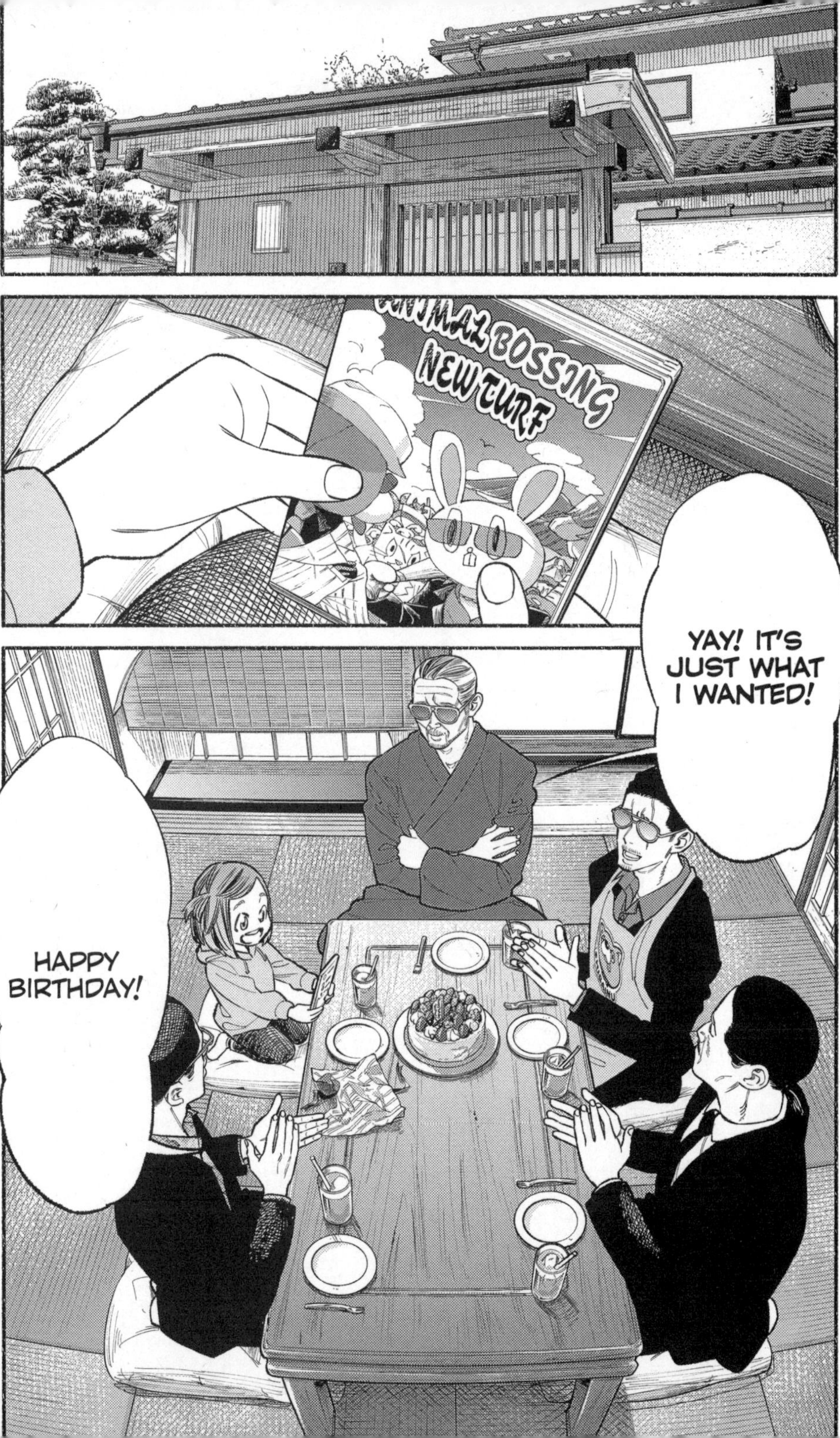
BOSSING
NEW TURF
YAY! IT'S JUST WHAT I WANTED!
HAPPY BIRTHDAY!

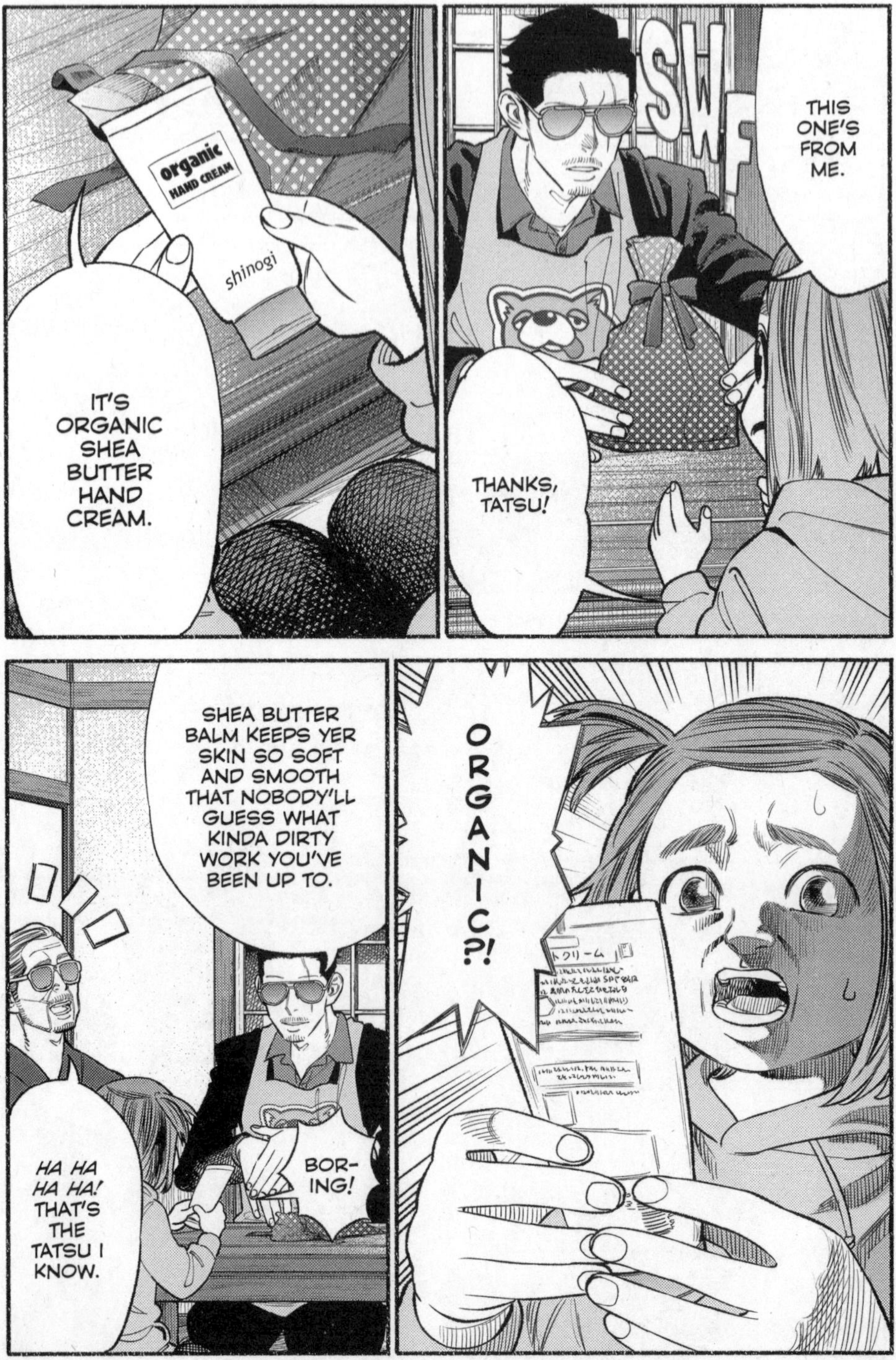
SWF
THIS ONE'S FROM ME.
THANKS, TATSU!
Organic
HAND CREAM
shinogi
IT'S ORGANIC SHEA BUTTER HAND CREAM.
ORGANIC?!
SHEA BUTTER BALM KEEPS YER SKIN SO SOFT AND SMOOTH THAT NOBODY'LL GUESS WHAT KINDA DIRTY WORK YOU'VE BEEN UP TO.
BOR-ING!
HA HA HA HA! THAT'S THE TATSU I KNOW.

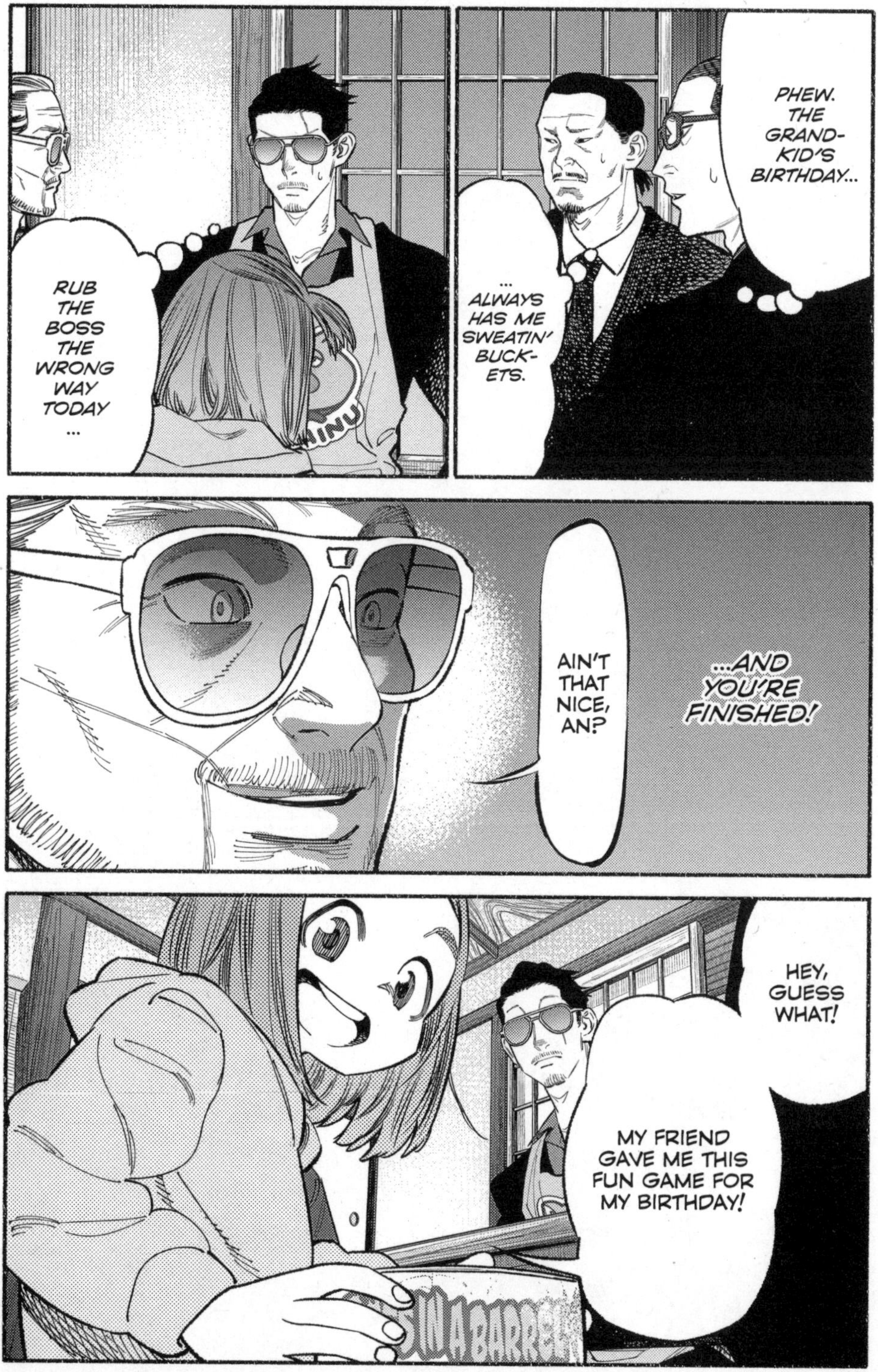
PHEW. THE GRAND-KID'S BIRTHDAY...
...ALWAYS HAS ME SWEATIN' BUCK-ETS.
RUB THE BOSS THE WRONG WAY TODAY ...
...AND YOU'RE FINISHED!
AIN'T THAT NICE, AN?
HEY, GUESS WHAT!
MY FRIEND GAVE ME THIS FUN GAME FOR MY BIRTHDAY!
INU
IN A BARREL

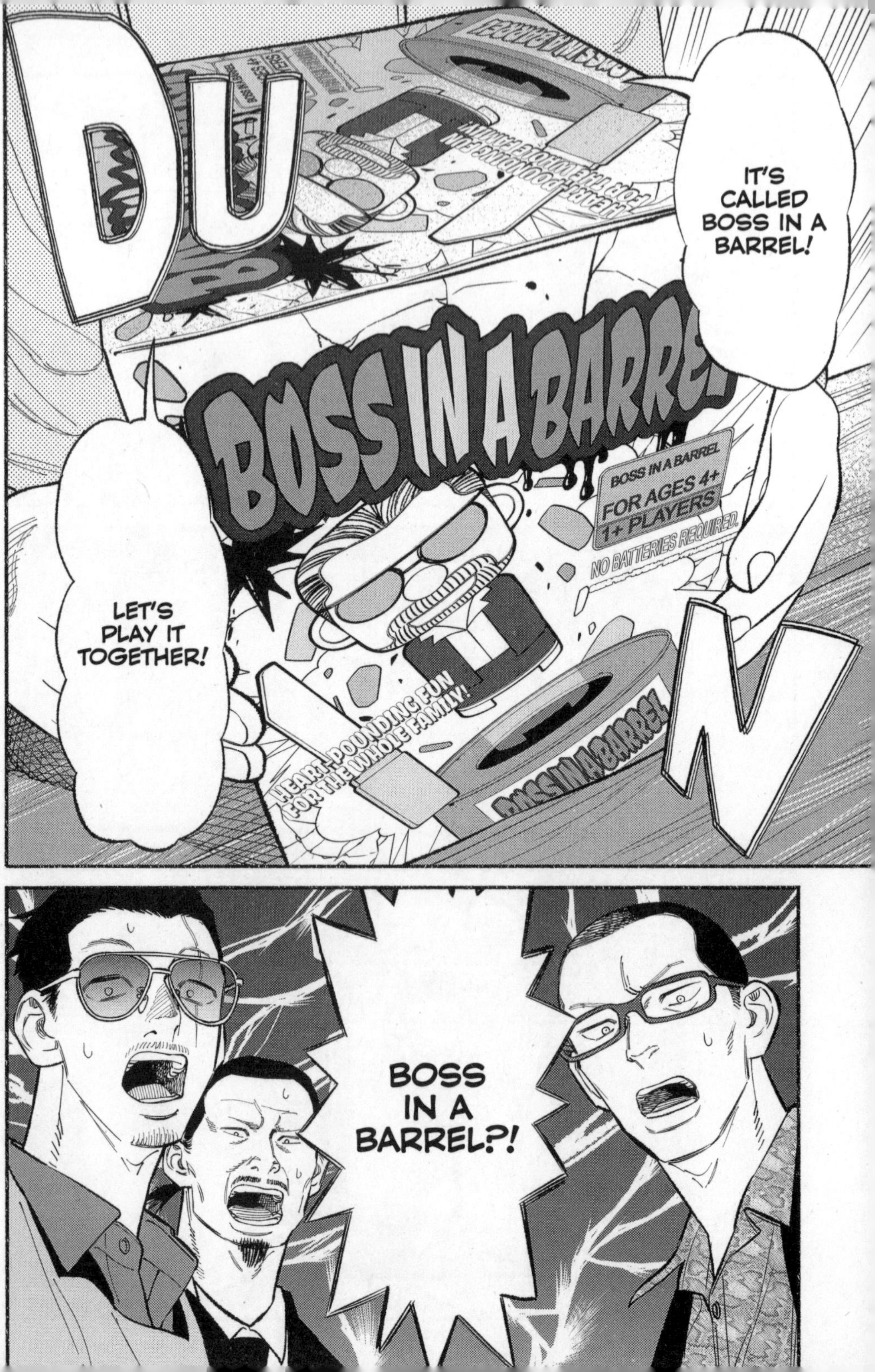
IT'S CALLED BOSS IN A BARREL!
DUN
BOSS IN A BARREL
BOSS IN A BARREL
FOR AGES 4+
1+ PLAYERS
NO BATTERIES REQUIRED.
HEART-POUNDING FUN FOR THE WHOLE FAMILY!
BOSS IN A BARREL
LET'S PLAY IT TOGETHER!
BOSS IN A BARREL?!

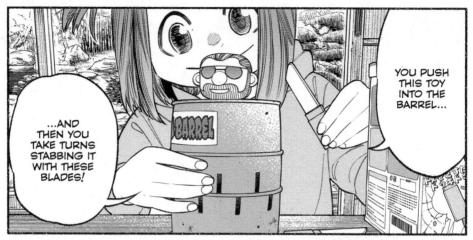

YOU PUSH THIS TOY INTO THE BARREL...
BARREL
...AND THEN YOU TAKE TURNS STABBING IT WITH THESE BLADES!
LOOK AT THE TOY!
HE LOOKS EXACTLY LIKE MY GRAMPA!
AHA HA HA HA HA!
HA...
HA HA HA HA HA HA!

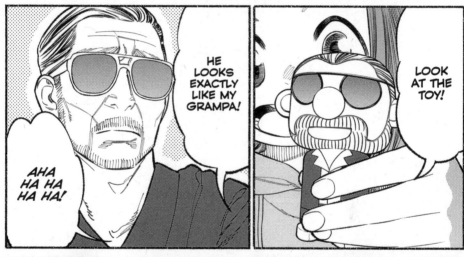

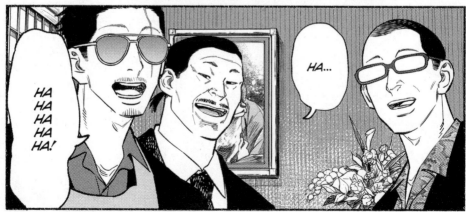

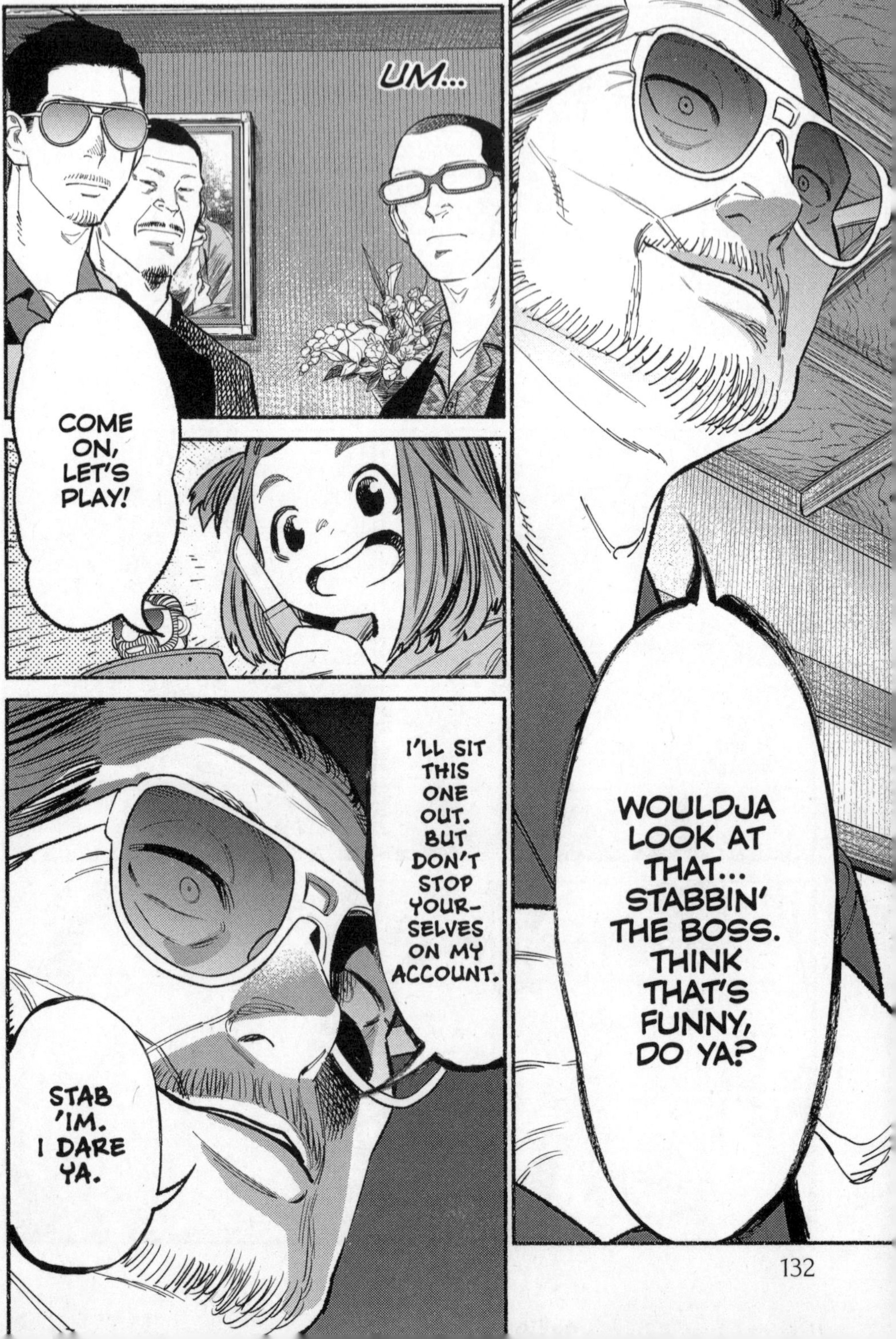
WOULDJA LOOK AT THAT... STABBIN' THE BOSS. THINK THAT'S FUNNY, DO YA?
UM...
COME ON, LET'S PLAY!
I'LL SIT THIS ONE OUT. BUT DON'T STOP YOUR-SELVES ON MY ACCOUNT.
STAB 'IM. I DARE YA.

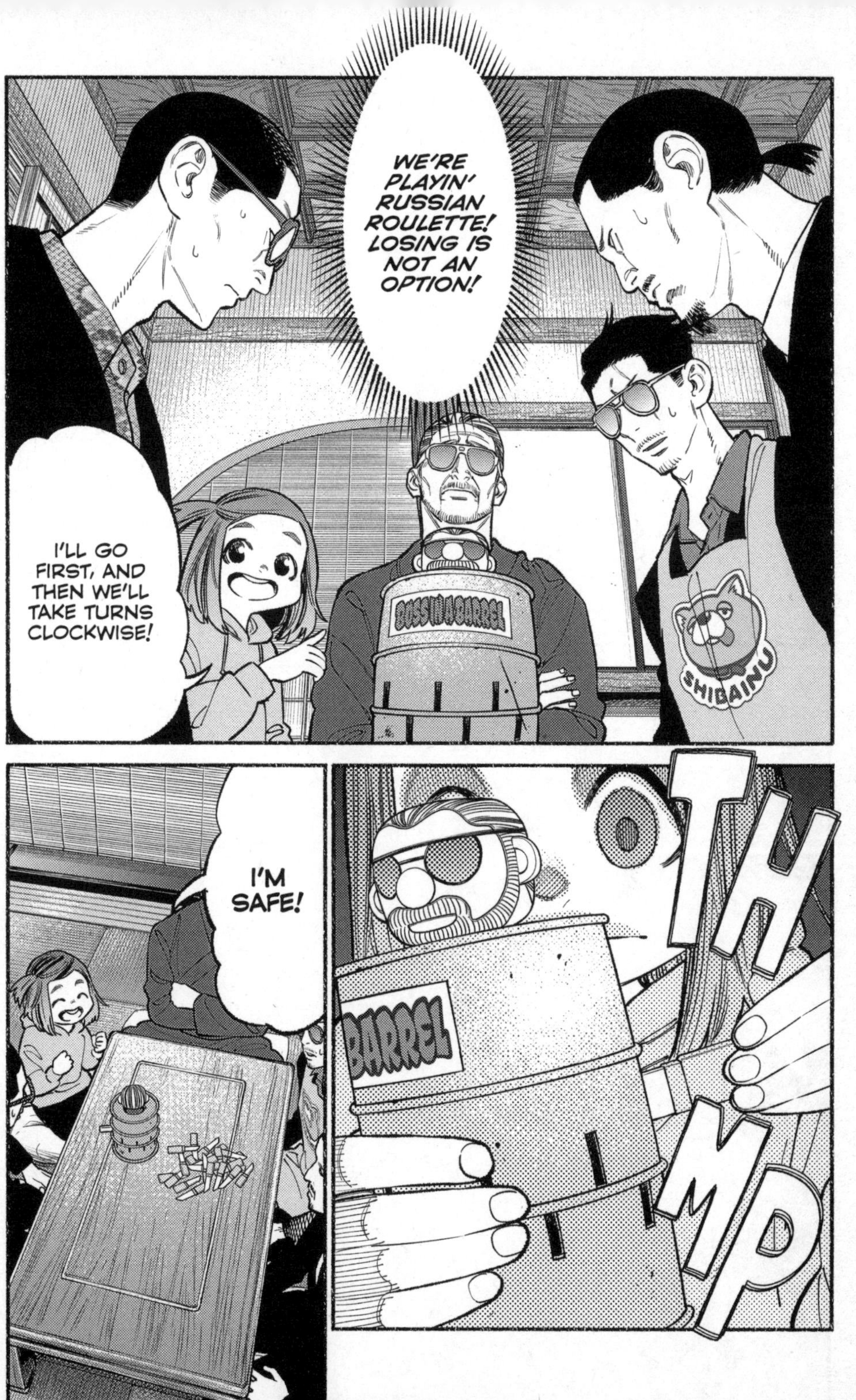
WE'RE PLAYIN' RUSSIAN ROULETTE! LOSING IS NOT AN OPTION!
I'LL GO FIRST, AND THEN WE'LL TAKE TURNS CLOCKWISE!
SHIBAINU
THUMP
BARREL
I'M SAFE!

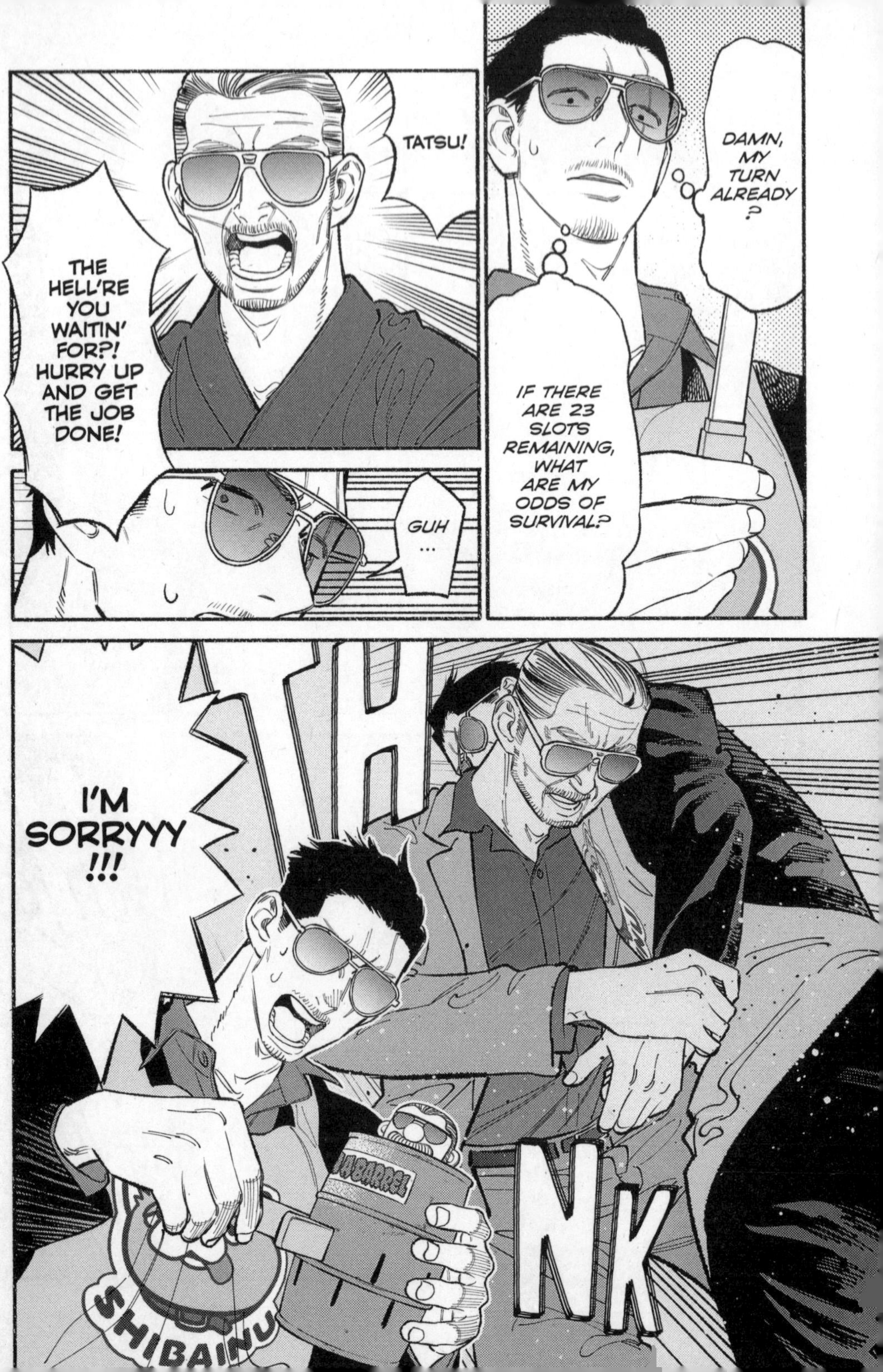
DAMN, MY TURN ALREADY?
IF THERE ARE 23 SLOTS REMAINING, WHAT ARE MY ODDS OF SURVIVAL?
TATSU!
THE HELL'RE YOU WAITIN' FOR?! HURRY UP AND GET THE JOB DONE!
GUH ...
I'M SORRYYY!!!
NK
SHIBAINU

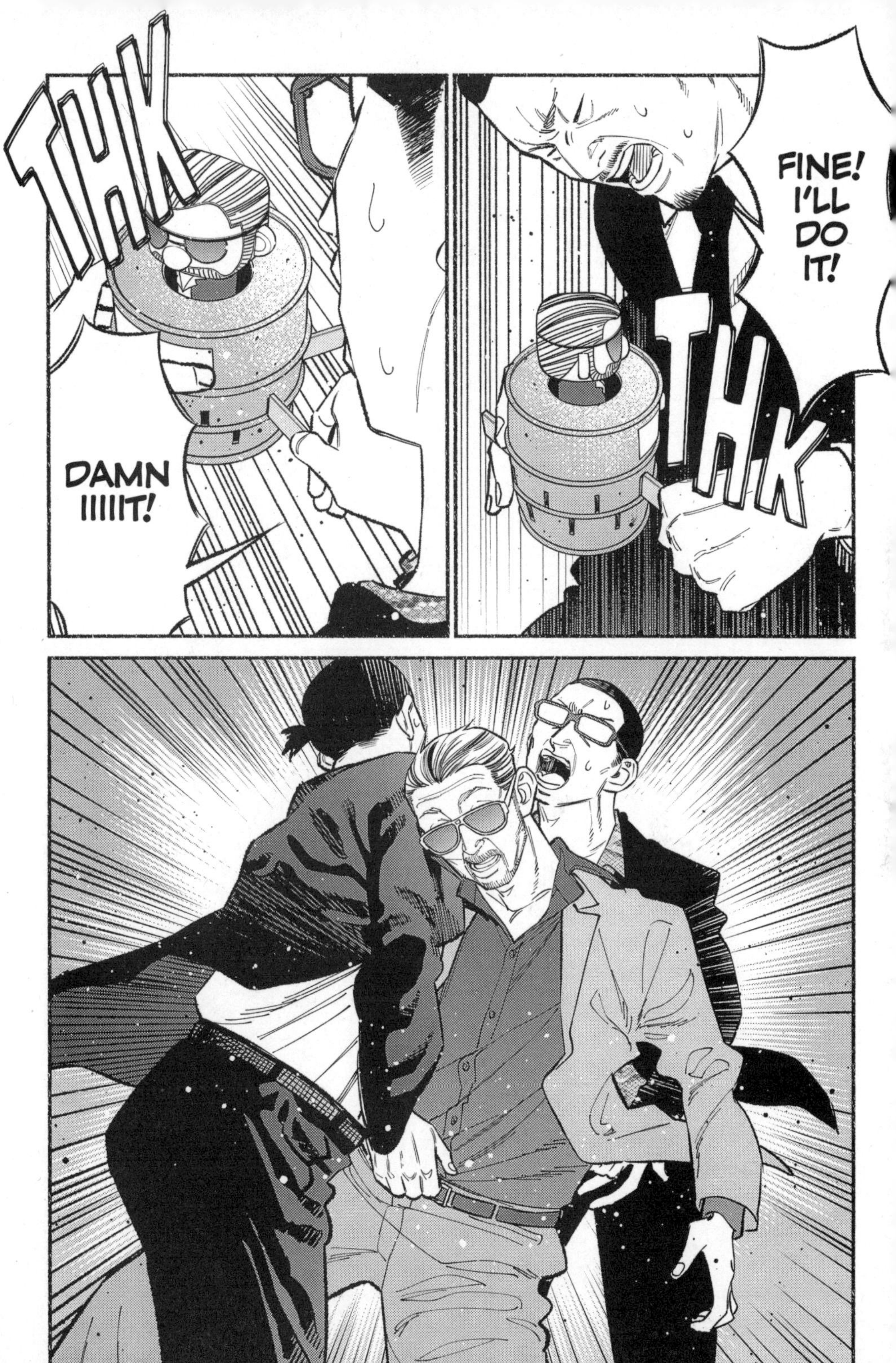
FINE! I'LL DO IT!
THK
THK
DAMN IIIIIT!

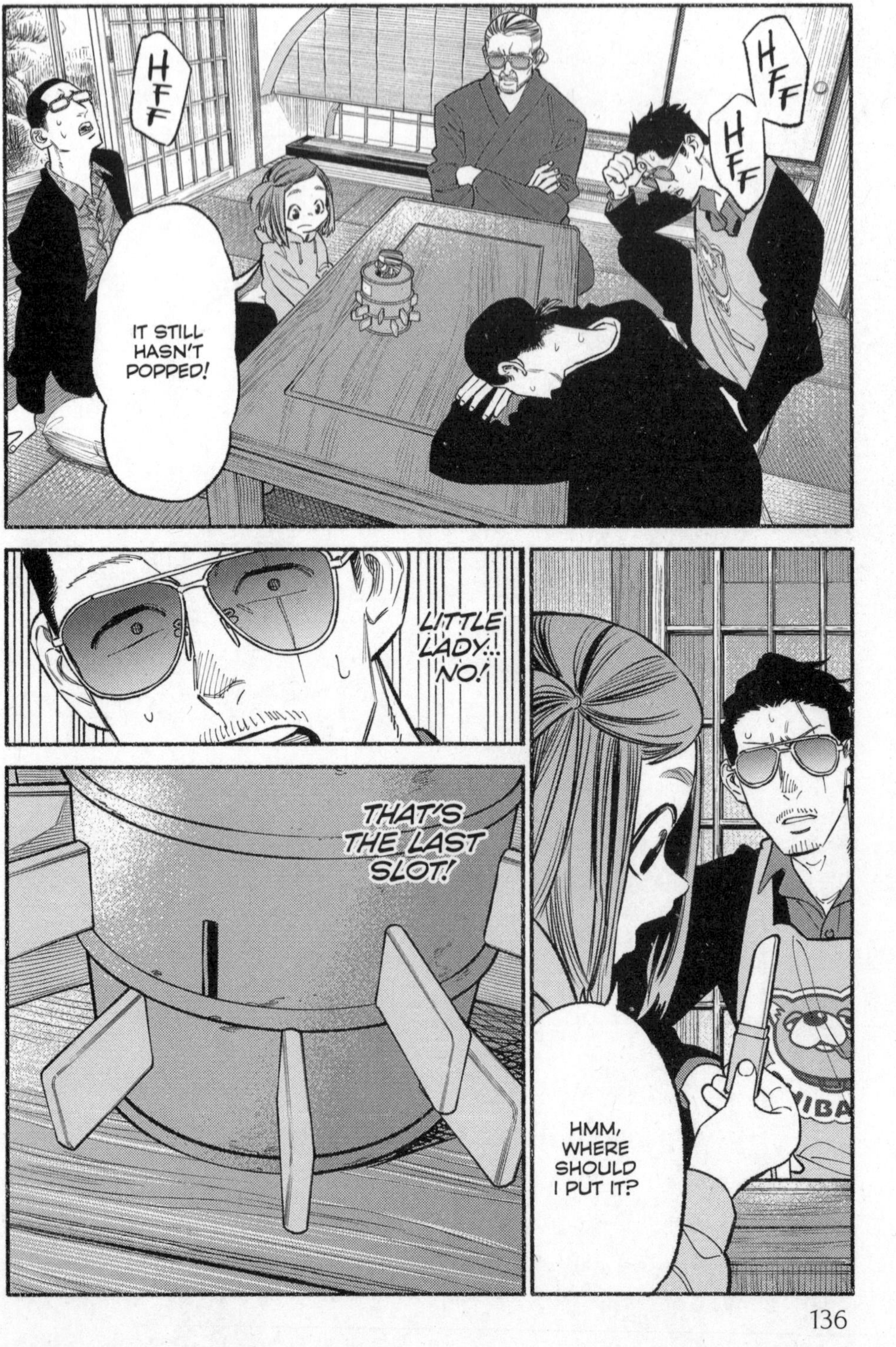
HFF HFF
HFF
IT STILL HASN'T POPPED!
HMM, WHERE SHOULD I PUT IT?
LITTLE LADY... NO!
THAT'S THE LAST SLOT!

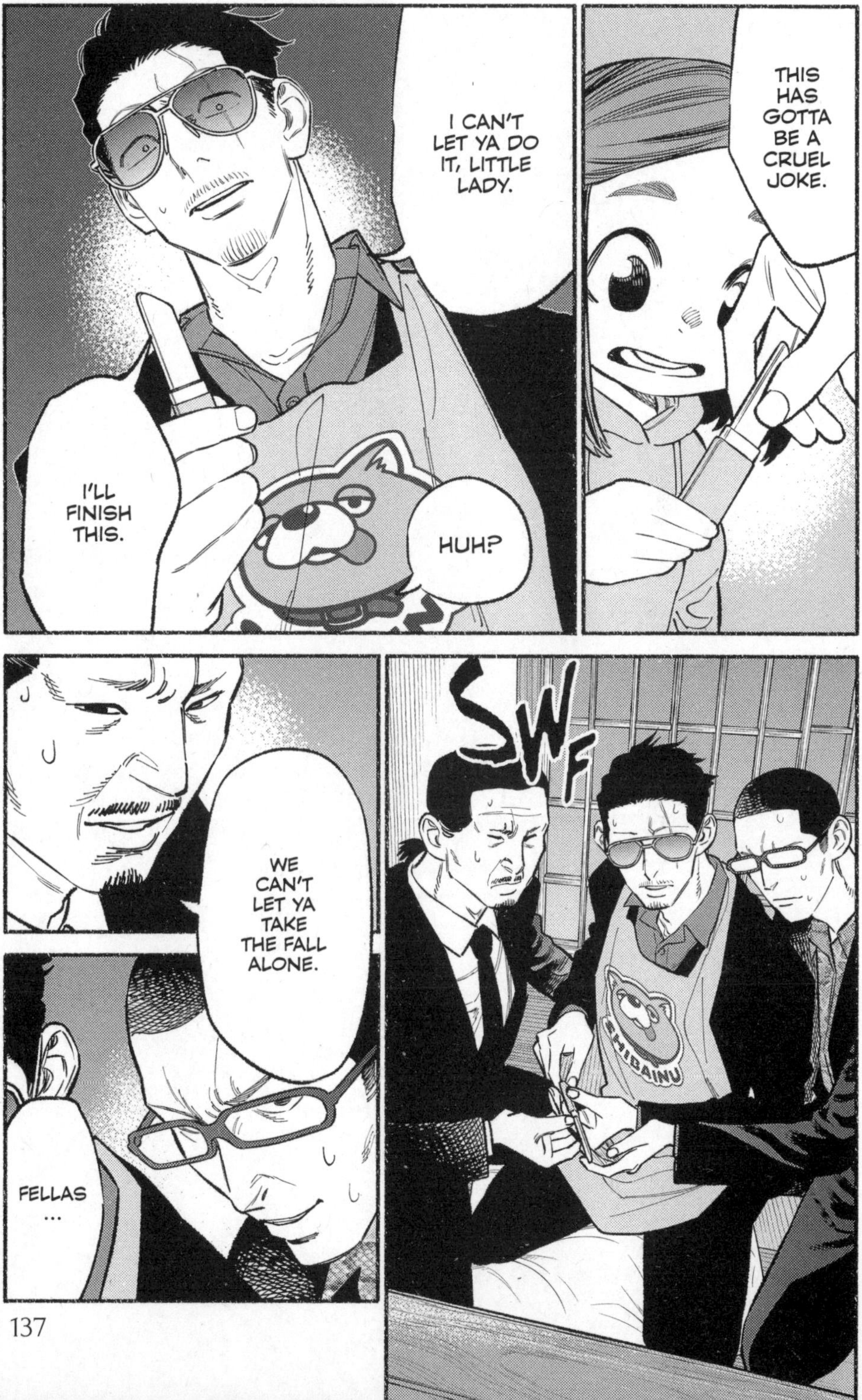
THIS HAS GOTTA BE A CRUEL JOKE.
I CAN'T LET YA DO IT, LITTLE LADY.
I'LL FINISH THIS.
HUH?
SWF
WE CAN'T LET YA TAKE THE FALL ALONE.
FELLAS ...

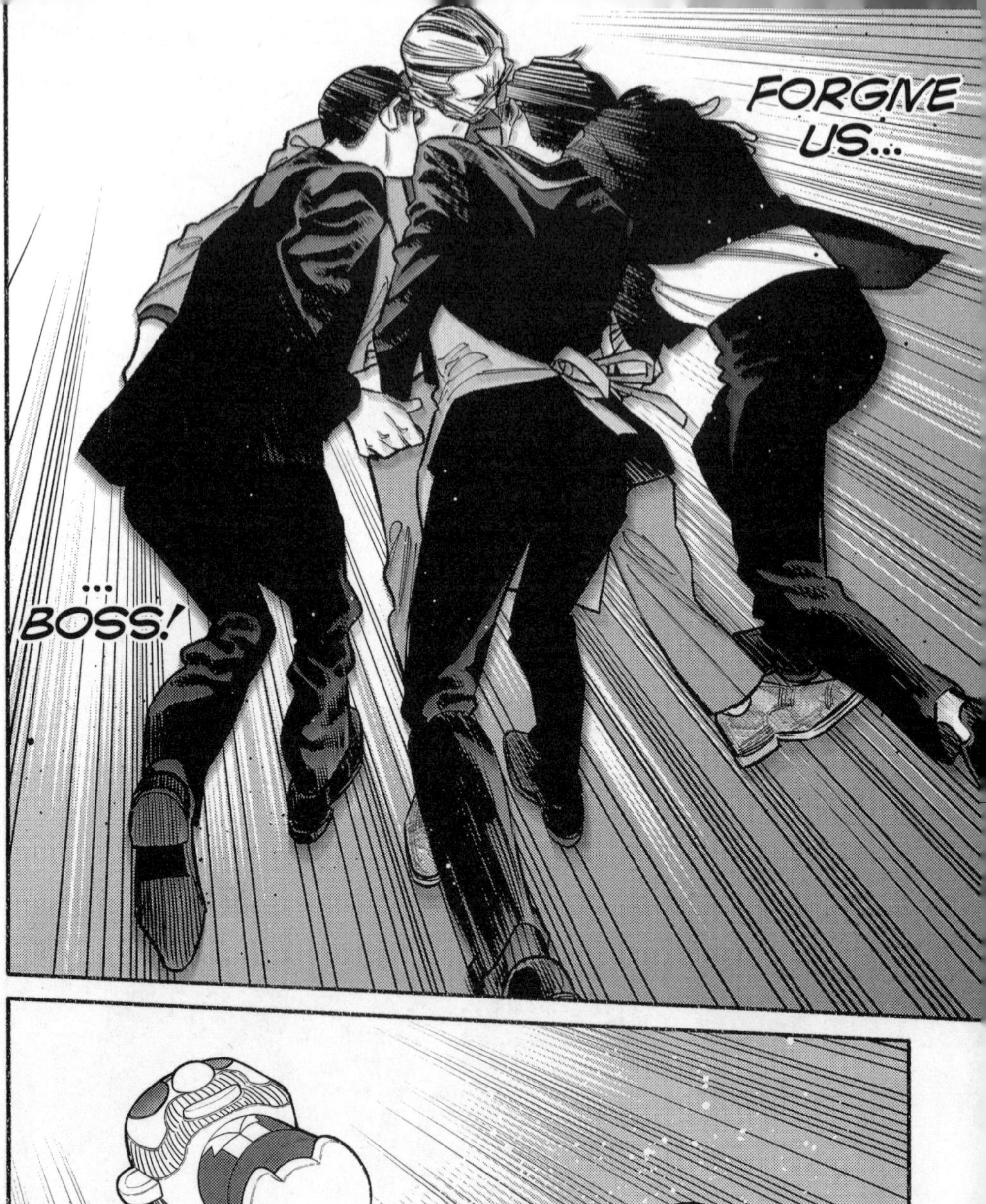
FORGIVE US...
...BOSS!
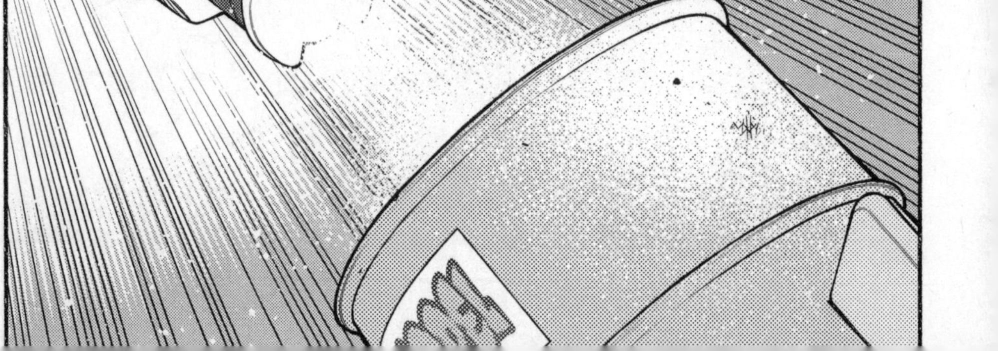

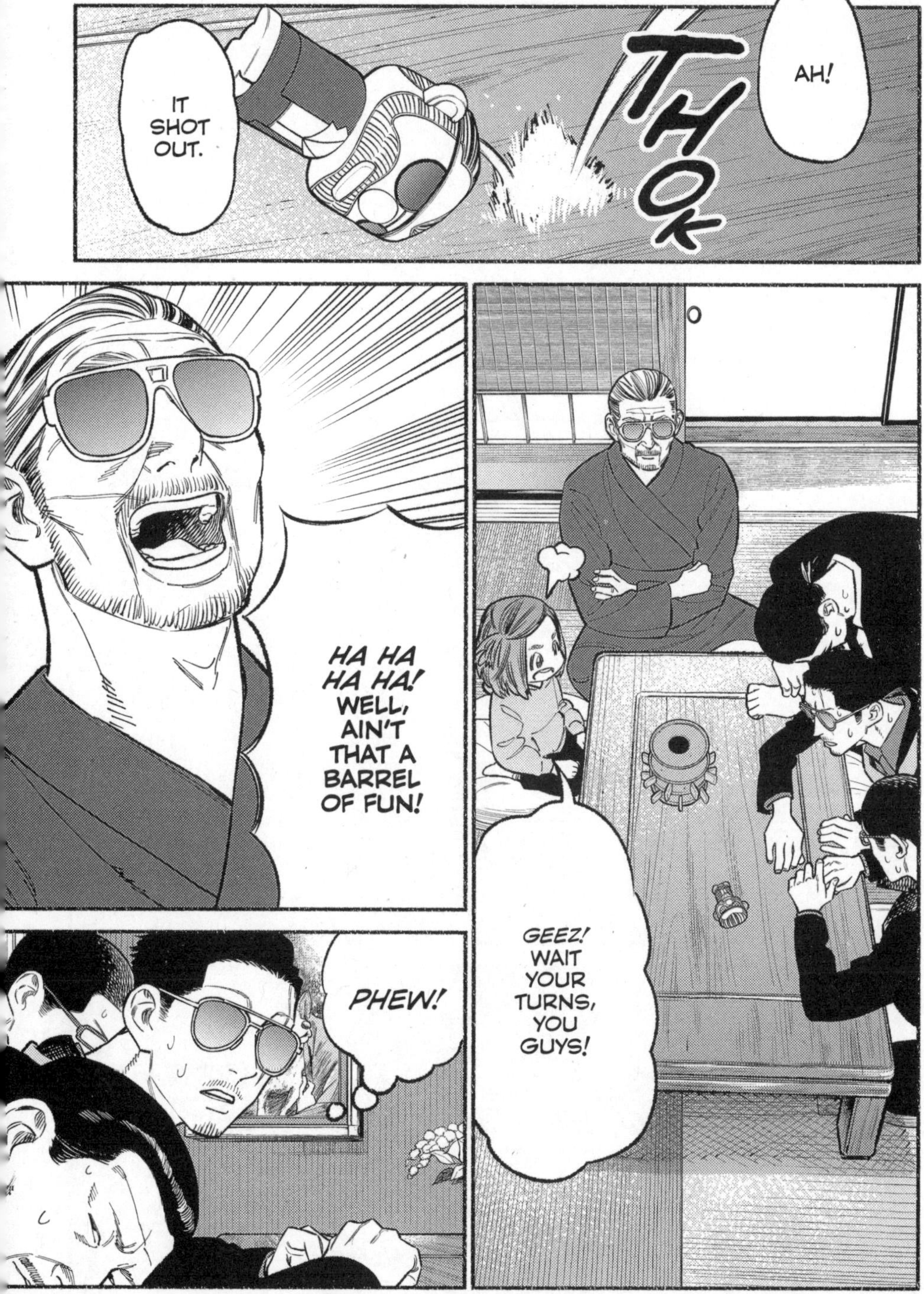
AH!
THOK
IT SHOT OUT.
GEEZ! WAIT YOUR TURNS, YOU GUYS!
HA HA HA HA! WELL, AIN'T THAT A BARREL OF FUN!
PHEW!

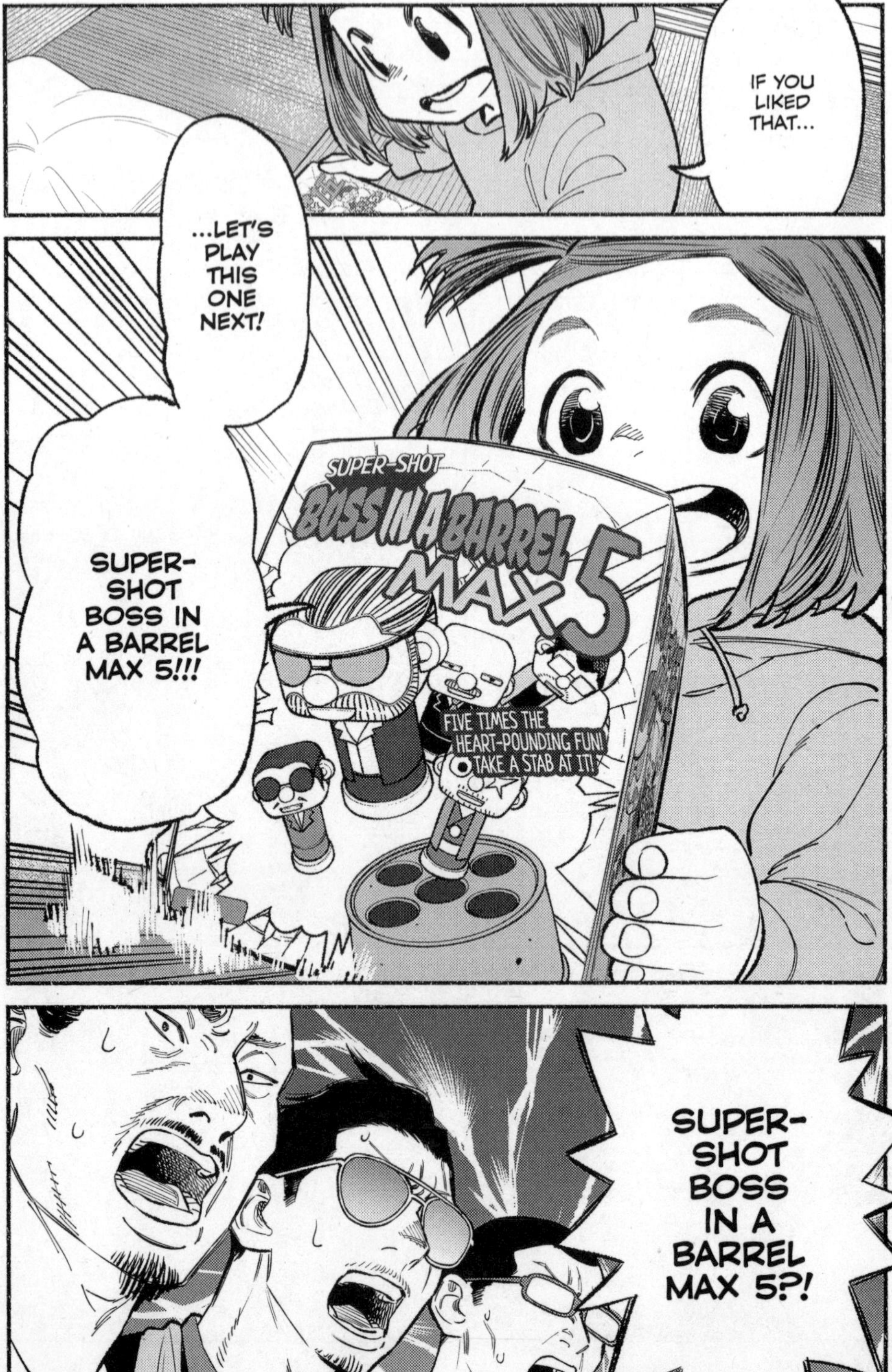
IF YOU LIKED THAT...
...LET'S PLAY THIS ONE NEXT!
SUPER-SHOT
BOSS IN A BARREL
MAX 5
FIVE TIMES THE HEART-POUNDING FUN! TAKE A STAB AT IT!
SUPER-SHOT BOSS IN A BARREL MAX 5!!!
SUPER-SHOT BOSS IN A BARREL MAX 5?!
THE WAY OF THE HOUSEHUSBAND ⑩ END

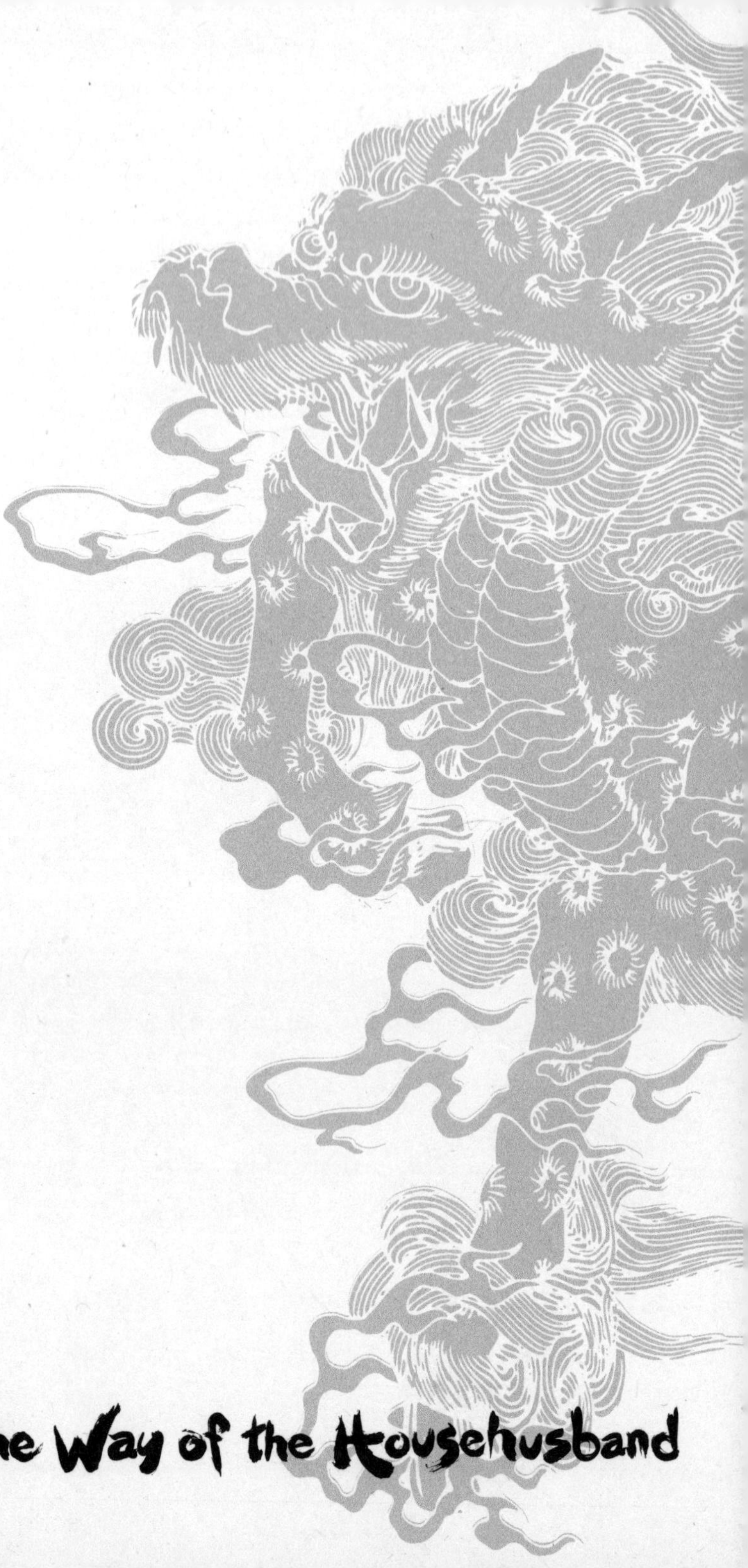

The Way of the Househusband

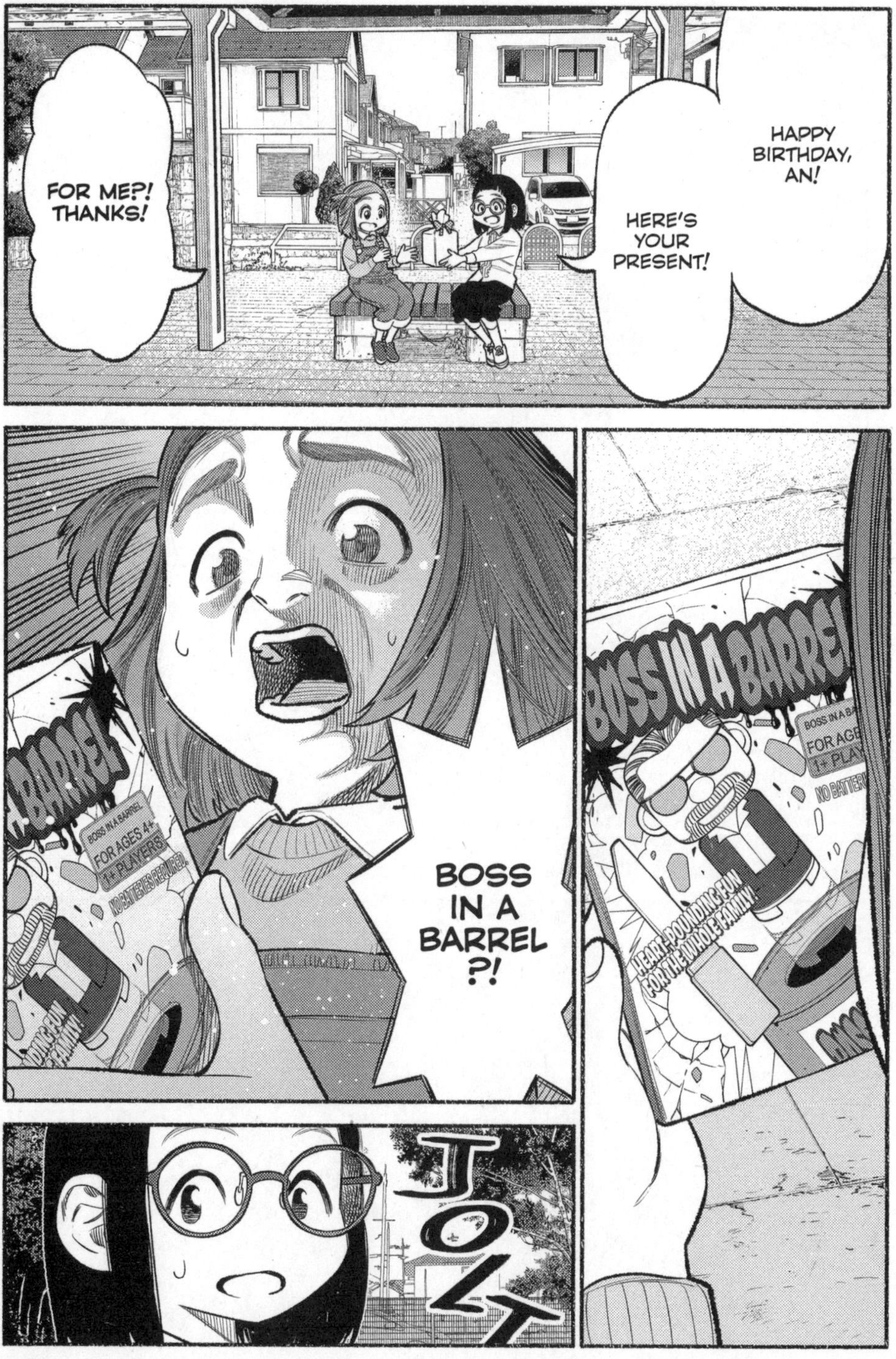
HAPPY BIRTHDAY, AN!
HERE'S YOUR PRESENT!
FOR ME?! THANKS!
BOSS IN A BARREL
HEART-POUNDING FUN FOR THE WHOLE FAMILY.
BOSS IN A BARREL
FOR AGES 4+
1+ PLAYERS
NO BATTERIES REQUIRED
BOSS IN A BARREL ?!
JOLT

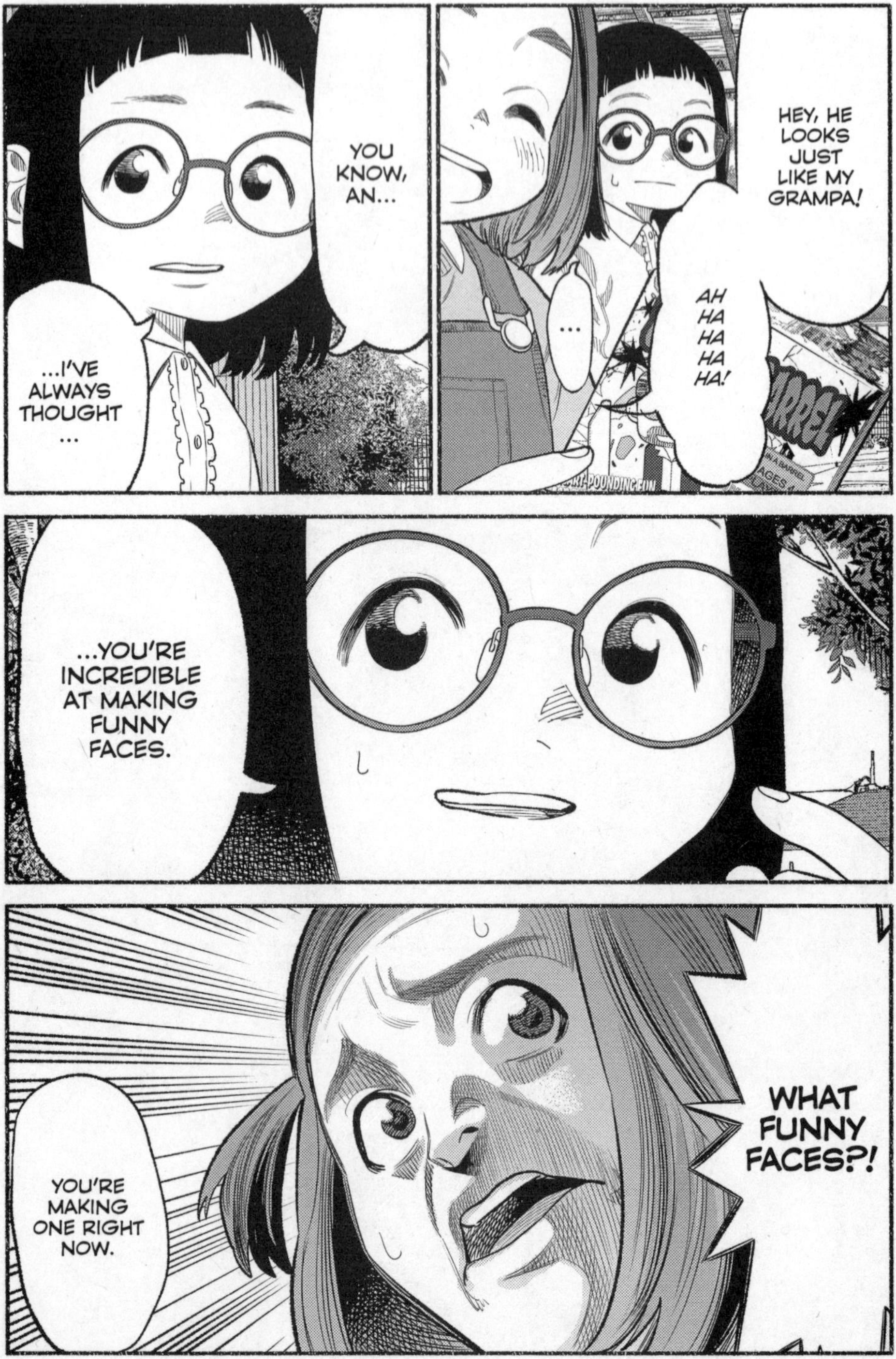
HEY, HE LOOKS JUST LIKE MY GRAMPA!
AH HA HA HA HA!
...
YOU KNOW, AN...
...I'VE ALWAYS THOUGHT ...
...YOU'RE INCREDIBLE AT MAKING FUNNY FACES.
WHAT FUNNY FACES?!
YOU'RE MAKING ONE RIGHT NOW.

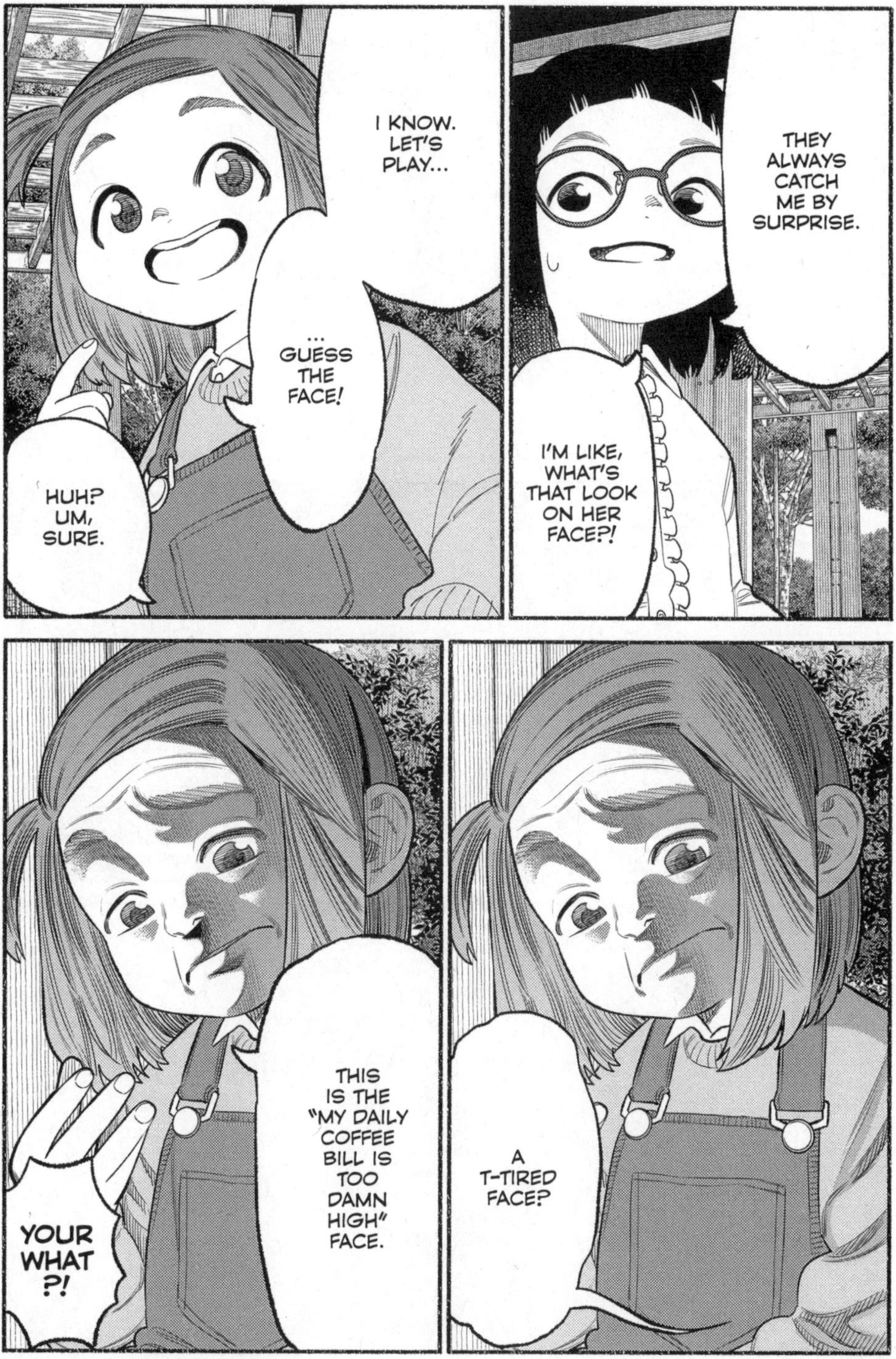
THEY ALWAYS CATCH ME BY SURPRISE.
I'M LIKE, WHAT'S THAT LOOK ON HER FACE?!
I KNOW. LET'S PLAY...
... GUESS THE FACE!
HUH? UM, SURE.
A T-TIRED FACE?
THIS IS THE "MY DAILY COFFEE BILL IS TOO DAMN HIGH" FACE.
YOUR WHAT?!

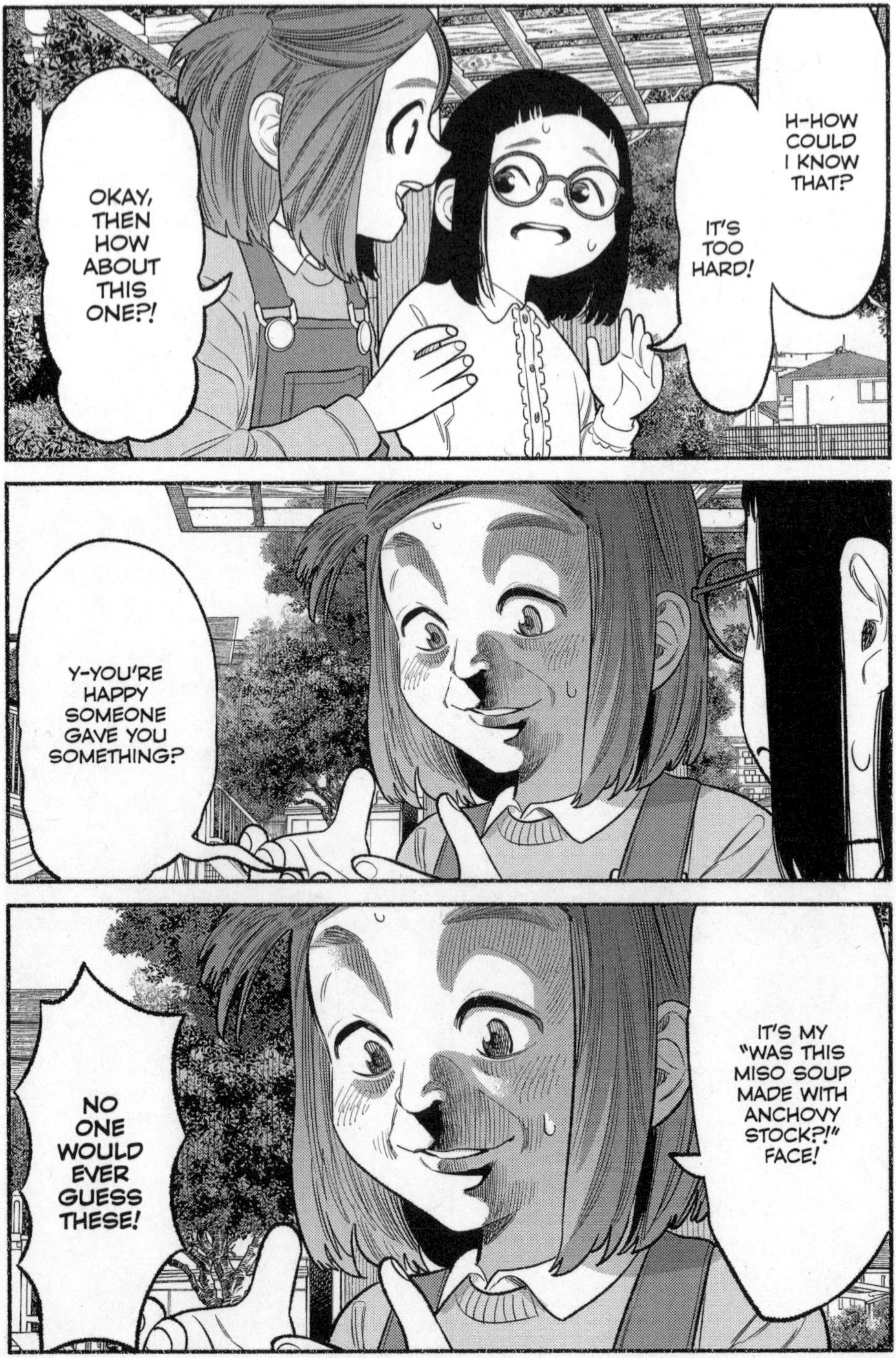
H-HOW COULD I KNOW THAT?
IT'S TOO HARD!
OKAY, THEN HOW ABOUT THIS ONE?!
Y-YOU'RE HAPPY SOMEONE GAVE YOU SOMETHING?
IT'S MY "WAS THIS MISO SOUP MADE WITH ANCHOVY STOCK?!" FACE!
NO ONE WOULD EVER GUESS THESE!

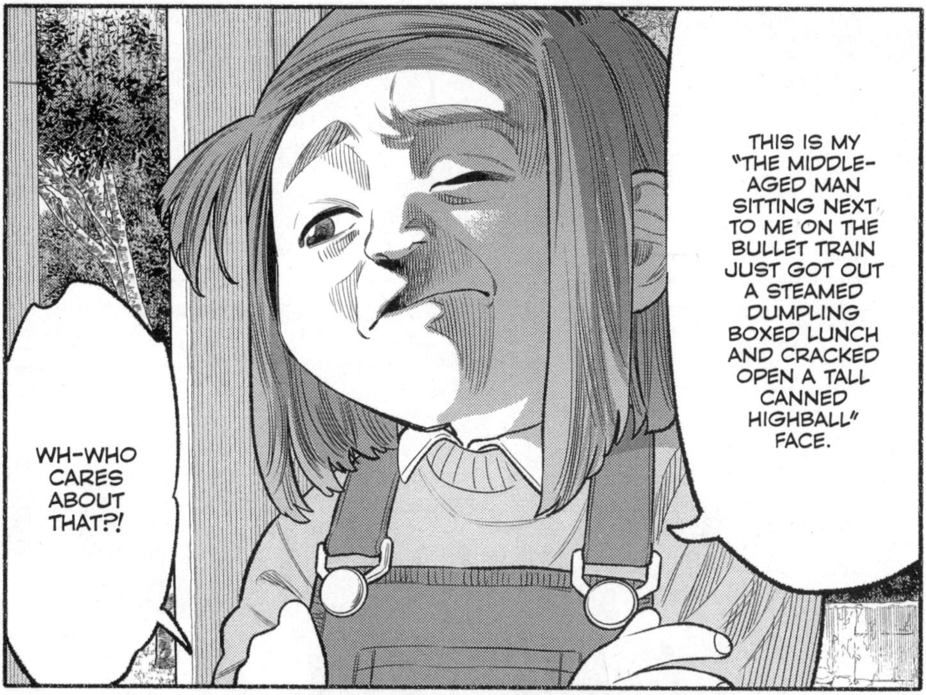
THIS IS MY "THE MIDDLE-AGED MAN SITTING NEXT TO ME ON THE BULLET TRAIN JUST GOT OUT A STEAMED DUMPLING BOXED LUNCH AND CRACKED OPEN A TALL CANNED HIGHBALL" FACE.
WH-WHO CARES ABOUT THAT?!
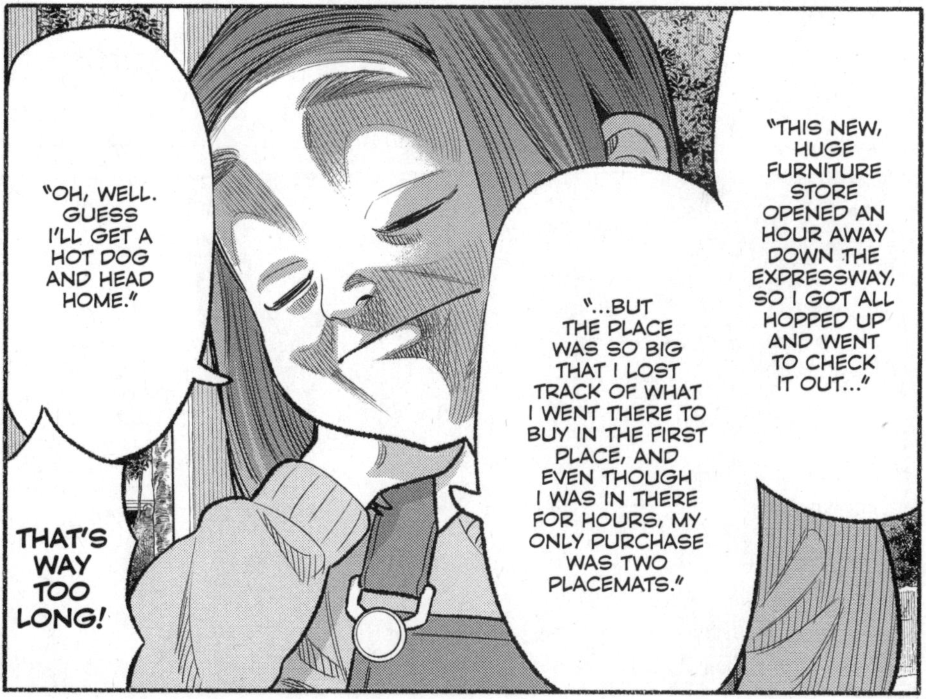
"THIS NEW, HUGE FURNITURE STORE OPENED AN HOUR AWAY DOWN THE EXPRESSWAY, SO I GOT ALL HOPPED UP AND WENT TO CHECK IT OUT..."
"...BUT THE PLACE WAS SO BIG THAT I LOST TRACK OF WHAT I WENT THERE TO BUY IN THE FIRST PLACE, AND EVEN THOUGH I WAS IN THERE FOR HOURS, MY ONLY PURCHASE WAS TWO PLACEMATS."
"OH, WELL. GUESS I'LL GET A HOT DOG AND HEAD HOME."
THAT'S WAY TOO LONG!

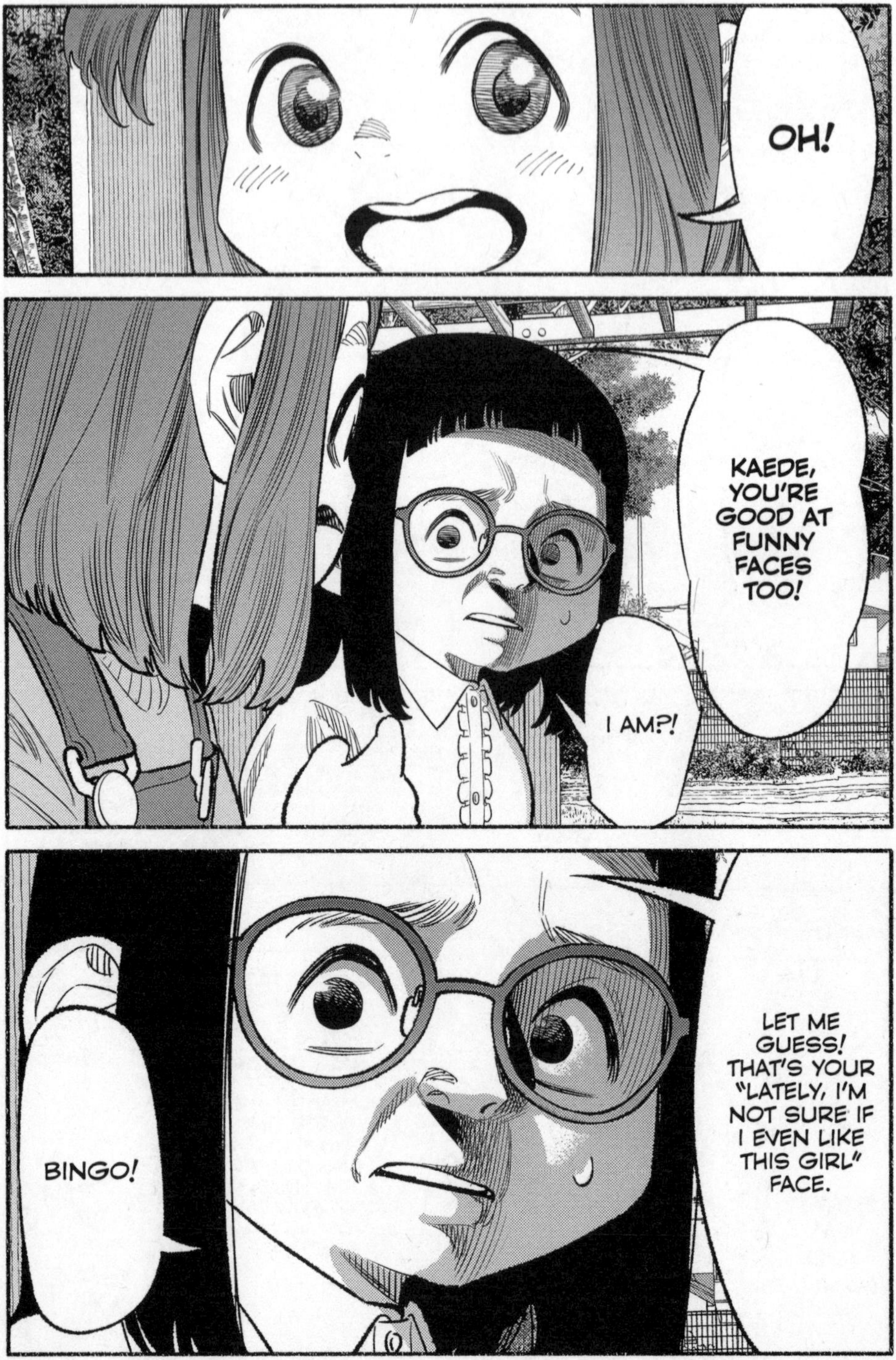
OH!
KAEDE, YOU'RE GOOD AT FUNNY FACES TOO!
I AM?!
LET ME GUESS! THAT'S YOUR "LATELY, I'M NOT SURE IF I EVEN LIKE THIS GIRL" FACE.
BINGO!

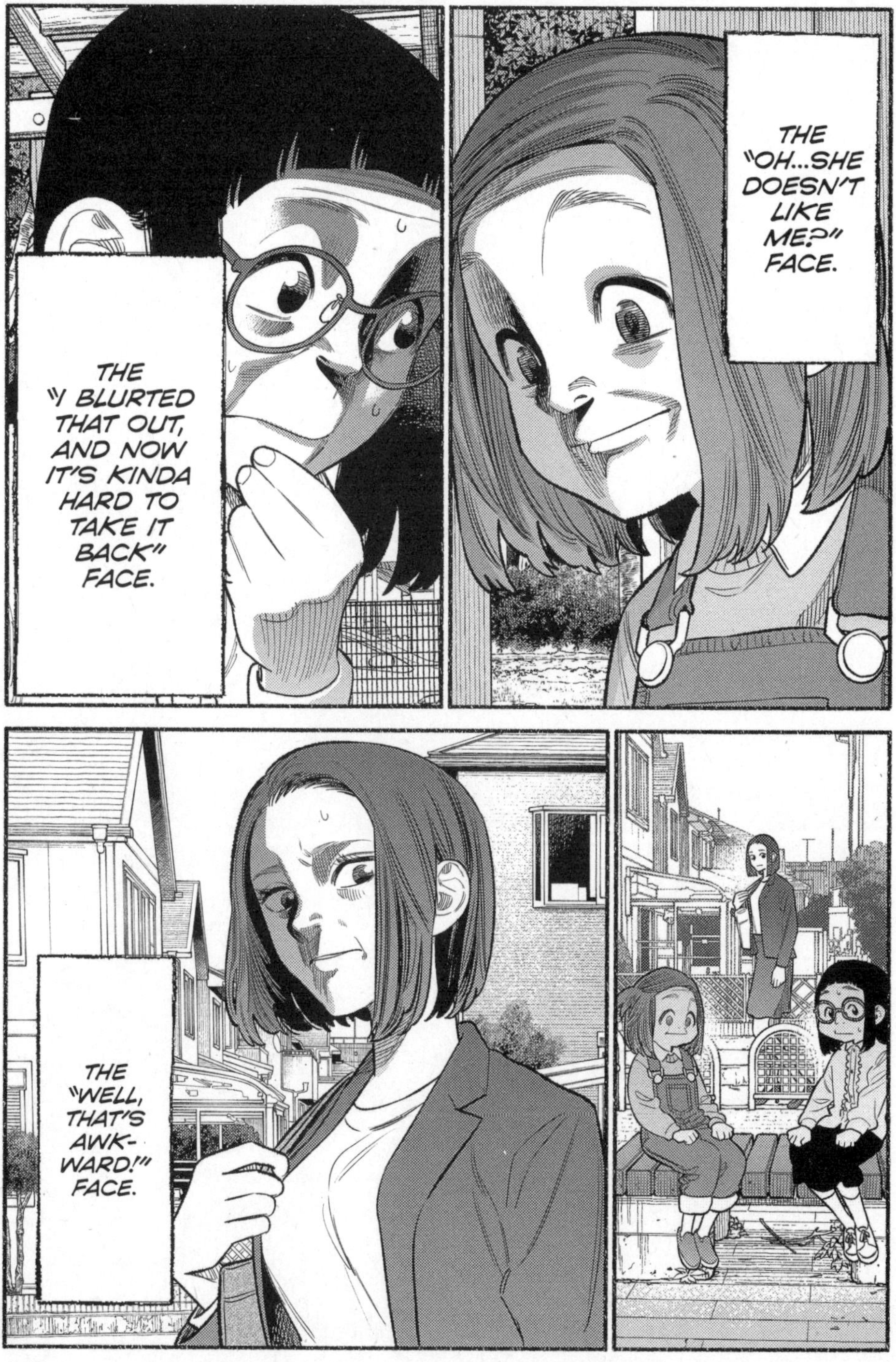
THE "OH...SHE DOESN'T LIKE ME?" FACE.
THE "I BLURTED THAT OUT, AND NOW IT'S KINDA HARD TO TAKE IT BACK" FACE.
THE "WELL, THAT'S AWK-WARD!" FACE.

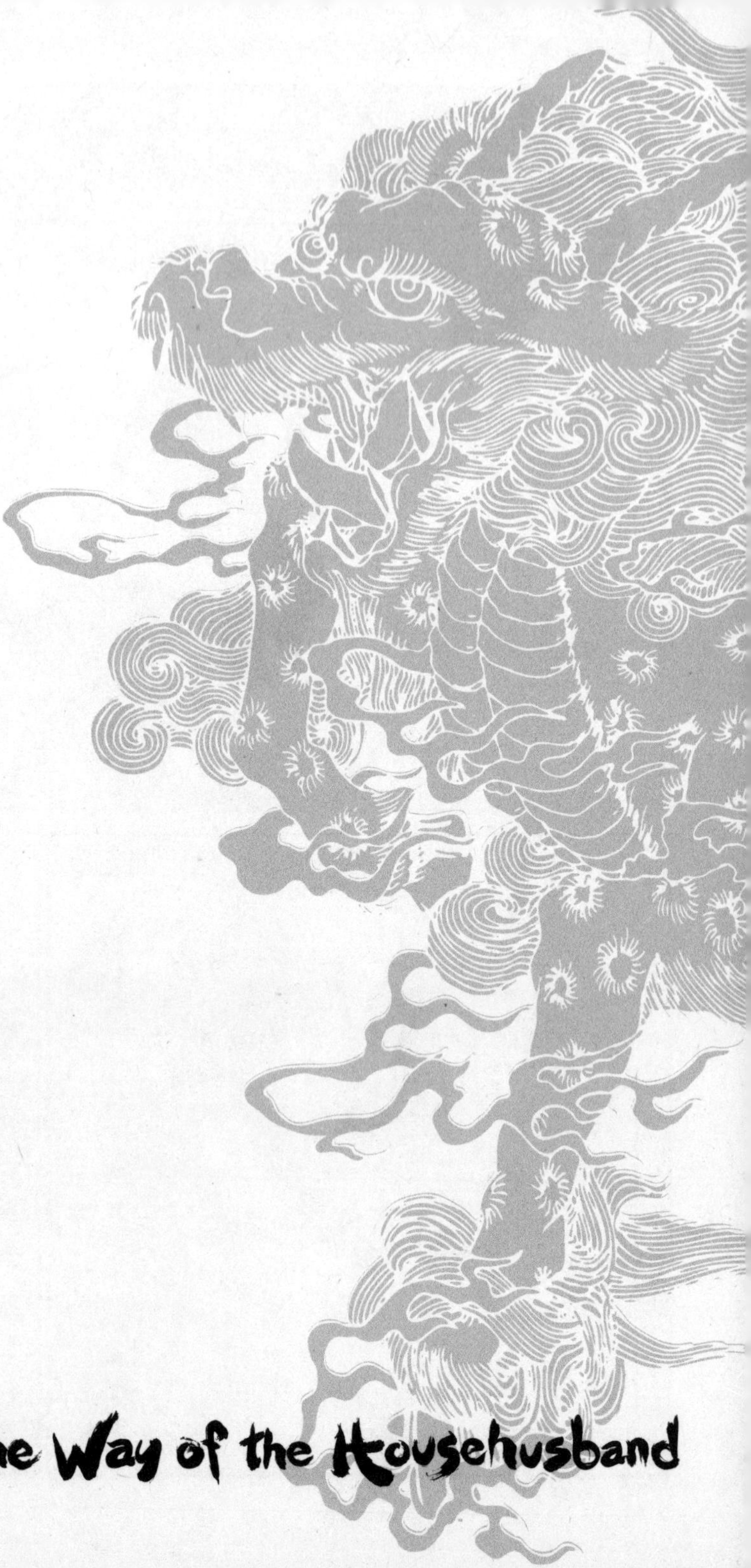

The Way of the Househusband

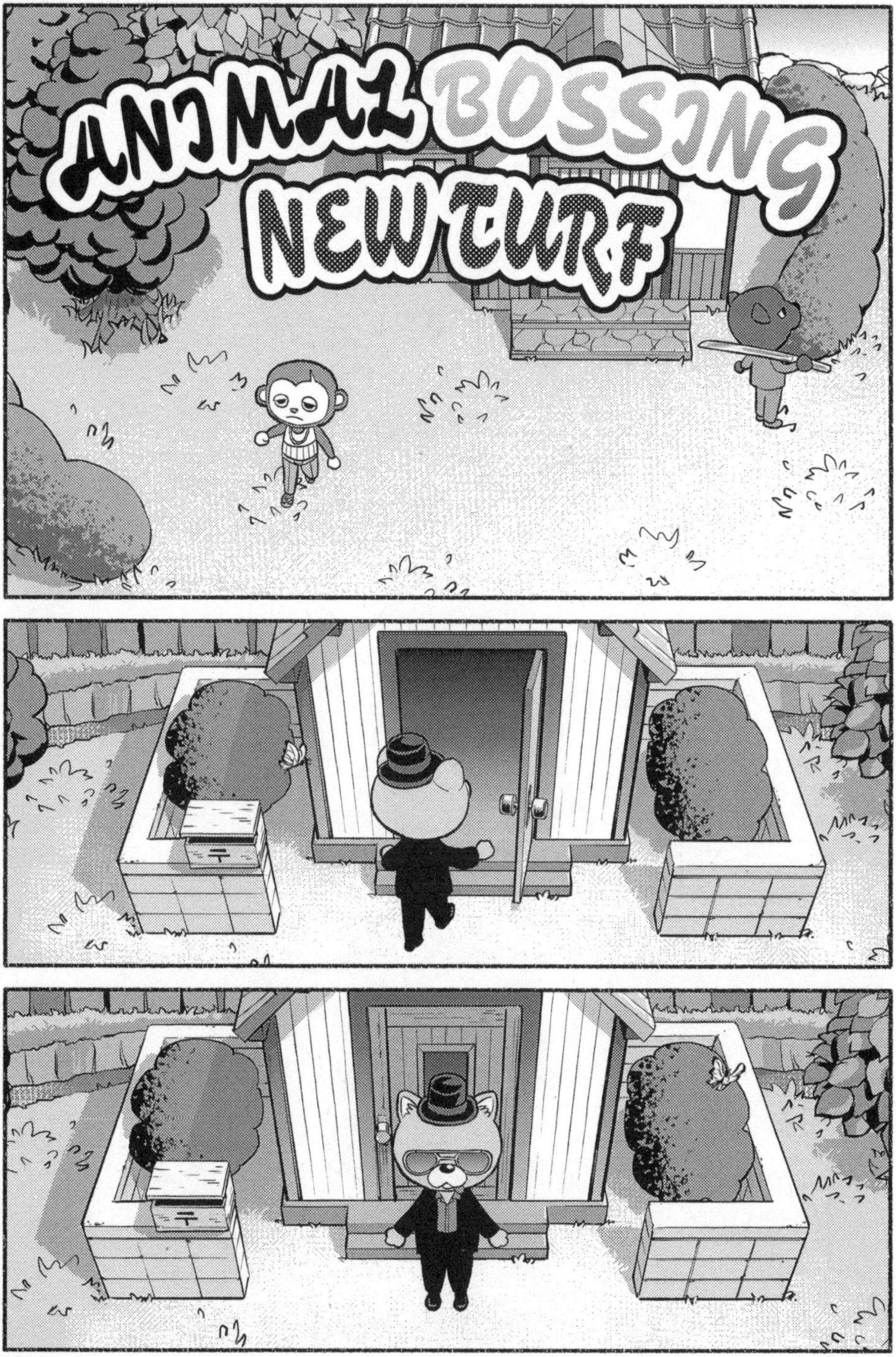
ANIMAL BOSSING
NEW TURF

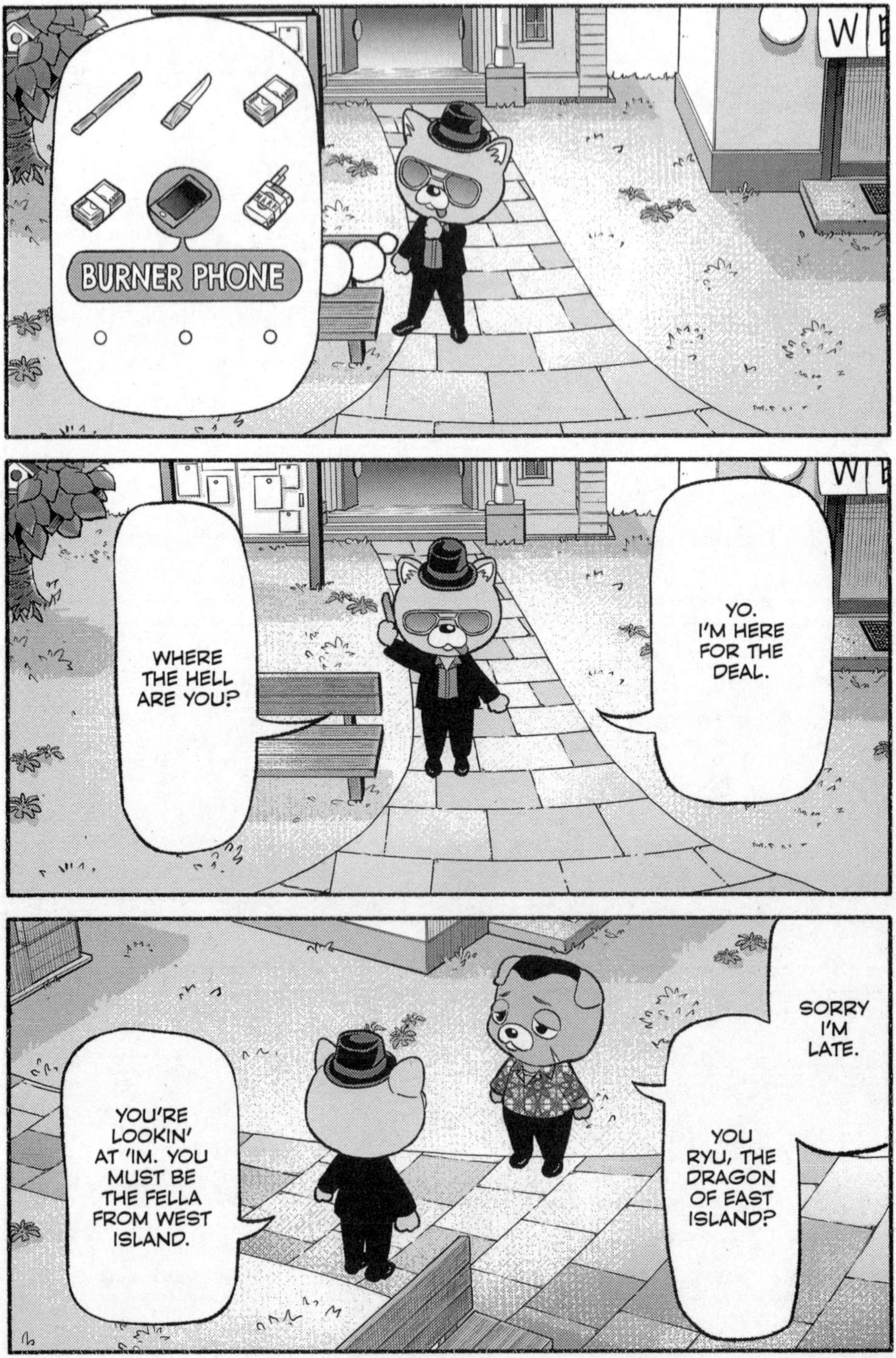
BURNER PHONE
YO. I'M HERE FOR THE DEAL.
WHERE THE HELL ARE YOU?
SORRY I'M LATE.
YOU RYU, THE DRAGON OF EAST ISLAND?
YOU'RE LOOKIN' AT 'IM. YOU MUST BE THE FELLA FROM WEST ISLAND.

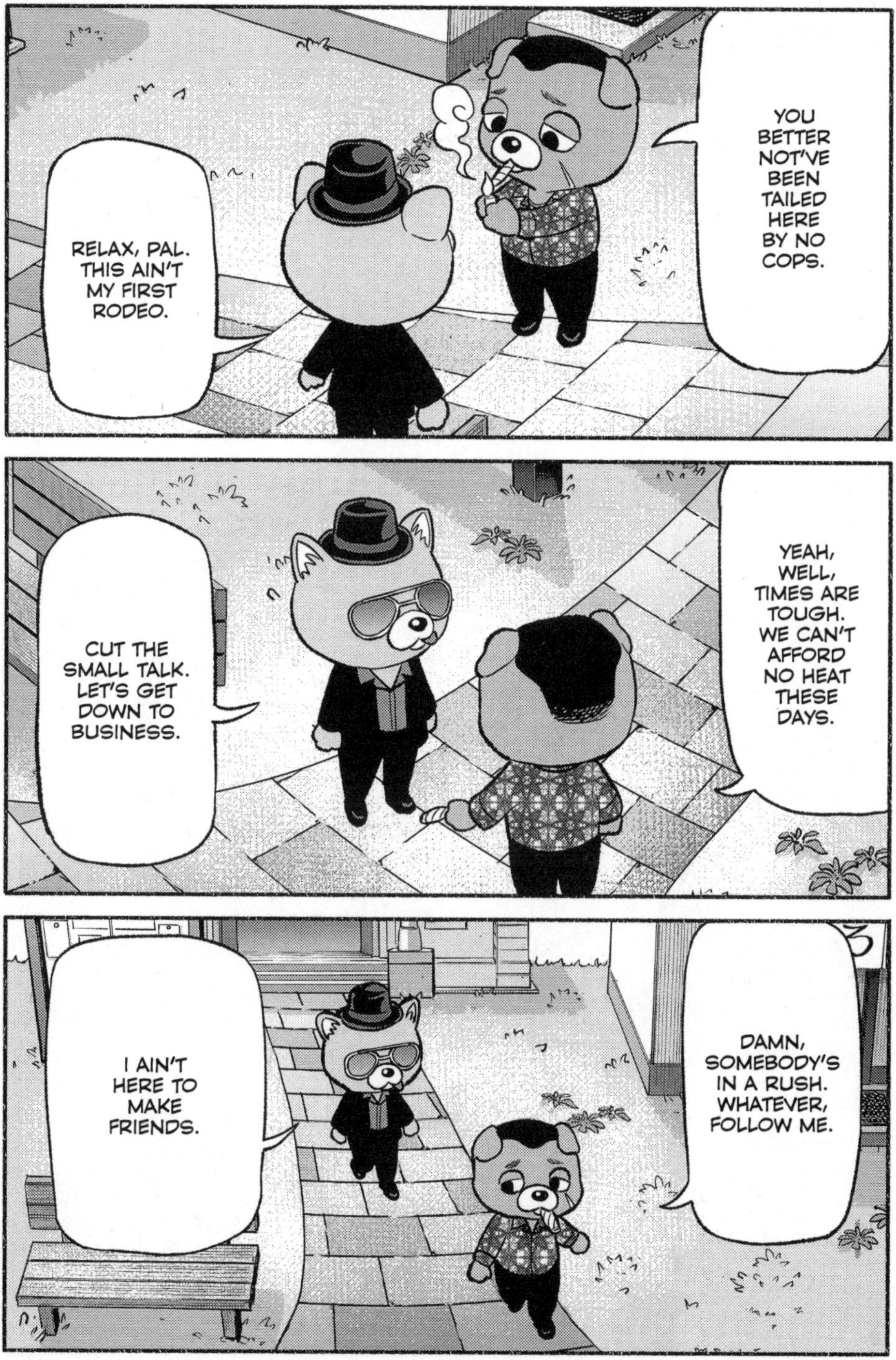
YOU BETTER NOT'VE BEEN TAILED HERE BY NO COPS.
RELAX, PAL. THIS AIN'T MY FIRST RODEO.
YEAH, WELL, TIMES ARE TOUGH. WE CAN'T AFFORD NO HEAT THESE DAYS.
CUT THE SMALL TALK. LET'S GET DOWN TO BUSINESS.
DAMN, SOMEBODY'S IN A RUSH. WHATEVER, FOLLOW ME.
I AIN'T HERE TO MAKE FRIENDS.

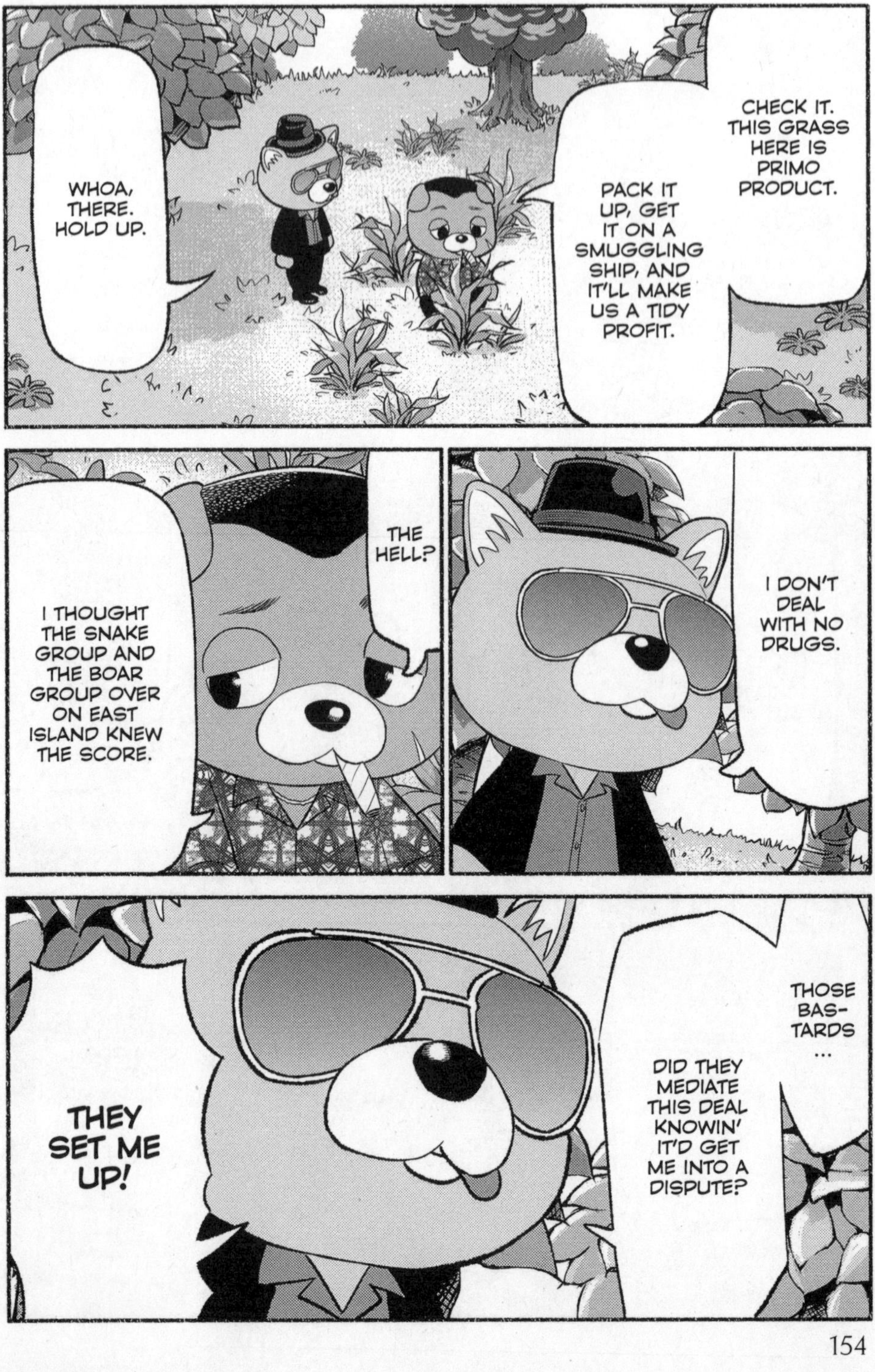
CHECK IT. THIS GRASS HERE IS PRIMO PRODUCT.
PACK IT UP, GET IT ON A SMUGGLING SHIP, AND IT'LL MAKE US A TIDY PROFIT.
WHOA, THERE. HOLD UP.
I DON'T DEAL WITH NO DRUGS.
THE HELL?
I THOUGHT THE SNAKE GROUP AND THE BOAR GROUP OVER ON EAST ISLAND KNEW THE SCORE.
THOSE BAS-TARDS...
DID THEY MEDIATE THIS DEAL KNOWIN' IT'D GET ME INTO A DISPUTE?
THEY SET ME UP!

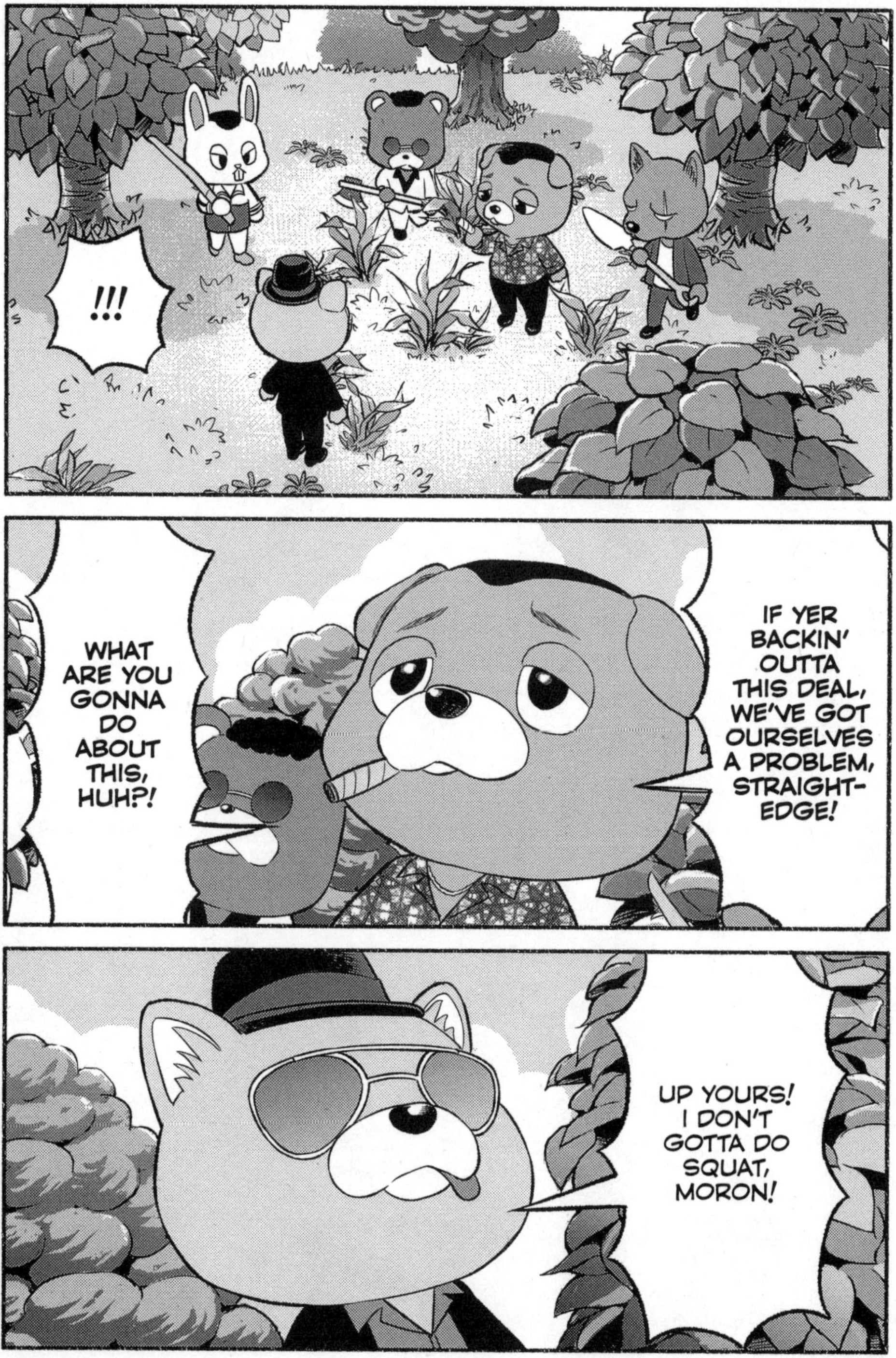
!!!
IF YER BACKIN' OUTTA THIS DEAL, WE'VE GOT OURSELVES A PROBLEM, STRAIGHT-EDGE!
WHAT ARE YOU GONNA DO ABOUT THIS, HUH?!
UP YOURS! I DON'T GOTTA DO SQUAT, MORON!

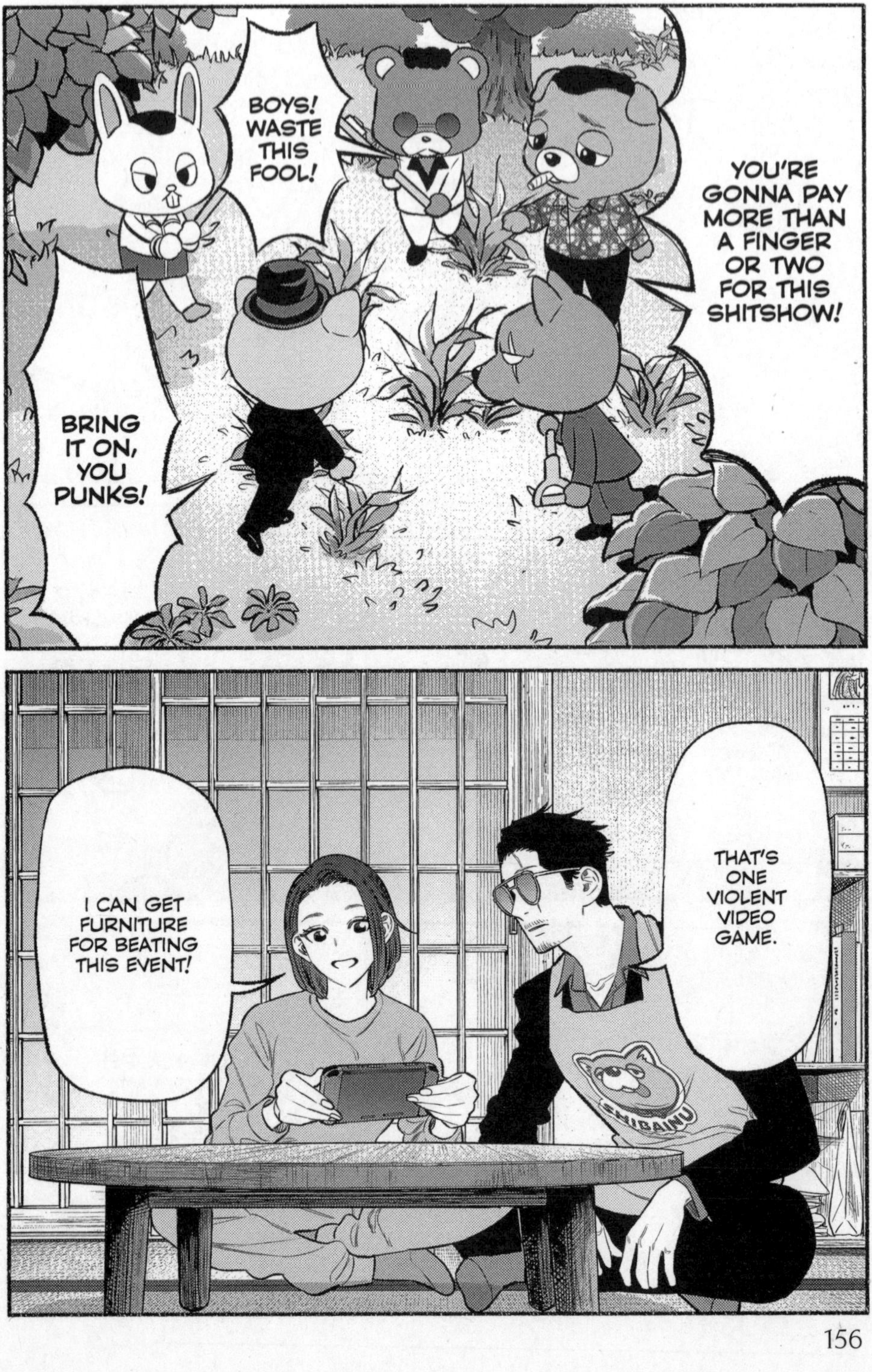
BOYS! WASTE THIS FOOL!
YOU'RE GONNA PAY MORE THAN A FINGER OR TWO FOR THIS SHITSHOW!
BRING IT ON, YOU PUNKS!
THAT'S ONE VIOLENT VIDEO GAME.
SHIBAINU
I CAN GET FURNITURE FOR BEATING THIS EVENT!

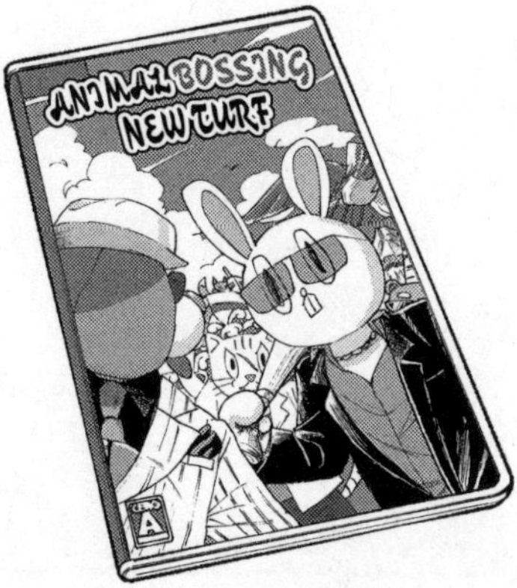
ANIMAL BOSSING
NEW TURF
A

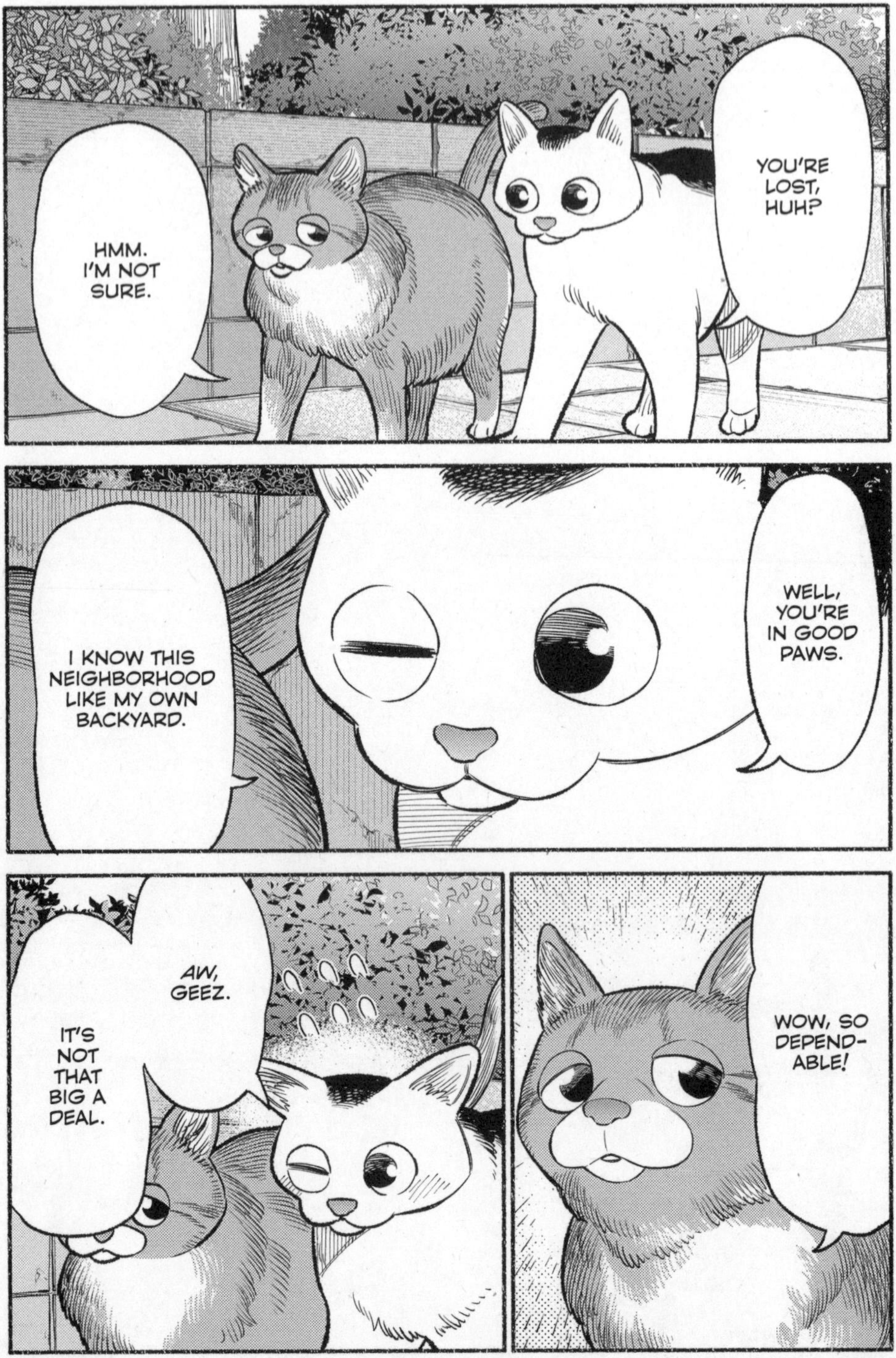
YOU'RE LOST, HUH?
HMM. I'M NOT SURE.
WELL, YOU'RE IN GOOD PAWS.
I KNOW THIS NEIGHBORHOOD LIKE MY OWN BACKYARD.
WOW, SO DEPEND-ABLE!
AW, GEEZ.
IT'S NOT THAT BIG A DEAL.

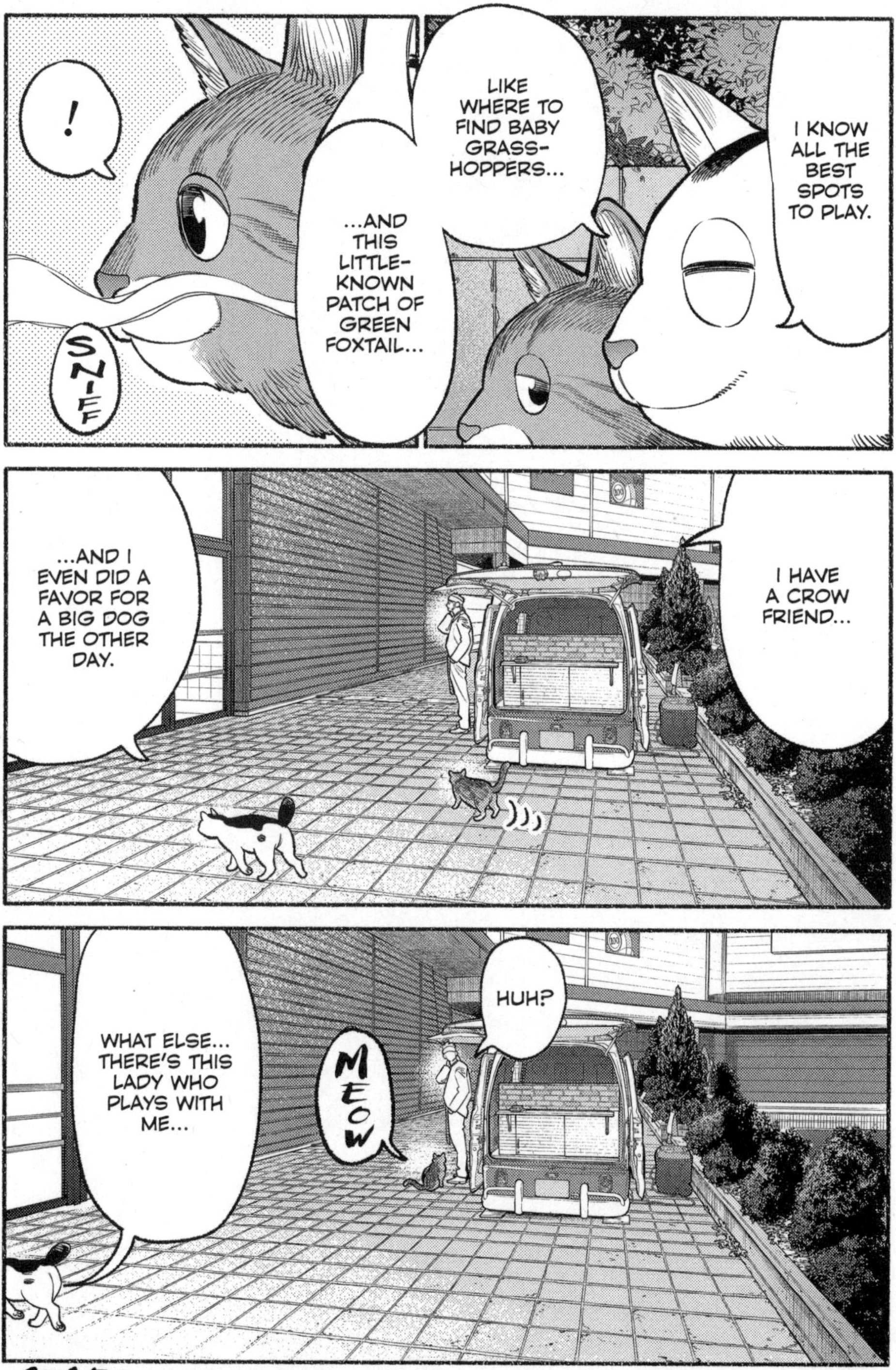
I KNOW ALL THE BEST SPOTS TO PLAY.
LIKE WHERE TO FIND BABY GRASS-HOPPERS...
...AND THIS LITTLE-KNOWN PATCH OF GREEN FOXTAIL...
!
SNIFF
I HAVE A CROW FRIEND...
...AND I EVEN DID A FAVOR FOR A BIG DOG THE OTHER DAY.
HUH?
MEOW
WHAT ELSE... THERE'S THIS LADY WHO PLAYS WITH ME...

GIN'S THE TYPE WHO WOULD DRUNKENLY RAMBLE ABOUT HIS HEROIC EXPLOITS. DON'T MISS VOLUME 11!

STAFF- MIDORINO, HIROE SPECIAL THANKS- KIMU

We've hit the double digits.
The serialization has been
running for four years now.
That's 32 years in dog years—
the age when getting called
"old man" makes you jump.

KOUSUKE OONO

Kousuke Oono began his professional
manga career in 2016 in the manga
magazine *Monthly Comics @ Bunch*
with the one-shot "Legend of Music."
Oono's follow-up series, *The Way of
the Househusband*, is the creator's first
serialization as well as his first English-
language release.

The Way of the House Husband

VOLUME 10
VIZ SIGNATURE EDITION

STORY AND ART BY
KOUSUKE OONO

TRANSLATION: Amanda Haley
ENGLISH ADAPTATION: Jennifer LeBlanc
TOUCH-UP ART & LETTERING: Bianca Pistillo
DESIGN: Alice Lewis
EDITOR: Jennifer LeBlanc

GOKUSHUFUDO volume 10
© Kousuke Oono 2018
All Rights Reserved
English translation rights arranged
with SHINCHOSHA Publishing Co., Ltd.
through Tuttle-Mori Agency, Inc., Tokyo

Printed in the U.S.A.

Published by VIZ Media, LLC
P.O. Box 77010
San Francisco, CA 94107

10 9 8 7 6 5 4 3 2 1
First printing, August 2023

VIZ MEDIA   VIZ SIGNATURE

viz.com   vizsignature.com

GANGSTER COOKING RECIPE vol.3

TODAY'S DISH: GRILLED SHIITAKE MUSHROOM WITH GINKGO NUTS

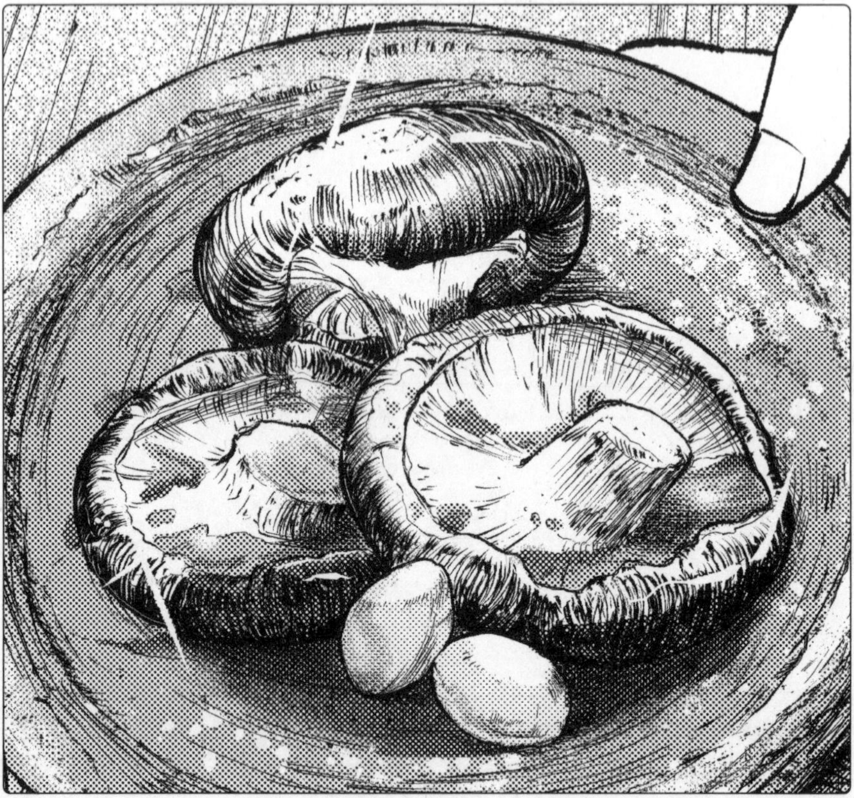

INGREDIENTS (SERVES 1)

- 3 shiitake mushrooms (grown in Tokushima Prefecture)
- 15 grams ginkgo nuts (grown in Aichi Prefecture)
- Salt and soy sauce to taste

DIRECTIONS

1. Deshell the nuts. Heat a drizzle of oil in a frying pan and add ginkgo nuts. Cook, stirring until toasted. Season with salt.
2. Trim mushroom stems. Grill mushrooms on both sides.
3. Transfer the mushrooms to a plate. Drizzle with soy sauce, garnish with ginkgo nuts, and it's done! Goes great with sake.

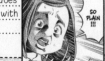

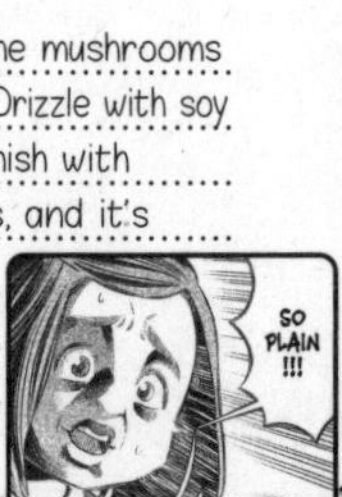
SO PLAIN !!!

Sophisticated and Delicious!

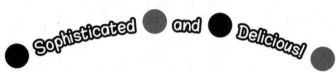

Lamb Terrine de Campagne with Velouté Sauce

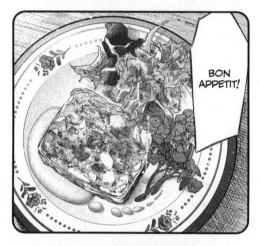

BON APPETIT!

GANGSTER COOKING

Six short stories that set the scene for the best-selling *BEASTARS* series!

BEAST COMPLEX

Story and Art by Paru Itagaki

In these six stories from the creator of the Eisner-nominated, best-selling series BEASTARS, a menagerie of carnivores and herbivores grapple with conflicts based on their differences and—sometimes—find common ground.

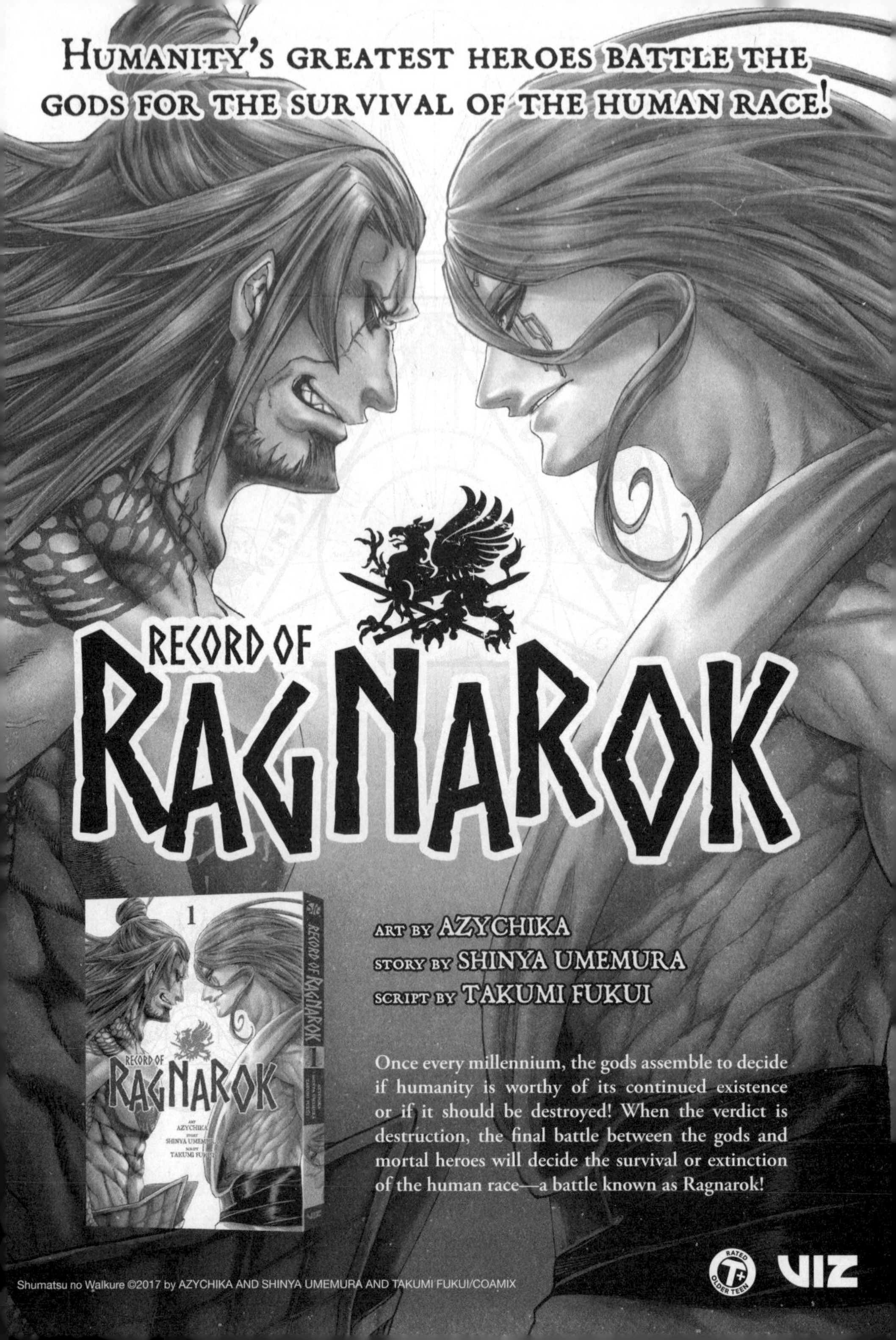

HUMANITY'S GREATEST HEROES BATTLE THE GODS FOR THE SURVIVAL OF THE HUMAN RACE!

RECORD OF RAGNAROK

ART BY AZYCHIKA
STORY BY SHINYA UMEMURA
SCRIPT BY TAKUMI FUKUI

Once every millennium, the gods assemble to decide if humanity is worthy of its continued existence or if it should be destroyed! When the verdict is destruction, the final battle between the gods and mortal heroes will decide the survival or extinction of the human race—a battle known as Ragnarok!

CHILDREN OF THE WHALES

In this postapocalyptic fantasy, a sea of sand
swallows everything but the past.

In an endless sea of sand drifts the
Mud Whale, a floating island city
of clay and magic. In its chambers a
small community clings to survival,
cut off from its own history by the
shadows of the past.

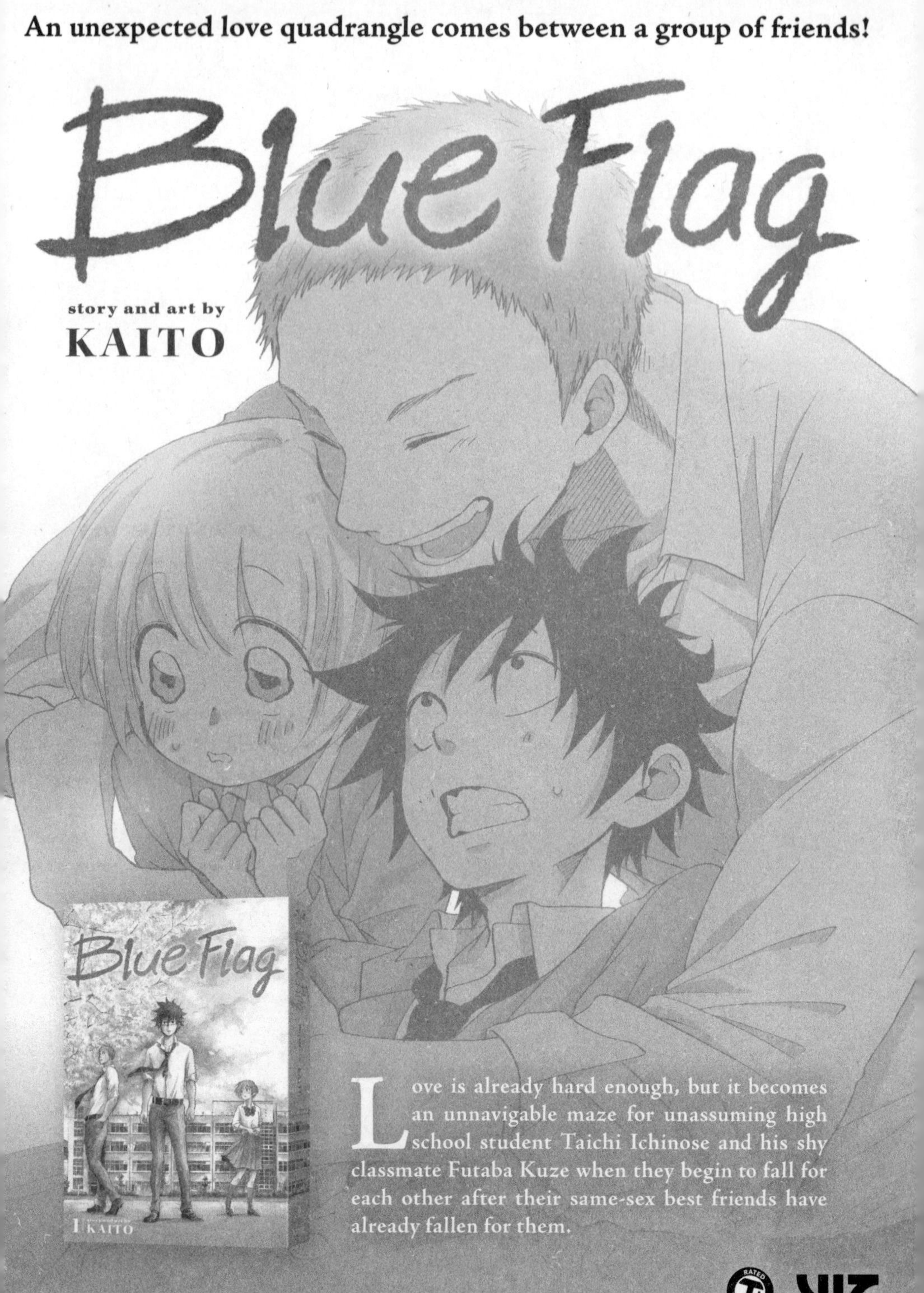

An unexpected love quadrangle comes between a group of friends!
Blue Flag
story and art by
KAITO
Blue Flag
1 KAITO
Love is already hard enough, but it becomes an unnavigable maze for unassuming high school student Taichi Ichinose and his shy classmate Futaba Kuze when they begin to fall for each other after their same-sex best friends have already fallen for them.
RATED T+ OLDER TEEN
VIZ